Yuchi Indian
Histories
Before the
Removal Era

Yuchi Indian Histories Before the Removal Era

Edited and with an introduction by

JASON BAIRD JACKSON

University of Nebraska Press   Lincoln & London

Library of Congress Cataloging-in-Publication Data

Yuchi Indian histories before the removal era / edited and
with an introduction by Jason Baird Jackson.
p. cm.
Includes bibliographical references and index.
ISBN 978-0-8032-4041-4 (pbk.: alk. paper)
1. Yuchi Indians—History. 2. Yuchi Indians—Social conditions.
3. Yuchi Indians—Social life and customs.
I. Jackson, Jason Baird, 1969–
E99.Y9Y83 2012
305.897'9—dc23
2012006240

Set in Sabon by Bob Reitz.

FIGURE 1. "An Indian woman weaving a basket of reed." Pictured on the colonial frontier of Georgia in 1736 by Philip Georg Friedrich von Reck or someone in his retinue. NKS 565 4° (Von Reck's drawings), No. 48. The Royal Library, Copenhagen, Denmark.

For discussion of this image and the collection from which it comes, see Hvidt, *Von Reck's Voyage*, 112–13. The image is online at http://www.kb.dk/permalink/2006/manus/22/eng/No.+48/?var=.

Dedicated to the Yuchi women whose long labors across five centuries—while barely observed by the colonial recorders whose experiences inform this volume—have helped insure a bright future for their people.

For the support of its historical preservation efforts, the Euchee (Yuchi) Tribe of Indians has been named as the direct beneficiary of any author royalties generated through the sale of this volume.

Contents

~

List of Illustrations

~

List of Maps

~

Tables

~

Introduction
On Studying Yuchi History

⁓

The Yuchi (alternatively Euchee) are a native North American people with a compelling story to tell. Yuchi people today, in the twenty-first century, still speak their own unique indigenous language,
one unrelated to any known language of the Americas. While many
Yuchi people are proud of their non-Yuchi ancestors just as they are
proud of their Yuchi ones, there are today Yuchi people who know
themselves to be—in the unfortunate language of U.S. Indian policy—"full-blood" Yuchis. The Yuchi people are led today, as in
times past, by hereditary chiefs who govern towns that are both
autonomous sociopolitical units and nodes in a broader social network that both constitutes a wider Yuchi society and situates Yuchi people for participation in a regional social system linking them
through relations of reciprocity and exchange with indigenous communities stretching from the Iroquois longhouses of Canada to the
dance grounds and chickee camps of the Florida Seminoles. The Yuchi people have not only survived the terrors of the past five hundred years; they enter the second decade of the twenty-first century as a thriving people. That is all story enough, but the narrative
gets strange. The vital people whom I have just described have been
characterized in some authoritative published works as extinct, and
despite having all the hallmarks associated with such status, they

are unrecognized in every way that counts by the federal government of the United States and by the Muscogee (Creek) Nation, the Native American polity that possesses the authority to speak and act on their behalf in contemporary formal and legal contexts. For some observers, the Yuchi do not exist; for others they are not supposed to. The chapters gathered in this volume aim to advance the project of making sense of how these two stories—persistence and marginalization—are braided together and rooted in the wider story of what happened to the Yuchis and other indigenous peoples in the years that followed the arrival of European and African peoples in eastern North America. The chapters gathered here are resolutely provisional and occasionally contradictory. They represent our best efforts at starting work that needs to be pursued more vigorously, carefully, and systematically than has been possible so far. They are a start.

While Yuchi individuals live today throughout the United States, the Yuchi people whose history is the focus of this modest volume can be found living in distinct and distinctive communities in what are today Creek, Tulsa, and Okmulgee Counties in east-central Oklahoma.[1] For modern Yuchis today, these contiguous town communities, which together are thought of as Yuchi country, represent home. But Yuchis are also quite aware that Oklahoma is not the old country from which their ancestors were forced by the government of the United States in the 1830s. Living on the South's northwestern margins, Yuchi families today preserve oral traditions of the hardships endured during removal, and these stories provide a link to a deeper past and to eastward places that many Yuchis hope to have a chance to visit—the Savannah, Flint, and Chattahoochee River Valleys in present-day Georgia and Alabama; the Appalachian Mountains of Virginia, Tennessee, and the Carolinias; the pine woods and swamps of Florida.[2] As the contributors to this volume begin to reveal, these places, like eastern Oklahoma, are places where Yuchi people were actors not only in their own histories but also in those of other much better known Native peoples and of the European colonizers and forcefully dislocated peoples of African ancestry with whom all Native peoples of eastern North America peoples have had to contend since the sixteenth century.

In the surviving documents from which histories of eastern North America after European colonization can be and have been written, there appear the names of hundreds of Native American communities. About some of these groups we now know quite a lot, but for most, little knowledge is available to us. Scores of Native peoples who once possessed distinctive identities and ways of life that represented unique local configurations of regionally distributed practices and beliefs were destroyed through the combination of introduced diseases, enslavement, military conquest, and the social disruption wrought by European colonization. Other peoples, more fortunate, found a range of creative ways of coping with these devastating disruptions. Some moved vast distances seeking new locales better positioned to enable them to survive and, ideally, thrive in the context of social change. Some radically altered their ancestral ways of life to develop new strategies more attuned to life in colonial contexts. Some entered into confederation with former neighbors—and sometimes former enemies—so as to create viable new societies better adapted to a new era. In a dynamic social process, some peoples sought refuge among neighbors. When this happened, sometimes they assimilated the languages, cultures, and social customs of their more powerful hosts. In other instances, recognizably distinct and new peoples emerged through the process known as ethnogenesis, wherein diverse source communities combine to create a new society with a hybrid or creolized culture and, often, novel social arrangements. The contributors to this volume share an interest in the diversity of ways that the Native peoples of eastern North America sought to position themselves in the stream of history after contact with Europe. Here, the almost completely unexamined case of the Yuchi people provides a productive vantage point on these broader questions.[3]

In a phrase that resonates with the whole problematic of this volume, then newly arrived German colonist Johann Bolzius, writing of colonial Georgia in 1734, commented: "One of the other nations, who are called Uchees, are much inclined to robbing and stealing, but these Creeks are honest, serviceable and disinterested."[4] It would seem that such "othering" opinions, offered parenthetically in published accounts largely concerned with "other" matters, are almost all that we yet have by way of Yuchi history before removal. Long an obvious need, the near complete absence of reliable, published work on Yuchi history has now become an obstacle, both to contemporary Yuchi community interests and to the growing and ever richer scholarly literatures on the Native Southeast, the American South, and the history of eastern North America more generally. By drawing together scholars from a range of fields whose research has intersected with Yuchi matters, the goal of this volume is to locate Yuchi history in space and time, in preliminary fashion, thereby fostering what might eventually become a robust Yuchi national historiography. In advancing such a goal, I am grateful for the contributors' willingness to take time away from other projects—projects more central to their long-term scholarly careers—to participate in this undertaking. We all share the hope that the work gathered here will serve as a starting point, and perhaps also an inspiration, for a more sustained and comprehensive study of Yuchi history in all its dimensions, eventually including consideration of cultural, social, economic, political, and other questions. The Euchee (Yuchi) Tribe of Indians, the contemporary community organization representing pan-Yuchi interests, is also very eager to promote such studies, as evidenced by its own recent work compiling sources on tribal history, its sponsoring of a Yuchi history symposium in 2010 at which several of the contributors to this volume presented their work, and its endorsement of the project that has resulted in this collection.

Other Work to Do

That the Yuchi have received so little historical attention is a complex puzzle in light of the considerable amount of sophisticated effort that has now been devoted to historical studies of Native, colonial, and early American history in the American South and the wider Atlantic world. In the course of their investigations, the authors represented in this volume suggest some of the factors that have contributed to this neglect—a limited but daunting corpus of historical sources, long-standing misunderstandings propagated in early and foundational scholarship, confusion over synonymy (i.e., ethnic group names), and an overreliance on certain typological models of Native societies (e.g., chiefdom, confederacy, nation, tribe) and of social change within them (e.g., coalescence, ethnogenesis, colonization). While much of the best work being done in this field is strongly multidisciplinary in orientation, a great deal of research continues to be pursued in isolation by historians and archaeologists working separately, and there have been too few cultural anthropologists, linguists, human geographers, and folklorists available and interested to participate in the broader project of writing the social and cultural history of the region. Bringing the work of a varied group of scholars together here is a further nod in the direction of cross-disciplinary work, but given its particular challenges, a *bona fide* project focused on Yuchi history (as one pressing example) will require a more integrated and collaborative approach. Such work remains the incompletely fulfilled promise of the interdisciplinary field of ethnohistory.[5]

To the extent that the Yuchi people have appeared in the annals of history over the long haul, they have done so as bit players in other peoples' dramas. The contemporary Yuchi community and the contributors to this volume would all be quick to acknowledge the ways that the Yuchi have always been well networked. In criticizing the marginalization of the Yuchi people in the extant histories, I am not advocating a view that would move them to the center of the frame without attending to their linkages to other peoples. My work as an ethnographer and ethnologist is aimed at understanding Yuchi cultural practices and social relations within a wider regional frame that accounts for the ways in which Yuchi social ties (some persistent, some changing) to other groups play a role in sustaining the distinctive *configuration* of both unique and more widely shared elements that Yuchi people understand as their traditional culture.[6] The problem has not been understanding Yuchi history vis-à-vis the histories of other peoples; the problem has been inattentiveness to the positioning of the Yuchi within such histories. Put more simply, sources on Yuchi history have either misrepresented them as no longer existing as a people (and thus as either completely extinct or as fully assimilated, culturally and socially, into a homogenized Muscogee [Creek] Nation) or have been built uncritically upon the biases of sources, particularly elite Muscogee nationalists but also colonial observers, who have sought in their words and actions to subjugate Yuchi autonomy to advance personal agendas and Muscogee national (or colonial) projects.

The preceding Bolzius quotation serves two useful purposes in the present context. It is advantageous in that it is a useful reminder that non-Yuchi observers sometimes *did* acknowledge the Yuchi, not only as the autonomous and distinctive people that both the contemporary Yuchi community and past generations of Yuchi people understood themselves to be but, going further, as a "nation" alongside and distinct from the Creek nation and other native societies.[7] It is useful, if also disheartening to Yuchis and their friends, in that it—in the space of a sentence—stands as an illustrative token of the type of anti-Yuchi discourse that has dominated their treatment in historical works colored by elite Creek narratives and a scholarly preoccupation with the careers in time of the so-called five major Indian Nations—Creek, Cherokee, Choctaw, Chickasaw, and Seminole—to the neglect of the dizzying diversity that did, and still does, characterize the lived realities of American Indian peoples in the South and in eastern North America more broadly. As the contributors to this volume suggest, the colonial South was a place where the honesty, serviceablity, and disinterested status of individuals and groups—as well as robbing and stealing—were very much part of the human experience, but these characteristics hardly mapped neatly onto bounded societies easily understood as uncontested nations. In the historical literature, unsympathetic descriptions of the Yuchi people (what Joshua Piker characterizes in his chapter as the "Yuchis are thieves" narrative) have been easier to locate than more nuanced or charitable ones. The authors of the essays gathered here have made important efforts to find and deploy sources that offer a richer picture even as some of them have faced the challenge of making sense of this historically dominant discourse.[8]

The most famous dissent to such opinions documented for the pre-removal era is that offered by the naturalist and proto-ethnographer William Bartram in his *Travels*. Bartram was favorably impressed with the Yuchi town on the Chattahoochee River, which he visited in summer 1775, describing it as the "largest, most compact and best situated Indian town I ever saw" with homes that were "large and neatly built." The town plan and domestic architecture that so impressed Bartram were home to a community that struck him as "populous and thriving, full of youth and young children." He understood the town's population of 1,000–1,500 citizens to be capable of mustering "five hundred gun-men, or warriors." Despite the brevity of his encounter with the Yuchi and the uncertainty that he, and we, experience in characterizing Creek-Yuchi relations, Bartram was at pains to note his awareness of the manner in which the Yuchi were typically on the receiving end of Muscogee (Creek) "jealousy," how the Yuchi "do not mix with" their Creek neighbors, and how the Yuchi were "usually at variance" with them.[9]

I am an ethnographer rather than a historian, and this experience colors my concerns and reactions to the state of Yuchi historiography. More obviously, my rich personal relationships with the Yuchi people of today motivate me to promote the view that scholars can do better than simply recount the slander of those period elites who brought their own biases and agendas—often hegemonic—to their accounts of and dealings with the Yuchi people. Focused as they are on the present and the recent past, my previous writings on Yuchi topics add little to the historical discussion, but my hope is that they provide some motivation for new scholarly work on Yuchi history.[10] In a simple sense, I hope that my ethnographic work at least serves as a corrective to views such as those recycled in many secondary sources. I am close enough to contemporary Yuchi people to know something of what it is like for them to live in a world still shaped by such talk. I also know that there are today still Creek elites who

speak and think of the Yuchi in this way.[11] My point is not to crit-
icize past scholars, although I wish they had been more nuanced,
given the long shelf life that scholarly writings on little-known peoples typically enjoy. My purpose instead is to evoke a set of research
problems that, while they are perhaps obvious, have remained unexamined and that—given the recent advances made by students
of Creek history on the one hand and of Yuchi ethnography on the
other—are more and more blatantly in need of attention.

At a minimum, some future student of Yuchi or Muscogee (Creek)
history could tackle, in more systematic fashion, the problem of Creek
and European perceptions of the Yuchi through time. Accessible
sources obviously exist and the exercise would prove very helpful.
This venture would generate more important follow-up questions,
such as assessing continuity and change through time and grappling
with the motivations that might underlie these pronouncements.

Stepping back to survey bigger problems, the disdain found in primary and secondary sources makes clear that despite recent advances, we still do not quite know how to characterize the changing social landscape of the Native Southeast. Perhaps we are almost there,
but our new and more complex models of Creek country through
time still reduce the Yuchi to footnote status and presume their assimilation into what was, and is, an essentially Creek cultural, political, and economic system. Despite noting Creek cultural hetero-
geneity, the current tendency is still to treat the Yuchi as structurally
equivalent with Nuyaka, Coweta, or some other Creek *italwa* (tribal
town). I have previously attributed this to the lack of readily accessible historical data, but I am increasingly convinced that such views
are largely the residue of past conventional wisdoms that have not
yet been completely scrutinized through fresh research.[12] Even if the
contemporary Yuchi community was not doing everything possible
to proclaim its continued existence as a distinct people with a unique
language, a characteristic culture, and their own understanding of
both their past and their relationship to Creek people, how could
scholars, when presented with the chronicle of disdain conveyed by
Creek and European elites, go on writing, and not writing, of the

Yuchi in history, as we have been doing? The contributors to this volume make important contributions aimed at turning this tide.

The broader interests of anthropology and history are today centered, in part at least, on what we might broadly characterize as narratives of resistance. I can think of no surviving Native North American people who better epitomize successful resistance, or to phrase it more positively, successful persistence, than the Yuchi.[13] While each of this volume's contributors seeks to make a contribution to a provisional telling of Yuchi history before removal, all of us would welcome someone taking up this work in a fulltime way. Speaking in the most instrumental terms, the next new book on a topic in pre-removal Creek or Cherokee history will certainly find interested readers in a growing community of scholars and students concerned with the history of the Native South, but some talented researcher still has the opportunity to complete the first book-length contribution on Yuchi history.[14] The present volume is intended, in part, to help clear the way for such an undertaking. I am confident that each of its contributors would welcome the chance to assist scholars interested in contributing to such work. If, despite my reservations, such a researcher must begin with the assumption that the Yuchi of, say, Benjamin Hawkins's day were just another township in Creek country, so be it. One has, in Joshua Piker's fine book on Okfuskee, an up-to-date model for researching a town-centered social history.[15] I hope all the contributors to this volume can offer further resources for such a project. Best of all, a modest and diligent historian willing to undertake serious work on Yuchi history will gain engaged allies among the Yuchi people. Yuchi interest in historical research stems from many sources, from the genealogist's impulse to understand one's personal past better to the politician's need to understand how the Yuchi came to be so disempowered, even by the standards found in Indian country. Contact with the generous Yuchi community of today will certainly raise suspicions about how their ancestors have been portrayed.

What modest progress that has been made recently, with respect to Yuchi history, has largely taken the form of corrective notes and a broader dismantling of provisional hypotheses that had, in light of John Swanton's scholarly prominence, become accepted interpretations.[16] Because Verner Crane and Swanton published their debate on Yuchi-Westo affiliations, scholars, faced with uncertainty, have traditionally approached this linkage more cautiously. John T. Juricek productively examined the Westo problems in the early 1960s, and more recently Eric Bowne has been pursuing new Westo work allowing us to tackle other thorny problems of synonymy and social history.[17] Most influential and problematic among these is Swanton's linkage of the Yuchi with the people known in colonial-era sources as the Chisca.

This matter is especially embarrassing for me, as Amos Wright's *Historic Indian Towns in Alabama, 1540–1838* was not the only book published in 2003 that almost certainly erred in accepting Swanton's long-standing Chisca proposals. Despite the fears expressed in the endnote buried on its page 291, I proceeded in *Yuchi Ceremonial Life* as if this linkage were firm.[18] No sooner was the book fixed in type than John Worth provided a convincing analysis suggesting that this is not so. My only consolation comes in noting that a Bancroft Prize–winning author can commit the same error that I did. Like me, Alan Gallay reproduced almost the whole of Swanton's rickety Chisca-Yuchi analysis, although to his credit, he did so while laying the groundwork for a useful account of a crucial event in Yuchi history, the destruction of Chestowee town in 1714.[19] Over the decades, countless scholars of note have built complex narratives atop Swanton's Chisca-Yuchi proposal, thereby confusing the literature and associating the Yuchi with unpleasantness in which they likely had no hand.

In the *Southeast* volume of the *Handbook of North American Indians*, Worth offers an account of the Chisca that contains a summary of his position on this matter. Thirty-four years in the making, this long forsaken tome saw the light of day only in 2004. While the *Handbook* is now available for consultation, I think the present volume can be strengthened by reiterating Worth's Chisca findings here, especially as they relate to his chapter in this volume directly and, generally, to the subject of the volume as a whole. After sketching what is known of the Chisca (I preserve his parenthetical citations), he notes:

> Though some authors have equated the Chisca with both the Yuchi and the Westo (or Chichimeco) Indians (e.g. Swanton 1922:288–308; Hann 1988:78–79, 1996:238–40), [recent] ethnohistorical work suggests that all three groups were distinct (Worth 1995a:52, 54; 1998:208). The Yuchi were noted separately from the Chisca under the names Uchi and Huchi during the Juan Pardo expedition in 1567, both being part of an anti-Spanish plot hatched by allies of the paramount chief of Coosa in the Ridge and Valley district west of the Appalachian summit (Hudson 1990:223–24, 270). Furthermore both French and English sources report Yuchis still in the Tennessee River valley in the early eighteenth century, their last town there being destroyed by Cherokees in 1714 (Bauxar 1957:389–96, 433–34; McDowell 1955:24, 53–57), and it was only a little before that time that Yuchis first migrated into the Savannah River valley and among the Lower Creeks of western Georgia (Worth 2000:285; "Yuchi," this volume). The Westo Indians, who invaded Guale province in 1661, have now been demonstrated to be a band of immigrant Erie Indians who slaved for the Virginians after 1659 (Swanton 1922:305; Worth 1995a:15–18; B. G. Hoffman 1964; W. Greene 1998; Bowne 2000).[20]

The good news in all this is that having grappled with the Chisca, Worth is now in a position, as indicated by his contribution to this volume, to confront the data, both historical and archaeological, that might tell us something positive about the "Uchi" themselves during the early contact period.

The Earliest Yuchi History

To the extent that the complexities of pre-removal Yuchi history in time and space can be arrayed in linear fashion, this volume proceeds in a roughly chronological order, beginning with Mary S. Linn's work on the linguistic affiliation of Yuchi and its implications for social and cultural history. We can hope that historical linguistics and archaeology will offer new insights into the Yuchi story before contact and that historians and historical archaeologists will find ways to enrich our knowledge of the period since. In my experience, Yuchi people have a high level of interest in the possibilities of such new research. They would welcome the discovery of new sources and would listen to new interpretations with great interest. While Linn's contribution reaches back to consider the time before European colonization of the Southeast, the remaining contributors to this volume present findings related to the period from the contact era through the removal era, which in the case of the Florida Seminoles considered by Brent Weisman comes to a close at a later period than for some other southeastern Indian peoples.[21]

While Yuchi people have conveyed great interest in the possibility of academic histories of their people, they also possess stories that scholars should listen to if such work is to proceed in the most fruitful fashion. It is historically paradoxical, but culturally quite reasonable, that the history Yuchi narrators know best is the oldest Yuchi story, the history of their creation as a people. In concluding this introduction and beginning the volume's work in earnest, I wish to summarize these accounts briefly, and I conclude with some observations on their relevance to our purposes.

As Yuchi elders past and present have described it, in the time of creation, Tsoyaha, the child of the Sun and Moon, sprang from celestial blood to become the first Yuchi man. At the heavenly square ground, which we of this world see as the rainbow, he was taught the most basic tribal rituals—purification through scratching, fasting, and the consumption of redroot and snakeroot medicines. To cure his loneliness, his mother removed one of his ribs, from which his wife was fashioned. When they then established the Yuchi people in this world, he was instructed to pass on these rites—the rituals of the Green Corn Ceremony. Today these powerful, complex, beautiful ceremonies remain the central defining force of distinctly Yuchi life today. Later in ancestral time, additional aspects of their patrimony were revealed to the Yuchi. Oral history thus recounts

the revelation of Cedar and Tobacco as additional sacred medicines, the bestowal by the White Crane of the Feather Dance songs,
and the tragic but ultimately heroic and instructive origins of the
Lizard Dance. In dramatic form, the Green Corn Ceremony enacts
this ancient history and maintains it as a vital force in contemporary Yuchi life.[22]

It is beyond the scope of this volume to say more about the narratives that Yuchi historians and cosmologists continue to recount
and that the three modern Yuchi towns enact in ritual. For our purposes, it is enough to note that these histories not only provide a
warrant for Yuchi peoplehood—they also charter the possibility
for the contributors to undertake historical work seeking to disen-
tangle the Yuchi from the Creek and colonial narratives in which
they have become caught. Yuchi tradition acknowledges the quite
separate origin stories possessed by the Muskogean peoples, stories
not of a descent from the heavens but of an emergence from a pri-
mordial underworld.[23] There is no reason to presume that these different origin narratives are modern fabrications. At the very least,
they reflect what eighteenth-century sources knew, that the Yuchi
and Creek are quite different peoples. In the present I would similarly note what Lester Robbins first observed in his early 1970s
Creek fieldwork. No so-called Lower Creek town today preserves
its Green Corn Ceremony, while their neighbors the Yuchi remain
devoted to the ceremonies of their own towns.[24] According to Yuchi
customary belief, it is a good thing for non-Yuchis that they do, as
the Sun looks down each day to see if his or her children remain in
this world. Similarly, each summer the Sun observes the Yuchi Green
Corn Ceremonies. When the Yuchi are no longer here, or when they
no longer perform the ceremonies with which they were entrusted,
the end time will come and everyone and everything will perish.[25]

Just as modern Yuchis do not deny the relevance of their Creek
neighbors and kinspeople to their own lives, I am not proposing that
we ignore the place of the Yuchis in Creek history or vice versa. As
an ethnographer, rather than a historian, I am only suggesting that
the ongoing persistence of cultural difference and social separation,

coupled with patterns of social differentiation rather than straight-forward incorporation, suggest to me that we can do better in accounting for the Yuchi past before, during, and after the time of their encompassment by their more numerous and at times domineering neighbors. So far the story has been a default one in which progressive assimilation into an ever more homogeneous Creek society has been presumed. While the archaeological record has pointed to commonalities in material life, Yuchi tradition and post-removal ethnography suggest that there may be other stories to tell. This book is a step toward such an investigation.

Acknowledgments

I wish to record my deep appreciation to the officers of the Euchee (Yuchi) Tribe of Indians, including the Yuchi town chiefs, for their support of this and related projects. Thanks are due as well to the staff of the University of Nebraska Press for its constant support of this book. I am particularly appreciative of the volume's authors for their valuable contributions. They, along with the engaged reviewers selected by the press, and the wider circle of "friends of Yuchi history"—including Pamela Wallace, John T. Juricek, Robbie Ethridge, David Chang, Kathryn E. Holland Braund, and Stephen Martin—have begun a collective project of historical investigation that I hope will flourish in the years ahead. Crucial in all my work is the support of my wife, Amy Jackson.

Notes

1. A summary of Yuchi history and ethnography is provided in Jason Baird Jackson, "Yuchi," in *Handbook of North American Indians*, vol. 14: *Southeast*, ed. Raymond D. Fogelson (Washington DC: Smithsonian Institution, 2004), 415–28.

2. Readers of this introduction and this volume will find a number of characterizations of the regional frames within which Yuchi culture and history can be understood. Arising out of the field of history, there is a contemporary argument that stresses the gains that come with referring to the region most at issue in this book as "the South." Characterizing the Yuchi or the Yamasee or the Chickasaw as Native peoples of the South thereby aligns discussions of

southern Indian history with broader studies of the American South, a powerful regional construct in the intellectual and cultural history (and historiography) of the United States. This is particularly important because Native societies have been systematically written out of a southern history that is too frequently misframed in biracial (black and white) terms. Thus studies of southern Indian history stand to contribute to, and improve, general historical knowledge of the region as a place that is infinitely more complex than conventional wisdom and conventional historical narratives have described.

This view—quite reasonable in its own terms—suggests that the anthropological cultural area designation "Southeast," which has most often framed discussions of the region's Native peoples, unhelpfully sets them outside the line of southern history and of thinking about the region generally. The argument suggests abandoning the term *Southeast* in lieu of *South*. I serve on the editorial board of the journal *Native South*, the venue in which the case for southern Indian studies has been sustained most clearly, and I am sympathetic to the motivations that prompt this effort. As long as the South is itself treated as a problematic and unstable category that has frequently been essentialized, then I support the cause of working vigorously to situate the story of the region's Native societies within a broader history of the South.

Beyond the inclusion argument though, I am concerned with the ways that cultural areas have been characterized in recent discussions focused on the Indigenous peoples of eastern North America. Building on the account of the southeastern culture area that I authored for the introduction to the *Southeast* volume of the *Handbook of North American Indians* (co-authored with Raymond D. Fogelson, Washington DC, 2004), I have drafted an essay—still in manuscript—that explores these issues further. It is beyond the scope of this note to address these issues here. For purposes of this volume it is noted that all the authors whose work is gathered here are, to various degrees, aware of the "South or Southeast" question. Many also pursue their work within a framework attentive to the broader Eastern Woodlands and Atlantic world contexts. While a diversity of regional framings are found in this book, all of the authors share a common concern with situating Yuchi history in wider contexts that include regional patterns and interethnic relations.

3. Key collections reconsidering the transformation of native societies in eastern North American during the colonial period include Marvin Smith, Robbie Franklyn Ethridge, and Charles H. Hudson, eds., *The Transformation of the Southeastern Indians, 1540–1760* (Jackson MS: University Press of Mississippi, 2002); Thomas J. Pluckhahn and Robbie Franklyn Ethridge, eds., *Light on the Path: The Anthropology and History of the Southeastern Indians* (Tuscaloosa: University of Alabama Press, 2006); Charles M. Hudson

and Carmen Chaves Tesser, eds., *The Forgotten Centuries: Indians and Europeans in the American South, 1521–1704* (Athens: University of Georgia Press, 1994); and Gregory Waselkov, Peter H. Wood, and M. Thomas Hatley, eds., *Powhatan's Mantle: Indians in the Colonial Southeast*, rev. and expanded ed. (Lincoln: University of Nebraska Press, 2006). Contributions to these volumes, along with much other recent ethnohistorical work, explore confederation, disease-prompted demographic collapse, slavery, assimilation, missionization, and other modalities of social transformation experienced in the region during the colonial period. For the concept of ethnogenesis, see William C. Sturtevant, "Creek into Seminole," in *North American Indians in Historical Perspective*, ed. Eleanor Burke Leacock and Nancy Oestreich Lurie (New York: Random House, 1971), 92–128; and Jonathan D. Hill, ed. *History, Power, and Identity: Ethnogenesis in the Americas*, 1492–1992 (Iowa City: University of Iowa Press, 1996). The historical anthropology of cultural *persistence*, a framework that seems particularly suitable to the story of the Yuchi, is found in the work of Edward Spicer. See: Edward H. Spicer, "Persistent Cultural Systems," *Science* n.s. 174 (1971): 795–800, and Edward H. Spicer and Rosamond B. Spicer, "The Nations of a State," *boundary 2* 19 (1992): 26–48. Many contributors to this volume attend to the ways that the brutal trade in Native slaves transformed the colonial South and the Indigenous peoples who called it or came to call it home. A touchstone work on this question is Robbie Ethridge and Sheri M. Shuck-Hall, eds. *Mapping the Mississippian Shatter Zone: The Colonial Indian Slave Trade and Regional Instability in the American South* (Lincoln: University of Nebraska Press, 2009). Continuity and change in practices of enslavement in southern Indian country are the focus of a recent study by Christina Snyder, *Slavery in Indian Country: The Changing Face of Captivity in Early America* (Cambridge MA: Harvard University Press, 2010).

4. Charles Jones, *Historical Sketch of Tomo-chi-chi, Mico of the Yamacraws* (Albany NY: J. Munsell, 1868), 47.

5. One of the great merits of ethnohistory as a conceptual meeting ground linking several disciplines is that it is not understood by practitioners in monolithic terms. Debating the nature of the project is one tradition that energizes the field, and not all contributors to this volume understand the field in the same way. My own orientations have been shaped by my teachers, including two past presidents of the American Society for Ethnohistory (ASE), Raymond D. Fogelson and Raymond J. DeMallie. Their approach to the field is illustrated in their respective presidential addresses: Raymond D. Fogelson, "The Ethnohistory of Events and Non-Events," *Ethnohistory* 36 (1989): 133–47, and

Raymond J. DeMallie, "'These Have No Ears': Narrative and the Ethnohistorical Method," *Ethnohistory* 40 (1993): 515–38. Many of the chapters gathered in this volume were initially presented in a panel focused on Yuchi history held at an ASE meeting in Chicago on 28 October 2004.

6. This the particular aim of several of my works, including Jason Baird Jackson, *Yuchi Ceremonial Life: Performance, Meaning, and Tradition in a Contemporary American Indian Community* (Lincoln: University of Nebraska Press, 2003); Jason Baird Jackson and Victoria Lindsay Levine, "Singing for Garfish: Music and Woodland Communities in Eastern Oklahoma," *Ethnomusicology* 46 (2002): 284–306; Jason Baird Jackson, "East Meets West: On Stomp Dance and Powwow Worlds in Oklahoma," in *Powwow*, ed. Clyde Ellis, Luke Eric Lassiter, and Gary H. Dunham (Lincoln: University of Nebraska Press, 2005); Gregory A. Waselkov (with Jason Baird Jackson), "Exchange and Interaction since 1500," in *Handbook of North American Indians*, vol. 14: *Southeast*, ed. Raymond D. Fogelson (Washington DC: Smithsonian Institution, 2004), 694–96.

7. As I hope my remarks suggest, my highlighting this colonial characterization of the Yuchi as a nation is not meant to suggest that I understand the category of nation as unchanging or unproblematic. In the fields of cultural anthropology and Native American and Indigenous studies, much important work is being directed at carefully disentangling conceptions of nation vis-à-vis Native American and European societies and Native and European social thought. Enriched and critical understandings of the associated notion of sovereignty are central to this work. While present-day Yuchis still speak more often of "Yuchi people," "Yuchi community," and "Yuchi tribe," their own ongoing nation-building project (shaped in part by broader trends in Indian country and by the history being evoked here) is reflected in the fact that contemporary Yuchi people also increasingly speak of the "Yuchi nation." For treatments of nation and sovereignty in the Native South, see Circe Sturm, *Blood Politics: Race, Culture, and Identity in the Cherokee Nation of Oklahoma* (Berkeley: University of California Press, 2002); Jessica Cattelino, *High Stakes: Florida Seminole Gaming and Sovereignty* (Durham NC: Duke University Press, 2008); Valerie Lambert, *Choctaw Nation: A Story of American Indian Resurgence* (Lincoln: University of Nebraska Press, 2009).

8. Although I wish he had been more circumspect in publishing it in the form that he did, Amos Wright has assisted students of Yuchi history in publishing a kind of greatest hits compilation of historical criticisms of the Yuchi. Understanding anti-Yuchi discourse in the colonial, early American, and more recent periods remains a historical project worthy of sustained work. A

scholar taking up this project can begin with the sources gathered by Wright in his *Historic Indian Towns in Alabama, 1540–1838* (Tuscaloosa: University of Alabama Press, 2003), 171. He writes:

> The Uchee had a terrible reputation, probably deserved, based on some of the following comments. George Stiggins, a Natchez Indian, described them around 1831 as being "more indolent, more thievish, more dissipated, and depraved in their morals" than any other tribe. They were settled on both Big and Little Uchee Creeks and were related to the Shawnee. "They were the most savage in the Creek nation, cling closely to their tongue and culture, not mixing with others. They only marry among their own."

For Stiggins's Yuchi comments, of which Wright is citing just a portion, see George Stiggins, *Creek Indian History: A Historical Narrative of the Genealogy, Traditions, and Downfall of the Ispocoga or Creek Indian Tribe of Indians* (Birmingham AL: Birmingham Public Library Press, 1989), 31–33. Wright goes on to provide additional critical commentary on the Yuchi from Creek elites Alexander McGillivray (in 1787) and Alexander Cornells (in 1831) as well as from clergymen Bolzius (in 1734) and John Wesley (in 1737) and Indian agent Benjamin Hawkins (in 1897).

This may be my only opportunity to record the understandably ironic feelings evoked among Yuchi Methodists—many of whom have been especially interested in the study of early Yuchi history—when they encounter the founder of their faith tradition speaking of their ancestors as people whom he believed to be "indeed hated by most and despis'd by all the nations, as well for their cowardice, and for out-lying all the Indians upon the continent." As Christians, the Yuchi Methodists are understanding people who practice a doctrine of forgiveness, but they also preach about the virtues of honest and modest speech. Wesley's tone suggests to me one reason why his missionary work among the Indians of Georgia ended in failure.

Wright's sources are John Walton Caughey, *McGillivray of the Creeks* (Norman: University of Oklahoma Press, 1938), 158; C. L. Grant, *Letters, Journals and Writings of Benjamin Hawkins*, vol. 2 (Savannah GA: Beehive Press, 1980), 518, 631; Trevor R. Reese, *Our First Visit to America: Early Reports from the Colony of Georgia, 1732–1740* (Savannah GA: Beehive Press, 1974), 60. For an additional historical account emphasizing thievery as a distinctly Yuchi quality, see Jones, *Historical Sketch of Tomo-chi-chi*, 45. The quotation from John Wesley derives from volume 3 of *The Works of the Reverend John Wesley* (New York: J. Emory and B. Waugh for the Methodist Episcopal

Church, 1831), 50. Wright's quotation of Wesley does not quite match that given in this source.

9. William Bartram, *William Bartram on the Southeastern Indians*, ed. Gregory A. Waselkov and Kathryn E. Holland Braund (Lincoln: University of Nebraska Press, 1995), 90. Similarly, if we consult Thomas Foster's edition of Hawkins's writings, we learn that his views of the Yuchi were more complex than the brief quotation excerpted by Wright (see note 7) would suggest. Benjamin Hawkins, *The Collected Works of Benjamin Hawkins, 1796–1810*, ed. H. Thomas Foster (Tuscaloosa: University of Alabama Press, 2003).

10. I did bring my ethnographic experiences and ethnological studies to bear on a historical inquiry in Jason Baird Jackson, "A Yuchi War Dance in 1736," *European Review of Native American Studies* 16 (2002): 27–33.

11. For a historical consideration of Yuchi identity and political action, vis-à-vis Muscogee (Creek) understandings of Yuchi subordination during in the twentieth century, see Pamela Wallace, "Yuchi Social History since World War II: Political Symbolism in Ethnic Identity," PhD diss., University of Oklahoma, 1998, and Pamela S. Wallace, "Indian Claims Commission: Political Complexity and Contrasting Concepts of Identity," *Ethnohistory* 49 (2002): 743–67.

12. Jackson, "A Yuchi War Dance in 1736," 27; Jason Baird Jackson, "Introduction," in *Ethnology of the Yuchi Indians* by Frank G. Speck (Lincoln: University of Nebraska Press, 2004), v–xvi.

13. The dangers common to scholarly treatments of resistance are taken up in Michael F. Brown, "On Resisting Resistance," *American Anthropologist* 98 (1996): 729–35. For persistence see Spicer, "Persistent Cultural Systems"; Spicer and Spicer, "The Nations of a State"; and George Pierre Castile and Gilbert Kushner, eds., *Persistent Peoples: Cultural Enclaves in Perspective* (Tucson: University of Arizona Press, 1981).

14. For a discussion of the Yuchi literature and the dearth of works relative to those dealing with the Creek and other groups, see especially Jackson, "Introduction," vi.

15. Joshua Piker, *Okfuskee: A Creek Indian Town in Colonial America* (Cambridge MA: Harvard University Press, 2004). For an additional town-level study set in the territory known as the Creek Nation, see Karl Langston Davis, "'Much of the Indian Appears': Adaptation and Persistence in a Creek Community, 1783–1854," PhD diss., University of North Carolina, Chapel Hill, 2003.

16. Jackson, "A Yuchi War Dance in 1736," 27–32; John T. Juricek, "First Georgia Reports of the Yuchis, 1733," *Yuchi History Notes* 7 (2004), http://jasonbairdjackson.com/2010/12/25/first-georgia-reports-of-yuchis-1733/, accessed December 24, 2010.

17. The key sources in the Crane-Swanton debate are Verner W. Crane, "An Historical Note on the Westo Indians," *American Anthropologist* 2 (1918): 331–37; Verner W. Crane, "Westo and Chisca," *American Anthropologist* 21 (1919): 463–65; John R. Swanton, "Westo," in *Handbook of American Indians*, Bureau of American Ethnology Bulletin 30, part 2, ed. Frederick Webb Hodge (Washington DC: Government Printing Office, 1910), 936; John R. Swanton, "Identity of the Westo Indians," *American Anthropologist* 21 (1919): 213–16; and John R. Swanton, *Early History of the Creek Indians and their Neighbors*, Bureau of American Ethnology Bulletin 73 (Washington DC: Government Printing Office, 1922). The later sources are John Juricek, "The Westo Indians," *Ethnohistory* 11 (1964): 134–73; Eric E. Bowne, "The Rise and Fall of the Westo Indians: An Evaluation of the Documentary Evidence," *Early Georgia* 28 (2000): 56–78; and Eric E. Bowne, *The Westo Indians: Slave Traders of the Early Colonial South* (Tuscaloosa: University of Alabama Press, 2005).

18. Wright, *Historic Indian Towns in Alabama*, 171. Jackson, *Yuchi Ceremonial Life*, 19–27, 291.

19. Alan Gallay, *The Indian Slave Trade: The Rise of the English Empire in the American South, 1670–1717* (New Haven CT: Yale University Press, 2002), 319. For a further discussion of the Chestowee incident, see Brett Riggs's contribution to this volume.

20. John Worth, "Chisca," in *Handbook of North American Indians*, vol. 14: *Southeast*, ed. Raymond D. Fogelson (Washington DC: Smithsonian Institution, 2004), 176–77; the sources that Worth cites in his Chisca essay are given here in the order in which he cites them: Swanton, *Early History of the Creek Indians and their Neighbors*, 288–308; John H. Hann, "Florida's Terra Incognita: West Florida's Natives in the Sixteenth and Seventeenth Century" *Florida Anthropologist* 41 (1988): 61–107; John H. Hann, *A History of the Timucua Indians and Missions* (Gainesville: University Press of Florida, 1996), 238–40; John E. Worth, *The Struggle for the Georgia Coast: An Eighteenth-Century Spanish Retrospective on Guale and Mocama*, Anthropological Papers of the American Museum of Natural History, no. 75 (New York, 1995), 15, 18, 52, 54; John E. Worth, *The Timucuan Chiefdoms of Spanish Florida*, 2 vols., vol. I: *Assimilation*, vol. II: *Resistance and Destruction* (Gainesville: University Press of Florida, 1998), 208; Charles Hudson, *The Juan Pardo Expeditions: Explorations of the Carolinas and Tennessee, 1566–1568* (Washington DC: Smithsonian Institution Press, 1990), 223–24, 270; J. Joseph Bauxar, "Yuchi Ethnoarchaeology, Part I: Some Yuchi Identifications Reconsidered." *Ethnohistory* 4 (1957): 279–301; J. Joseph Bauxar, Yuchi Ethnoarchaeology, Part II: The Yuchi of Tennessee, Part III: The Mouse Creek Focus, Part IV: Correlation

of Ethnohistorical and Archaeological Data, Part V: Conclusions" *Ethnohistory* 4 (1957): 369–464; William L. McDowell Jr., ed., *Journals of the Commissioners of Indian Trade, September 20, 1710–August 29, 1718*, The Colonial Records of South Carolina, series 2, vol. 1 (Columbia: South Carolina Archives Department, 1955), 24, 53–57; John E. Worth, "The Lower Creeks: Origins and Early History," in *Indians of the Greater Southeast: Historical Archaeology and Ethnohistory*, ed. Bonnie G. McEwan (Gainesville: University Press of Florida, 2000), 267–98; Jackson, "Yuchi," 415–28; Bernard G. Hoffman, *Observations on Certain Ancient Tribes of the Northern Appalachian Province*, Bureau of American Ethnology Bulletin 191 (Washington DC: Government Printing Office, 1964); William Greene, "The Erie/Westo Connection: Possible Evidence of Long Distance Migration in the Eastern Woodlands during the 16th and 17th Centuries," paper presented at the Southeastern Archaeological Conference, Greenville SC, 1998; Bowne, *The Westo*.

21. Other organizational schemes for this volume could have been devised and a different range of contributions could have been assembled. The theory motivating the choices reflected here can be described overtly. The volume reflects a desire to proceed in multidisciplinary fashion, with contributions from the fields of historical linguistics, history, historical anthropology, and archaeology. It also works from the assumption that in addition to regarding it for different temporal periods, Yuchi history is also effectively viewed (given the provisional state of its study) from the vantage point of the better known Native peoples with whom the Yuchi have had sustained contact. As is reflected in this volume, these are the Muscogee (Creek), Shawnee, Seminole, and Cherokee. As an ethnographer I can note that these four groups are also the Native peoples with whom the present-day Yuchi community maintains the closest relationships. It is important to stress that with the exception of the Yuchi story in the context of the Seminole Wars and associated Seminole removals, this volume does not take up the Yuchi story during the Removal era, including the time of the Creek Civil War that preceded it. Sources for the writing of such a history are available, and Yuchi removal is the crucial link connecting the colonial and early American period to post-removal history in Indian Territory and is thus a particularly pressing matter for historical investigation.

22. Jackson, *Yuchi Ceremonial Life, passim*, especially 206–40; Speck, *Ethnology of the Yuchi Indians*, 102–31; Albert Gatschet, "Some Mythic Stories of the Yuchi Indians," *American Anthropologist* 6 (1893): 279–82; Günter Wagner, *Yuchi Tales* (New York: G. E. Stechert and Company, 1931).

23. See Warren, this volume, and Greg Urban and Jason Baird Jackson, "Mythology and Folklore," in *Handbook of North American Indians*, vol.

14: *Southeast*, ed. Raymond D. Fogelson (Washington DC: Smithsonian Institution, 2004), 707–19.

24. Lester Eugene Robbins, *The Persistence of Traditional Religious Practices among Creek Indians*, PhD diss., Southern Methodist University, 1976, 5. Many Upper Creek towns continue, like the Yuchi, to maintain the institution of tribal town chieftainship and the practice of an annual ceremonial cycle in which the Green Corn Ceremony is the most important event. While I have written in this introduction of anti-Yuchi hostility expressed by Creek leaders, I also want to stress that the Yuchi have, in Oklahoma, long maintained close ties with numerous tradition-minded Creek towns, especially among the Upper Creek towns preserving Green Corn Ceremonialism. Visiting patterns between the Yuchi and these towns are discussed in Jackson, *Yuchi Ceremonial Life, passim*. There are also some contemporary Creek political leaders sympathetic to Yuchi concerns.

25. The link between the world's fate and Yuchi ritual obligations is discussed in various ethnographic sources and is articulated by Yuchi ceremonialists today. For an instance, see Speck, *Ethnology of the Yuchi Indians*, 107. As reflected by my pronoun usage here, there is some disagreement across time and individual narrators as to the gender of the Sun in Yuchi cosmology. Instability in the understood gender of the Creator is a theme in Shawnee ethnography as well. This matter is explored in the work of Carl F. Voegelin and Erminie Wheeler Voegelin, including their "The Shawnee Female Deity in Historical Perspective," *American Anthropologist* 46 (1944): 370–75. Voegelin and Voegelin specifically discuss the relationship between Shawnee beliefs and those of the Yuchi, Iroquois, and Christian Europeans with whom the Shawnee have been in sustained contact.

1. Deep Time and Genetic Relationships
Yuchi Linguistic History Revisited

~

Comparative linguistics is concerned with establishing groups of languages that share a genetic affiliation. Except in extreme cases where the speakers of one language have shifted to an unrelated language, such as the shift to English experienced by many indigenous communities today, establishing the linguistic genetic affiliation entails confirming biological genetic relatedness among groups of people and thus a common, inherited history. Historical and comparative linguistics and the reconstruction of ancestral forms of languages give us information about what prehistoric people were doing, where they had been, with whom they were acquainted, and what the nature of this contact was. As Terrence Kaufman, a specialist in Mesoamerican linguistics, states: "While archeology, genetics and comparative ethnology will help flesh out and provide some shading in the picture of pre-Columbian [people], it is comparative linguistic study, combined with some of the results of cross-cultural study, that will supply the bones, sinew, muscles and mind of our reconstructed model of early folk and their ways."[1] Understanding the linguistic history of Yuchi will give us perhaps the greatest understanding of the most remote history of the Yuchi people.

The Yuchi language is considered a language isolate. This does not mean that the language was never related to any other language or language family. When a language is an isolate, two causes probably exist. First, the related languages may have suffered catastrophic loss through the death of entire populations of speakers. Second, speakers of the related languages may have shifted to other languages. This shift can be forced and can happen relatively quickly, often through slavery, or by subtle choices due to prestige of other languages and cultures. Most likely, combinations of these causes occurred over time.[2] A language isolate means that comparative-historical methodology cannot firmly establish a genetic relationship with any known language or language family at this time. It means that linguists must search for relationships that are deeper and more remote in time and that these have not yet been established for Yuchi.

Edward Sapir speculated that Yuchi may be a distant relative to the Siouan language family.[3] While the faults and merits of this speculation are still debated today, looking at the time depth of the Siouan-Catawban family can give us an idea of how far back in time linguists must look to establish any genetic relationship with Yuchi. Proto-Siouan is estimated to be 3,000 to 4,000 years old. In other words, the core Siouan languages (Mandan, Lakota, Osage, and Tutelo, to name a few) diverged about 1,000 BCE. The Catawban branch, made up solely of Catawba, probably diverged 1,000 years earlier.[4] Hence around 5,000 years ago the speakers all of these modern languages were one people, speaking what is referred to as a 'proto-language,' or Proto-Siouan-Catawban. If Yuchi were related to Proto-Siouan-Catawban, then the relationship must predate the Catawban split by a time depth great enough to obscure its obvious relationship to Proto-Siouan-Catawban. Thus we are looking at a time depth of at least 6,000 years, or 4,000 BCE, for any potential relationship, whether it turns out to be with Proto-Siouan-Catawban or another language family. This is approximately the same time depth of the well-documented Proto-Indo-European language family. The problem, then, is finding and proving a relationship at this time depth.

In this essay I will review the literature surrounding the genetic classification of the Yuchi language. The goal is not to critique the methodology or its practitioners past or present but to reveal some of the problems with Yuchi data in the application of the comparative method for distant genetic relationships.[5] This chapter does not have an answer to the ultimate question of Yuchi linguistic history; that is, to which other language or languages Yuchi is related. It does, however, clarify what we know about Yuchi linguistic history, what we can hope to know, and possible paths for continued research in this area.

The Yuchi Language

Following is a brief description of the Yuchi language, with particular focus on those elements that have been, or may continue to be, important in the search for genetic relationships.[6]

The languages of the Americas, on the whole, pattern typologically in different ways from languages in other areas of the world. Nearly all the information in a sentence is carried on the verb. Languages that mark information primarily on the verb are known typologically as head-marking languages.[7] Many are also considered polysynthetic, meaning that the rich verbal morphology allows the nouns to be dropped from the sentence, and when they do occur, there is much freer word order. Many of the languages also exhibit noun incorporation, a process whereby the direct object of a sentence can be compounded into the verb root to create words for common actions and to help regulate the flow of information.[8]

The Yuchi language broadly follows these typological patterns. Information that can be found as independent words in many languages, such as tense, aspect, the reflexive, and location, is attached to the verb. The verb also has obligatory pronominal information marked on it. In the case of Yuchi the pronouns are prefixes attached to the verb. These pronominal prefixes carry information about person, number, and the grammatical role of the nouns. Because pronominal information is on the verb, nouns may be freely dropped in discourse after first reference or whenever the reference is understood. A few lines from the traditional tale "The First Woman to Leave a Lazy Husband" illustrates the use of the attached pronoun and the ability to drop independent nouns when they are clear.[9]

1) koɫæne se-k'ą   nąte   ša   tʰæbi=he   sio-ɫa=he
   food   3SG.EF.AGT-make and   field into-LOC   3SG.EF.AGT-go=FREQ

   'She [Yuchi woman] made dinner, and when she went to the field'

(2) se-k'ątawenǫ   sio-'wete
    3SG.EF.AGT-spouse=DEF.NE   3SG.EF.AGT:APP-talk

    'to call her spouse [a pigeon]'

(3) 'yætakʰo ta s'æ=yo-čʰi   'ya-yo-kwa   se-ɫæ
    dead.tree on down=3SG.NE.AGT:APP-sit across=3SG.NE.AGT:APP-say 3SG.EF.AGT-find

    'she found him sitting on a tree stump singing.'

(4) sio-wæ   nę=k'ala   yo-k'ą   tę
    3SG.EF.AGT:APP-leave   NEG=thing   3SG.NE.AGT-work   ABLE.EMPH

    'She left him because he couldn't do any work.'

When independent nouns are given, normal word order in Yuchi is subject-object-verb (SOV).

The American Southeast patterns as a linguistic area. By the time of European contact, the peoples of the Southeast had been in contact with one another for thousands of years and had shared not only cultural and societal patterns but words, grammar, and semantic patterns as well. Yuchi shares some areal traits with its neighbors. Yuchi patterns with the Southeast in having retroflex sibilants, the pronunciation of 's' with the tip of the tongue pointing slightly back.[10] The demonstrative pronouns, such as 'this' and 'that,' precede the noun. This is an unexpected word order for an SOV language, yet all of the languages of the Southeast have it with the exception of Choctaw-Chickasaw and Catawba. The Yuchi language also shares many of the southeastern (and Mesoamerican) loan translations, such as 'house-mouth' for 'door' and 'skin of tree' for 'bark,' and loan borrowings, such 'peach' derived from 'plum' and 'pig' derived from 'possum.'

Yet despite its shared typological and borrowed patterns, Yuchi is a unique language. The sound system of Yuchi stands out in the Southeast, with a larger inventory of distinctive sounds (phonemes) than are found in the languages of their Muskogean and Shawnee

(Algonquian) neighbors. Yuchi has thirty-three distinctive consonants (C). Each stop ('p,' 't,' and 'k') and affricate ('ch' and 'ts') has a three-way distinction: a plain pronunciation, aspirated (with a puff of air), and glottalized. All fricatives (such as 'f' and 's') and resonants (such as 'w,' 'y,' and 'n') also have a plain and glottalized pronunciation. Yuchi has twelve vowels (V), including a set of nasal vowels. Unlike Shawnee and Southeastern Siouan languages, vowel length is not distinctive, although vowels can be lengthened through a process of deleting a syllable when words are shortened.

Syllables are simple in Yuchi. Syllables can have a cluster of only two consonants for their onset, and syllables are open, meaning they do not end with a consonant. Thus, the basic syllable is (C)CV.[11] The simplest words in Yuchi, called roots, are mostly made of one syllable. Thus Yuchi roots are small in form, and many noun and verb roots are the same. A sample of Yuchi roots is given below.

(5)
	'e	'lie down'
	čwę	'rub up against'
	ła	'arrow, bullet'
	p'a	'look at'
	k'o	'throat, swallow'
	tę	'cedar'
	şpa	'blackberry, be spread out'
	šo	'body, waist, be soft'
	s'æ	'land, earth, dirt'
	wą	'give'

While the set of noun and verb roots is closed and relatively small, many words are made from compounding roots. Noun compounding is profuse and often complex and continues to augment the Yuchi vocabulary.

Yuchi has a noun class system. Indefinite nouns are unmarked, but in order to make a noun definite ('the'), a noun class marker must be used. The noun class system is based on animacy. In Yuchi, animate nouns are capable of initiating motion; inanimate nouns cannot. Inanimate nouns are further categorized by position and shape: sitting (roundish or no definite shape), standing (long, horizontal), lying (long, vertical). Unlike other languages that are sensitive to position and shape, Yuchi has not extended the categories to include scattered or flexible objects. Animate nouns are rather famously divided into Yuchi people and all other animate beings. However, this category is likely a very new meaning shift from an honorific marking for non–family members that, by the late nineteenth century, began being used for referring to 'half-breed' Yuchi.[12] Yuchi people are then divided by male and female. An honorific system based on age and familial relationship, the forms of which change depending on whether the speaker is a male or female, has created a plethora of Yuchi class markers.

Nearly all the information in the sentence is carried by morphemes (meaningful parts) attached to the verb. In addition to the verb stem, the verb has four prefix slots, two proclitics (loosely attached morphemes), and one suffix. These morphemes are in strict order that may not change. The Yuchi verb template is shown in table 1.

TABLE 1. Yuchi verb template

Negative Proclitic	Inanimate Theme or Locative Proclitic	3rd Actor or Patient Prefix	1st & 2nd **Patient** Prefix	1st & 2nd **Actor** Prefix	Valence Prefix	**Verb Stem**	Aspect Suffix

Starting with the verb stem, there can be remnants of noun incorporation in some verbs, but incorporation is not productive today. These verb stems appear like compounds. A handful of verb roots, mainly locative and existential, have completely different forms (suppletive) in the singular and plural, and fewer still have a dual pronominal form. Some verb roots may be reduplicated to show consecutive and distributed actions. A set of irregular verb roots shows historical fusion with pronominal prefixes.

Moving to the left of the stem, the first slot is for morphemes that regulate the number of participants in the sentence. The valence slot may contain a comitative 'with someone,' a reciprocal 'with/to each other,' reflexive 'to oneself,' or a general applicative that adds one participant to an event.

Moving farther left of the stem, the next three slots are reserved for pronominal information about who is doing or undergoing the action. The prefixes distinguish person (including inclusive and exclusive), number (singular and plural), and gender (the animate/inanimate system already described in the noun). The pronominal prefixes also mark the role of the noun phrases. Yuchi is an active-stative language. This means there are two sets of pronominal prefixes. One set, the agent set, marks participants that are the subject instigators or doers of events and activities.

(6)   tsene-weno̧   we-ti-'nȩ
       dog-DEF.NE   3SG.NE.PAT-1SG.AGT-see
       '*I* saw the dog.'

(7)   *Tišti.*   '*I* dance.'

The patient set marks the semantic patient, the participant that is affected by the action or state. This set include the subject of stative verbs and the objects of event.

(8)   we-*tse*-wa
       3SG.NE.AGT-1SG.PAT-bite
       'He bit *me*.'

(9)   *Tzeyu.*   '*I* am sick.'

The agency of intransitive subjects cannot change depending on the degree of control or performance of the core participant, as it does in agent-patient grammatical relations, but is based on the inherent aspect class—state or non-state—of the verb. The agent and patient pronominal prefixes are also found on nouns to indicate possession. Yuchi, along with Cherokee, Catawba, and Biloxi, use the actor pronominal prefixes to indicate inalienable possession, or those things that are inherently possessed, such as body parts and familial terms. Most other languages that make this distinction use the patient marking for inalienable.

Yet a third 'set' a pronominal prefixes exists as well. Günter Wagner and W. Lewis Ballard analyze these as a set to mark indirect objects.[13] However, this approach leaves a unacceptable number of direct objects using the supposed indirect object forms. Nicklas analyzes these forms as having been fused with a historical marker of the beneficiary, a participant who benefits from the action of the verb.[14] Following this lead, I reanalyzed these forms as the actor set historically fused with an applicative, a marker that adds one participant, but not necessarily always the beneficiary, to the event. In order to interact with the pronominal prefixes and create the phonological fusion seen today, placement of this morpheme would have been in the same slot that contains other valence prefixes. These can be seen in the preceding examples (2) and (4). The verb *'wede* 'talk' would normally take the agent prefix *se-* 'she,' but the use of the agent plus applicative *sio-* 'she' indicates the more transitive 'call someone.' Similarly, the verb *wæ* 'leave' is generally intransitive, but with *sio-* the verb can be read as 'leave someone.'[15]

The verb stem also has a small number of aspect suffixes marking repetitive actions, habitual actions, and immediate completion of actions. One of these, the frequentative, can be seen in example (1).

Following the verb are modal and position auxiliaries and a variety of mood, tense, and aspect particles. These particles may be arranged in a variety of orders to create subtle nuances in meaning and effect. An example of the ability modal can be seen in example (4) and the stacking of the probability and ability modals in (10).

(10)	ko-tsę	hala	yǫ-čʰyą	læti'ęte	tę
	3SG.IMP.AGT-hair	all	2SG.PAT:APP-hard	PROB	ABLE
	'They might pull all one's hair out.'				

Historically, Yuchi marked subordinate clauses by using different forms for the past progressive tense, negation, and the particle *-čʰi* in subordinate positions. In example (3) the embedded clause 'he was singing' is unmarked. An example of marked subordination follows; the subordinate forms are italicized.

(11)	wahe-'ę	hi-ne-'yu'ǫda	hæ=sio-ła	šę=čʰi
	why-VB	3SG.INAN.PAT-2SG.AGT-know	NEG.SUB-3SG.EF.AGT-go	PAST.SUB=SUB
	'How do you know *that she didn't go*?'			

Establishing Distant Genetic Relationships

In the first step in determining linguistic families, comparative linguists establish cognates, or shared inherited vocabulary, between two or more potentially related languages. To do this they compare basic vocabulary, such as environmental terms, familiar relationships, body parts, and bodily actions and activities that all humans do. These words must exhibit plausible connection in both sound and meaning. Then, importantly, linguists compare sound segments from these words to establish sound correspondences or sounds changes between languages that follow regular phonological rules. If these correspondences cannot be made, the words cannot be firmly established to be inherited from a common ancestor. Whole words and grammar are also compared to determine shared morphological patterns. Each step requires meticulous linguistic work, broad knowledge of surrounding language families, and in-depth knowledge of the individual language.[16]

Comparative methodology works very well in time depths of 2,000 to 3,000 years ago but begins to struggle in more distant or remote relationships. In addition to establishing sound correspondences, one must rule out that the similarities in potential cognates are due to circumstances other than inheritance. These include borrowings, sound symbolism, onomatopoeic forms, and chance similarities. In establishing remote relationships, the potential cognates must be as close as possible in both articulation and meaning. While semantic shifts are normal in language (for example, the English word 'hound' used to mean 'dog' but now means a specific breed of dog), the potential for the similarity to be due to chance greatly increases if the slightest changes are accepted. The more time passes, the harder it is to weed out borrowings because we do not know the history of the people. While even one cognate, by definition, indicates a genetic relationship, when doing distant comparative work, it is difficult ever truly to rule out borrowings and chance.

This is why evidence of distant genetic relationships ultimately depends on the discovery of shared grammatical forms, mainly irregular morphological paradigms. Antoine Meillet expected morphological "peculiarities" to be the foundation of comparative-historical linguistics. He stated clearly that resemblances in vocabulary only orients research but that "grammatical correspondences are proof, and only they are rigorous proof."[17] Statistically, a set of morphological forms cannot be explained as chance and rarely as borrowing.

Finding grammatical evidence also has its pitfalls. Grammatical traits such as word order and the existence of noun classes are too broad to be used. Even a noun class system based on position, as it is in Yuchi, can be found in unrelated languages around the world.[18] Traits that are predictable from typology cannot be used to determine family relationships. For example, the fact that Yuchi has SOV word order predicts that there are more prefixes than suffixes and that the auxiliaries follow the main verb, to name only a few.[19] As in the Southeast linguistic area, characteristics such as the presence of alienable/inalienable and inclusive/exclusive distinctions in Yuchi are probably due its being a head-marking language.[20] Grammar is also not immune to borrowing, and longtime neighbors share structures. Thus, in addition to typological residue, areal features, if any, must be identified and weeded out.

To help resolve questions of genetic features from typological features, Johanna Nichols extends the morphological notion of paradigms to that of paradigmaticity, or the layering of probabilities.[21] Her results are instructive. The more parts of one structure that are found to be the same means a lower probability that their occurrence is due to chance or typology. Paradigmaticity can be found in structured sets of vocabulary (such as the numerals), sets of morphemes (their forms, placements, and meanings combined), and all the forms of an irregular verb (such as the Indo-European verb 'be'). Paradigmaticity can also be found in cognates that have multiple syllables. Paradigmaticity helps separate type-identifying features (TI) from individual-identifying (ID), or genetic, features. "It is my impression that what is offered as grammatical evidence in long range comparisons generally lacks paradigmaticity," she warns.[22]

Nichols draws from an impressive database of world languages to calculate the probability of a structure. She calculates the statistical probability that a like structure (a word, a set of lexical items, a morphological paradigm) could occur by chance in two or more separate languages. She calculates the individual language as 0.001 (or one in a few thousand of the world's languages) and multiplies this by statistical significance, or 0.01–0.05. The result is 0.00001, or one in one hundred thousand. Thus, a structure is ID if the probability of its occurring is two languages is 0.00001 or greater. If it is less, then the like structure could be due to chance.[23]

Nichols illustrates the probability that a vocabulary item with multiple syllables could exist in two languages by chance. She uses the Proto-Indo-European word *wydhewa* 'widow.' She gives the probability of one consonant appearing as 0.05, or one out of an average 20 consonant inventory. The string has four consonants *w, *y, *dh,* and *w,* so the calculation is 0.05[4]. The result is 0.000 006 25, which is well within the estimated ID range.

Nichols points out that the probability of a word that only shares two consonants significantly decreases to 0.0025, a number that is not ID. With roots made of only one open syllable, Yuchi is immediately at a loss. By way of illustration, if we apply this same statistical measurement to the proposed bisyllabic cognates between Proto-Siouan and Yuchi, the probability of chance increases even more. Using Mary Haas's Proto-Siouan form for 'two' as *nupa* and in Yuchi as *nowe,* the [n] is shared, so we can determine 0.05; vowels are calculated by Nichols at .2, and since they are not exactly the same at .2 x .2. The bilabial also is .05 x .05. Thus, 0.5 x .4 x .10 = 0.002, a number that is clearly not able to support a claim for genetic relationship.[24]

To summarize, probabilities do not just illustrate but codify the need for longer lexical forms, structured sets of vocabulary, and morphological paradigms in distant comparative work. Unfortunately, for cv stem languages like Yuchi, in which the longest roots are bisyllabic, the use of lexical items will never give the probability needed to confirm a genetic relationship. Most attempts to classify Yuchi have used only compared word lists in which resemblances pointed to a possibility of cognate sets, but the search for Yuchi distant relationships needs to concentrate on paradigmaticity.

Once enough family relationships and subgroupings are established, reconstruction of the proto-language can begin in earnest. The proto-language, including sound system, vocabulary, and morphology, is the proposed common language at deeper time depth. In order to propose and prove remote relationships, it is the proto-languages that must then be compared. Since Yuchi must be related to other languages at a deep time depth, serious considerations for Yuchi must work with proto-forms, not current language forms. This work has often not been done and so further hinders finding deep genetic relationships with Yuchi.

Early Classifications of Yuchi

Albert Gallatin's 1836 "synopsis" for the American Antiquarian Society was the first attempt to classify all the known languages of North America. The classification posited twenty-eight families from eighty-one languages. He classified as an isolate any language for which affiliation was not proven, and there was much that was not proven at that time. In the Southeast, for example, Cherokee was not yet determined to be Iroquoian, Choctaw was not definitively Muskogean, and no Southeast language was recognized as Siouan. Gallatin's classification was conservative, not speculative. Thus he classified Yuchi as an isolate. The system was revised in 1848 and 1854 to reach thirty-two families finally; Yuchi remained an isolate.[25]

Gallatin's classification was based on collected vocabulary lists called "schedules." The schedules were lists for the field worker to retrieve basic vocabulary (body parts and family relationship and environmental terms). They also included number systems, animals, cultural items, and pronouns. Gallatin's Yuchi data were collected by Nathaniel Ware around 1820, and Major John Ridge in 1826, a Cherokee Indian who was fluent in his language. Ware's word list is quite sound. Ridge's work is valuable because he was able to hear the distinctions in the stop consonants with more accuracy than was Ware, but he was not consistent in how he wrote vowels.

The next classification of Yuchi appeared in John Wesley Powell's definitive work on the classification of American Indian languages north of Mexico.[26] His classification yielded fifty-eight linguistic stocks, and later this figure was reduced to fifty-five. By this time a better picture of the Southeast was emerging, and Powell's classification now included the Southeastern Siouan languages. Powell classified Yuchi as a genetic isolate language, and he put the language in its own isolate branch named 'Uchean.'

Powell made his classification almost solely from word lists and the intuition of others.[27] His Yuchi data came from Gallatin's 1836 publication and the information collected by Albert Gatschet in Leonard, Indian Territory, in 1885. Powell's classification of Yuchi as an isolate was probably influenced by Gatschet, who stated in the introduction to his collection of Muscogee Creek tales, "From what we know of it [Yuchi], it shows no radical affinity [genetic relationship] with any known American tongue."[28] Despite its reliance on vocabulary, much of Powell's classification system has withstood the test of time.

The Siouan-Yuchi Proposal

For comparative linguistics the early twentieth century began a period of reductionism—a concerted effort to place many isolate languages and families within other established families. In 1913 Sapir proposed the Algonkian-Ritwan classification, linking the Algonquian languages of the Northeast, Great Lakes, and Plains to the Ritwan languages of Wiyot and Yoruk of California. Although considered preposterous at first, Algonkian-Ritwan, now called Algic, was proven to be a legitimate affiliation. Searching for other deeper relationships, and hoping to stimulate further research by making proposals based on little but phonetic inventories, broad morphological similarities, and speculation, Sapir proposed a new classification of North American Indian languages in 1921, revised in 1925 and 1929.[29]

Sapir's 1929 classification has been the most dramatic proposed reduction of Native North American language families into a few deeper stocks. Sapir's classification reduced Powell's fifty-eight fami-lies to six stocks.[30] Of the proposed six stocks, the largest in number of family subgroups, diversity of these families, and territory cov-ered was Hokan-Siouan. It covered languages from California, the Southwest, northern Mexico, the Plains, and the Southeast. Lan-guages of the Southeast were classified in three subgroups: Tunican (Tunica-Atakapa and Chitimacha), Iroquois-Caddoan, and the East-ern Group. Yuchi was placed in the Eastern Group along with Si-ouan and Muskogean. In Sapir's 1921 and 1925 classifications, Yu-chi was an equal branch next to Siouan and Muskogean. In other words, Yuchi was no more closely related to Siouan than to Musk-ogean. His early Eastern Group proposals are given in table 2.

TABLE 2. Sapir's Eastern Group, 1921 and 1925

Eastern Group, 1921	Eastern Group, 1925
(1) Siouan	(1) Siouan
(2) Yuchi	(2) Yuchi
(3) Muskogian	(3) Natchez-Muskogian
	(4) Timucua

Sapir's final revision of his Eastern Group, which appeared in the *Encyclopædia Britannica* in 1929, has had a lasting effect on Yu-chi studies. It was here that he published a Siouan-Yuchi subgroup equal with his Natchez-Muskogian subgroup, which tentatively in-cluded Timucua (table 3).

TABLE 3. Sapir's Eastern Group, 1929

Eastern Group, 1929	
(1) Siouan-Yuchi	(2) Natchez-Muskogian
a. Siouan-Catawban	a. Natchez
b. Yuchi	b. Muskogian
	c. Timucua (?)

Significantly, the 1929 revision places Yuchi in closer relationship to Siouan than with Muskogean. It is not known why Sapir did this. He may have done it simply to remove both Siouan and Yuchi from the Muskogean family, as they are clearly not related. His proposal may have relied on the similarity of the phonetic inventory to Siouan, especially the distinction of aspirated stops. However, recent work on Proto-Siouan has revealed that the aspirated stops in Siouan languages occurred well after their split from Catawaba and therefore after any possible relationship to Yuchi as well.[31] He may also have been intrigued by the active-stative marking attributed to Siouan languages and Yuchi. In Sapir's time, however, no distinction was made between active-stative languages and agent-patient languages. Today it is well documented that Siouan languages are agent-patient and Yuchi is active-stative.[32] His data, it is assumed, came from the existing word lists, but he left no records of any analysis, reasoning, or data supporting his Siouan-Yuchi proposal.

Sapir intended many parts of his classification to stimulate further research, not to be taken as fact.[33] Yet his success with establishing the Algic family created an aura of fact to his work. Speaking about the Southeast as a whole, and certainly true in regard to Yuchi, Haas reflected, "Whatever the final judgment may be about the eventual accuracy of Sapir's classification, the immediate result was unfortunate for Southeastern linguistics since it greatly over-simplified the picture and seemed to give assurances that the classificatory problems of the area had been settled."[34] Earnest comparative work on the southeastern languages stagnated until the 1940s when Haas began tearing down Sapir's grouping of the Southeast. She began a new era of reanalysis, splitting speculative stocks and searching for different groupings for the Southeast.

Attempts to Prove the Siouan-Yuchi Proposal

Hans Wolff, Mary Haas, James M. Crawford, and Robert Rankin have searched for evidence of a Siouan-Yuchi connection. It was not a primary undertaking for any of them. Wolff worked mainly on Proto-Siouan. Although he did some fieldwork on Yuchi in the 1940s, and published one Yuchi text with analysis, ultimately he did not include Yuchi in his Proto-Siouan reconstructions.[35]

Haas was working on establishing the Gulf family, a now abandoned proposal that included Muskogean languages, Natchez, Chitimacha, and Atakapa of the Southeast. In one of two articles presenting her evidence for Gulf, Haas uses the word for 'water' as an example of systematic correspondences and reconstruction able to be done on the Gulf languages.[36] Her reconstructed Gulf word for water is *(a)kwi(ni). Haas goes on to compare her proposed Gulf reconstruction to Proto-Siouan and Yuchi, using the Proto-Siouan form *mini ~ *wini from Wolff's text and her own Proto-Siouan reconstruction *m-ni. She finds that at least this one Proto-Siouan word is "certainly related" to Proto-Gulf. She then compares the Yuchi word for 'water,' tse. Haas doubted a genetic affiliation between the forms *(a)kwi(ni) and tse.[37] Haas concluded that the word for 'water' did not indicate a closer relationship between Yuchi and Siouan than between Yuchi and the Gulf languages. Without this connection between Yuchi and Gulf, there would be no way to suggest a relationship between the Siouan and Yuchi words. Aware that it is impossible to determine genetic relatedness based on one word, she presented four separate lexical items in Proto-Siouan (PS) and Yuchi that she believed might prove with further work to be cognates. The forms are PS *nupa, Yuchi nowe 'two'; PS *sepi, Yuchi ispi 'black'; PS *natu, Yuchi go-to 'head'; and PS *p-qa, Yuchi paga 'bitter.'[38] Ultimately, however, Haas left the Siouan-Yuchi connection 'inconclusive.'

In her paper "Athabaskan, Tlingit, Yuchi, and Siouan," Haas was once more in search of other possible family groupings. Here she presents a brief comparison of lexical resemblances of Proto-Athabaskan, Tlingit, Yuchi, and Proto-Siouan. Her reason for comparing these languages was the similarities in their consonant inventories. In particular she noted the unaspirated, aspirated, and ejective stops series found in all of the languages, but as already mentioned, sound inventories and especially a Siouan-Yuchi connection based on aspirated stops cannot be used as a basis for genetic relationships. In addition she noted a chance comparison of several words that looked similar. Her curiosity led her to the discovery and comparison of thirty-four lexical resemblances; only sixteen of them were resemblances between Yuchi and Proto-Siouan. Her suggestion was that these four language families could be related, but she gave no suggestion for internal groupings. She purposely did not hyphenate Yuchi with Proto-Siouan to place them in a closer relationship because "no systematic evidence has ever been presented to show that Sapir's assumption of an especially close relationship between Yuchi and Siouan family is valid."[39] Her compared segments actually show a higher degree of similarity and regular patterning between Yuchi and Proto-Athabaskan than between Yuchi and Proto-Siouan.[40] It was this kind of data that intrigued Haas.

Haas's work to find regular correspondences between these languages exemplifies many of the problems associated with comparative work at deep time depths. First, nearly all of the similarities are based on cv stems or combinations. In addition, Haas allowed the use of cv segments from longer forms to be compared with full forms. This reduces a longer form to a short form. As discussed earlier, only the longer form could be persuasive evidence for genetic relationship. Also, the possible sound correspondences Haas gives are often broad phonetic similarities. Haas does not compare any labial sounds (Tlingit does not have labials), few velars (such as /k/ or /x/), and one nasal. Most of the comparisons, then, are between alveolar (such as /s/ or /t/) to alveolar-palatal (such as /š/ or /ǰ/) segments. With any sound in the alveolar region, a legitimate comparison to any other alveolar sound at such a time depth must take phoneme frequency into consideration. Twenty out of the thirty-three consonants in Yuchi, or 60 percent, are alveolar or alveo-palatal sounds, and all of these sounds are legitimate syllable onsets in Yuchi. The Athapaskan and Siouan consonant inventories are similar in this percentage. The probability that the matches are due to chance multiplies with the frequency of the phonemes. Clearly, the number of phones in the alveolar region, and the similarities allowed in the comparisons, are candidates for chance.

Finally, Haas permits similar segments that have undergone semantic shifts. For example, the Yuchi word 'smash' is used in place of 'cut,' 'leaf' for 'feather,' 'leg' for 'bone,' and so on.[41] As mentioned, this sort of shift in meaning is permissible if a genetic relationship has been established, but such shifts cannot be accepted when trying to establishing a genetic relationship, as the likelihood of finding similar phonetic segments greatly increases when semantically nonequivalent forms are compared. However, Haas emphasized that the data were only the preliminary 'suggestions' from her initial inquiry.[42]

Crawford collected primary data on Yuchi, including a lexicon, with a Yuchi speaker living in Georgia and during fieldwork in Oklahoma in the 1970s. In a paper that he read at the Southern Anthropological Society annual meetings in 1970, he discussed potential cognates between Yuchi and data from the Southeastern Siouan languages Biloxi and Ofo. He had gathered ninety-one words in his comparative list, and then, reminiscent of Sapir's Hokan-Siouan, connected twenty-three of these to proposed Hokan words. He never worked with available Proto-Siouan data to help support his connection either of Yuchi to Siouan or of Siouan to Hokan. His comparisons, too, were extremely broad in place and manner of articulation and in semantics, and he tried to draw out systematic sound correspondences. However, he could establish no regular phonological rules and later retracted their conclusiveness. He expected to find some identity correspondences even at this time depth, but he recognized that a few segment matches were all he could find. Even in those, he could not rule out that the similarities were due to chance or borrowing.[43] Crawford expressed disbelief in any Siouan-Yuchi relationship and the inclusion of Yuchi in Wallace Chafe's proposed Siouan-Iroquoian-Caddoan.[44]

In the late 1990s, Robert Rankin began a search for grammatical proof supporting Proto-Siouan-Catawban (henceforth PSC) and Yuchi. He had worked for years on a comparative Siouan dictionary and thus had extensive knowledge of Proto-Siouan and access to the most accurate reconstruction of Proto-Siouan lexical items and grammar.[45] His work centered on three aspects of the grammar: a set of prefixes on nouns, the pronominal prefixes on the verb, and the order of prefixes on the verb.[46]

Rankin introduces a PSC noun classification system based on an animacy hierarchy. According to Rankin, in PSC this system is manifested in classificatory prefixes on the noun. Rankin compares these to Proto-Siouan prefixes to Yuchi morphemes: Proto-Siouan *wi- and Yuchi we- 'animate non-human,' and Proto-Siouan *ko- and Yuchi go- 'human.'[47] The system shows some regularity in his proposed subclasses as well. Yuchi uses the morpheme we- in the construction of three foodstuffs directly derived from animal products and some weather phenomena; the *wi- morpheme has been reconstructed for Proto-Siouan in some words of these same categories. In addition, a Proto-Siouan prefix *ra- found in body parts from the arms on up appears to be shared by the Yuchi morpheme da- used in many body parts associated with the face.

At first, these looks like prime candidates for paradigmaticity, and Rankin comments that the "idiosyncratic semantic division" in the *wi-/we- class is good evidence for genetic inheritance. However, these morphemes in Yuchi, unlike those of PSC, are not part of an ancient, static classification system. Instead, they are noun roots that have compounded with other noun roots and are more recently in the process of becoming bleached of clear rootlike meaning and becoming more like a classificatory prefix. In other words, they are lexical prefixes, a type of morpheme common in languages of the Northwest Coast and Alaska.[48] Thus the Yuchi morphemes that do act as a noun classification system are new, representing the initial stages in the process of grammaticalization from compounding to full lexical prefixes. This process probably began in the last one thousand years. As such, they cannot be compared to an old noun class system, as they have arisen thousands of years after a potential split between PSC and Yuchi.

If these morphemes do not represent a shared ancient classificatory system, then the case for paradigmaticity is gone as well. The sound-meaning correspondences of PSC *wi-, *ko-, and *ra- with the Yuchi we-, go-, and da- are simply three potential cognates, not paradigmatic. Hence they would be without the statistical force needed to help prove a relationship even if they were someday proved to be cognates. Finally, the inclusion of weather phenomena in an animate nonhuman class is common in animacy-based classification schemes, so it would not have been an idiosyncratic boost for the case of a unique paradigm.

Rankin also addresses PSC and Yuchi pronominal prefixes. Aware that pronominal forms are susceptible to consonant symbolism and similarity in their shortness, Rankin focuses on the verb stems with historically fused pronominal prefixes to reconstruct a paradigm in Yuchi, Catawban, and Proto-Siouan. This is the strongest morphological evidence in support of a genetic relationship to Proto-Siouan. The forms themselves are provoking. However, the paradigm includes no third person form for Yuchi, making it parallel to the lack of overt third person marking in Siouan languages. However, there is a third person inanimate *hi-* that appears to be an earlier general third person prefix. While the profusion of third person animate classes in Yuchi are arguably recent innovations, the *hi-* third person inanimate should be seriously considered in reconstruction. Rankin ends this section by cautiously pointing out that the paradigmaticity of his reconstructed Yuchi pronominal prefixes and those of PSC is in itself still not enough to prove a genetic relationship, given that a nearly identical pronoun paradigm has been shown between Proto-Miwok and late Proto-Indo-European, a similarity that is actually due to chance.[49]

The final argument Rankin presents is the order of prefixes on the PSC and Yuchi verb stems. This argument suffers greatly from inaccurate analyses of Yuchi. PSC, like many of its modern languages, had instrumental prefixes. Following Wagner's Yuchi grammatical sketch, Rankin posits *hi-* as an instrumental prefix on the verb in Yuchi. However, *hi-* is a third person inanimate prefix, and there is no evidence that it ever functioned as an instrumental prefix. In addition, Wagner erroneously analyzed comitative *k'ã-* 'with someone' that occurs next to the verb stem as an incorporated object *k'a*. This forces the inclusive/exclusive pronominal prefixes on the outer layer of verb prefixes. This placement also renders his proposed Yuchi verb template analogous to the Proto-Siouan template. Rankin admits that the inclusive/exclusive occurs inside in all cases but with the verb 'carry,' but he reminds readers that reconstruction work must rely on the exceptions. However, this verb is not an exception but quite regular when the *k'ã-* is rightly viewed as the comitative prefix and not an incorporated object *k'a* 'thing.'

With both the noun class and verb template arguments negated, the only potentially valid argument is the reconstructed pronominal prefixes. In his own words, Rankin states that this is not enough evidence by itself to prove the relationship.

Sapir's Eastern Group was easily dismantled, and his Hokan-Siouan stock is now universally abandoned. Yet in the case of his Siouan-Yuchi proposal, proposal became hypothesis, and hypothesis became accepted fact. Browsing through the American Indian reference books found at any library or mega-bookstore will leave the inquisitive convinced that Yuchi is a Siouan language. Even if Yuchi is someday proven to be related to Proto-Siouan-Catawban, it would still not be correct to call it a Siouan language, as the Catawban and Yuchi branches would have diverged from an earlier ancestor.

Other Proposals

Since it is clear that Yuchi is not related to any language in the Southeast at any easily analyzable time depth, the search should extend out in space and time. Searching for genetic relationships outside the Southeast can avoid some of the problems associated with determining borrowed forms. However, very few searches have been conducted for a relationship between Yuchi and languages outside the Southeast.

William Elmendorf proposed a connection between Siouan and Yukian, a small family that is made up of the Yuki and Wappo languages of California. In 1963 Elmendorf presented a list of ninety-five possible cognates to support his Siouan-Yukian hypothesis. To represent Siouan, he used Biloxi and Ofo from the Southeastern subgroup of Siouan, spoken in the lower Mississippi Valley and Mobile Bay respectively. He supported these data with Proto-Siouan data from Wolff's "Comparative Siouan I–II" study and personal communications from Haas. In this initial search he included ten Yuchi words that he thought could be cognates with Yukian (mainly

Wappo) words. His Yuchi data came from Wagner's "Yuchi" sketch and from Haas's "The Proto-Gulf Word for Water." He did not attempt any regular sound correspondences but asserted that the number and similarity of the words alone pointed to a genetic relationship between Yukian and Siouan, especially as the great distance between the families ruled out borrowing.[50]

A year later Elmendorf expanded his comparison of Yukian, Siouan, and Yuchi, including thirty-seven total Yuchi comparisons. The ten Yuchi words used in his original presentation were republished along with eleven more lexical resemblances among the three groups. He also added ten more Yuchi words with possible Yuki cognates and six more Yuchi words compared to Siouan as possible cognates. Nearly all forms were drawn directly from Haas's "Athabaskan, Tlingit, Yuchi, and Siouan" study and thus did not shed any new light on the Siouan and Yuchi debate. His proposed cognates are replete with the same problems that plagued Haas and Crawford: the words are either too small (cv), or the compared segments are too small (often just a c or cv part of a word), to be conclusive of genetic relationship. In addition, he allowed semantic shifts, some as far afield as his equation of 'excrement' with 'drip/drop.' In addition, Elmendorf's Yuchi data are replete with spurious forms.[51]

While Elmendorf was the first to attempt to find grammatical evidence in support of a possible genetic relationship to Yuchi, his morphological evidence relied mainly on cv combinations that he presented as an earlier lexical stem shared by the Yukian family. However, his stem sets have not been proven reconstructed morphemes for Proto-Yukian. So a Yuchi-Siouan-Yukian connection has never been established.

Crawford redirected his search to the southeastern isolates Atakapa and Tunica. At the end of his 1979 survey article on Timucua and Yuchi he provides a list comparing thirteen words between Yuchi and Atakapa and twelve words between Yuchi and Tunica. He states that he was open to the possibility of their being cognates. Of these, the Atakapa data are the most intriguing, with several grammatical morphemes (three pronouns and the dependent clause negation proclitic) and two bisyllabic words in which both syllables are similar, but neither list by itself is enough to stir further interest.[52]

As mentioned, Haas looked into a relationship between Yuchi, Proto-Siouan, and Athapaskan and Tlingit, which are far outside the Southeast. She found a handful of possible cognates. These have yet to be proven, and this line of inquiry has not been pursued further.[53] However, Haas's Yuchi and Athapaskan interest should be revisited with new Proto-Athapaskan or Na-Dene forms. Her hunch continues to be intriguing since the languages have a surprising degree of similarity in the kind and order of prefixes on the verb.

This can also be said of the Proto-Siouan-Iroquoian-Caddoan proposal, which Chafe suggested may also include Yuchi. While much of the lexical evidence originally used to support the hypothesis has been refuted, or is based on small CV segments, the similarity in the verb templates of the languages is still intriguing.[54] At the risk of following in the footsteps of my esteemed predecessors—tossing in ideas to stimulate thought but that cannot be taken even as a proposal—there are several Yuchi morphemes, including the third person inanimate and applicative, that are similar to Proto-Iroquoian in form, function, and placement. It may be that work in this area may lend support to the Siouan-Caddoan-Iroquoian proposal and of Yuchi being related to this proto-family. If Yuchi were part of this deep relationship, the language would not necessarily be any closer to Proto-Siouan-Catawban than to the other proto-languages. It would, however, show an early relationship between Yuchi and three large families that spread out across the Eastern Woodlands and Southeast.

Conclusion

The proposals for the genetic classification and attempts to establish undisputed genetic evidence for Yuchi have been bound up with the history of Americanist linguistics; Yuchi's classification as an isolate to a branch of the encompassing Hokan-Siouan family parallels more general trends of splitting and lumping in the endeavor to classify American Indian languages, sometimes to the neglect of sound methodology. The years of searching for cognates has yielded no regular sound correspondences between Yuchi and any other language or language family. At the time depth of any proposal, the search must concentrate on sets of grammatical evidence, especially sets of grammatical morphemes, or paradigmatic forms. For example, if the locative suffixes in Yuchi, taken together as a set in form, function, and meaning, could prove to be related to another set in form, function, and meaning, then the similarities could not be due to chance or borrowing. The search for morphological evidence and structured sets of vocabulary between Yuchi and any other American Indian language has just begun but has so far been inconclusive.

While Sapir's Siouan-Yuchi connection should be firmly put aside once and for all, a deeper connection between Proto-Siouan-Catawban, Yuchi, and other proto-languages should still be explored. With better Proto-Siouan-Catawban material available and a more complete Yuchi grammar, perhaps shared cognates and grammatical paradigms can be teased out. The search in this direction continues to yield interesting information about shared history, whether that history is genetic or indicates a long, presumably mostly friendly, relationship between two unrelated peoples.

With only very distant genetic relationships possible for Yuchi, there will never be an abundance of evidence. With innovative research on the stability of grammatical forms and the nature of borrowing, grammaticalization in polysynthetic languages, and careful reconstruction of proto-languages, a stronger case for a genetic relationship to Yuchi may someday be possible. There are many as yet unexplored historical connections to be made through linguistic enterprise. Until then, Yuchi is a genetic isolate.

Acknowledgments

This contribution to Yuchi history has its roots in a PhD examination paper in the Department of Linguistics at the University of Kansas. For this incarnation I would like to thank the American Philosophical Society Library for the ease of access to their holdings, and the National Science Foundation grant #0345694, titled

A Dictionary and Textbase of Euchee (Yuchi), which made it possible for me to do research at the APS and to continue research with the Yuchi community.

Notes

1. Terrence Kaufman, "Language History in South America: What We Know and How to Know More," in *Amazonian Linguistics,* ed. David L. Payne (Austin: University of Texas Press, 1990), 31.

2. Sarah Thomason, *Language Contact: An Introduction* (Washington DC: Georgetown University Press, 2001), 1–10.

3. Edward Sapir, "Central and North American Indian Languages," in *Encyclopædia Britannica,* 14th ed., vol. 5 (London, 1929), 138–41.

4. These dates are from Lyle Campbell, *American Indian Languages: The Historical Linguistics of Native America* (Oxford: Oxford University Press, 1997), 142. However, they differ from Robert Hollow and Douglas R. Parks, "Studies in Plains Linguistics: A Review," in *Anthropology of the Great Plains,* ed. W. Raymond Wood and Margot Liberty (Lincoln: University of Nebraska Press, 1980), 68–97. Hollow and Parks date Proto-Siouan at 2,000–3,000 years before present.

5. For an excellent and thorough history of Americanist comparative-historical linguistics and the problems of determining deep genetic relationships see Campbell, *American Indian Languages.*

6. Unless indicated otherwise, this description of Yuchi is based on a fuller account provided in *A Grammar of Euchee (Yuchi)* (Lincoln: University of Nebraska Press, forthcoming) that I prepared in collaboration with present-day Yuchi speakers. All data from this source are given in the Americanist Phonetic Alphabet; data from other sources are given in their original notation.

7. Johanna Nichols, "Head-marking and Dependent-marking Grammar," *Language* 62 (1986): 56–119.

8. There is a long literature on polysynthesis and noun incorporation, including Marianne Mithun, "On the Nature of Noun Incorporation," *Language* 62 (1986): 32–37, and Mark Baker, *The Polysynthesis Parameter* (Oxford: Oxford University Press, 1996).

9. This tale was collected by Jeremiah Curtain in 1885 and was retranslated into Yuchi by Maxine Barnett, Josephine Bigler, Josephine Keith, and Maggie Marsey in Sapulpa, Oklahoma, in the summer of 2005. I have presented only the morpho-phonemic line here. The spoken line contains some word shortenings. The abbreviations used are as follows: AGT agent subject; APP applicative; EF Yuchi Female; EMPH emphatic; FREQ frequentative; LOC locative; NE Non-Yuchi; NEG negative; SG singular.

10. Lewis Ballard, "Sa/ša/la: Southern Shobboleth?" *International Journal of American Linguistics* 51 (1985): 334–41, and T. Dale Nicklas, "Areal Features of the Southeast," in *Perspectives on the Southeast: Linguistics, Archeology, and Ethnohistory*, ed. Patricia Kwachka (Athens: University of Georgia Press, 1994), 1–15. The Yuchi grammatical information is from page 6. The calques are from Lyle Campbell, Terrence Kaufman, and Thomas Smith-Stark, "Meso-America as a Linguistics Area," *Language* 1986 (62): 530–70, quoted in Nicklas, "Areal Features of the Southeast," 12. The loan borrowings are from Cecil Brown, *Lexical Acculturation in Native American Languages* (Oxford: Oxford University Press, 1999), 130–39.

11. There can be a coda, filled by inserted nasal consonants following nasal vowels and /h/ in some environments, and /n/ utterance final position with the past perfective particle.

12. Albert Gathschet, "Yuchi Vocabulary, March 1885, Koncharty District, Creek Nation, Indian Territory," National Anthropological Archives, Smithsonian Institution, Manuscript 1440. I discuss the non-Yuchi category in Mary S. Linn, "Yuchi and Non-Yuchi: A Living Classification," *Florida Anthropologist* 50 (1997): 189–97.

13. Günter Wagner, "Yuchi," in *Handbook of American Indian Languages*, vol. 3 (New York, 1934), 291–384, and W. Lewis Ballard, "Aspects of Yuchi Morphophonology," in *Studies in Southeastern Languages*, ed. James Crawford (Athens: University of Georgia Press, 1975), 163–87.

14. T. Dale Nicklas, "Marking the Beneficiary in Muskogean, Dakota, and Yuchi," in *1994 Mid-American Linguistics Conference Papers*, vol. 2, ed. Frances Ingemann (Lawrence: University of Kansas, 1994), 611–23.

15. The *sio-* in line (1) on the verb "go" is irregular.

16. For an accessible introduction of the comparative method, see Robert Rankin, "The Comparative Method," in *The Handbook of Historical Linguistics*, ed. Brian D. Joseph and Richard D. Janda (Oxford: Oxford University Press, 2003), 183–12. S. P Harrison, "On the Limits of the Comparative Method," in the same volume, 213–43, defines the temporal limitations of the comparative method in general. Campbell, *American Indian Languages*, 206–59, gives the most thorough discussion of the problems encountered in doing deep comparative work in American Indian languages.

17. Antoine Meillet, *Linguistique historique et linguistique général*, vol. 8 (Paris: Champion, 1958), 91.

18. Laurel Watkins, "Position in Grammar: Sit, Stand, Lie," *Kansas Working Papers in Linguistics* 1 (1976): 16–41.

19. The seminal work on predictive typology is Joseph Greenberg, "Some

Universals of Grammar with Particular Reference to the Order of Meaningful Elements," in *Universals of Language*, ed. Joseph H. Greenberg (Cambridge MA: MIT Press, 1963), 339–41.

20. Johanna Nichols, *Linguistic Diversity in Space and Time* (Chicago: University of Chicago Press, 1992), 254.

21. Johanna Nichols, "The Comparative Method as Heuristic," in *The Comparative Method Reviewed: Regularity and Irregularity in Language Change*, ed. Mark Durie and Malcolm Ross (Oxford: Oxford University Press, 1996), 39–71.

22. Nichols, "The Comparative Method as Heuristic," 52.

23. Nichols, *Linguistic Diversity in Space and Time*, 49. Her calculation of statistical probability is based on perfect matches.

24. Nichols, *Linguistic Diversity in Space and Time*, 50, discusses perfect matches from non-perfect matches. If we use the more recently analyzed and more accurate Proto-Siouan form **rupa* (form from Robert Rankin, pers. comm.), the number increases because /r/ is not a perfect match with /n/. Thus the likelihood of the Yuchi and Proto-Siouan words being related decreases even more.

25. Albert Gallatin, *A Synopsis of Indian Tribes Living within the United States East of the Rocky Mountains, and in the British and Russian Possessions in North America*, Transactions and Collections of the American Antiquarian Society 2 (Cambridge: Cambridge University Press, 1836), Yuchi classification on 97. Comments on Gallatin's methodology can be found in Mary Haas, "Southeastern Languages," in *The Languages of Native America: Historical and Comparative Assessment*, ed. Lyle Campbell and Marianne Mithun (Austin: University of Texas Press, 1979), 299–326.

26. John Wesley Powell, "Indian Linguistics Families of America North of Mexico," reprinted in *Introduction to Handbook of American Indian Languages and Indian Linguistic Families of America North of Mexico*, ed. Preston Holder (1891; Lincoln: University of Nebraska Press, 1966), 83–221, Yuchi classification on 202–3.

27. Campbell, *American Indian Languages*, 61.

28. Albert Gatschet, *A Migration Legend of the Creek Indians* (Philadelphia PA: D. G. Brinton, 1884), 18.

29. Edward Sapir, "Wiyot and Yoruk, Algonkin Languages of California," *American Anthropologist* 15 (1913): 617–46. Sapir's series of classifications of all North American languages is found in "A Bird's Eye View of American Indian Languages North of Mexico," *Science* 54 (1921): 408; "The Hokan Affinity of Subtiaba in Nicaragua," *American Anthropologist* 27 (1925): 402–30,

491–527; and "Central and North American Indian Languages," *Encyclopædia Britannica*, 14th ed., vol. 5 (London, 1929), 138–41.

30. Only Joseph Greenberg's huge Amerind stock is a larger lumping effort, grouping all the languages of the Americas together with the exception of his Na-Dene (Athabaskan, Eyak, Tlingit, and Haida) and Eskimo family, proposed in *Language in the Americas* (Stanford: Stanford University Press, 1987).

31. Robert Rankin, pers. comm. to Lyle Campbell, cited in Campbell, *American Indian Languages*, 265. Mary R. Haas, in her *The Prehistory of Language* (The Hague: Mouton, 1969), 90–92, still used the aspirated stop series in Siouan and Yuchi languages as possible evidence for a genetic relationship.

32. Although the types of grammatical relations are related, there are clear differences. Marianne Mithun's "Active/Agentive Case Marking and Its Motivations," *Language* 67 (1991): 510–47, teased out the differences between the two types of split subject systems.

33. Campbell, *American Indian Languages*, 75–76.

34. Mary R. Haas, "The Southeast," in *Native Languages of the Americas*, ed. Thomas Sebeok (New York: Plenum Press, 1976), 573–612.

35. Hans Wolff, "Comparative Siouan I–II," *International Journal of American Linguistics* 16 (1950): 61–66, 113–21, and "Comparative Siouan III," *International Journal of American Linguistics* 17 (1951): 168–78. His "Yuchi Text with Analysis" appears in *International Journal of American Linguistics* 17 (1951): 48–53.

36. Mary Haas, "The Proto-Gulf Word for Water (with Notes on Siouan-Yuchi)," *International Journal of American Linguistics* 17 (1951): 71–79, and "The Proto-Gulf Word for Land (with a Note on Proto-Siouan)," *International Journal of American Linguistics* 18 (1952): 238–40. The PS and Yuchi forms and final quote given in the text are from Haas, "The Proto-Gulf Word for Water," 79. The title of these papers, with "Siouan-Yuchi" hyphenated as a family, is unfortunate and surprising because she clearly states that the relationship is only a proposal.

37. "The Proto-Gulf Word for Water (with Notes on Siouan-Yuchi)," 71–79, and "The Proto-Gulf Word for Land (with a Note on Proto-Siouan)," 238–40. Haas speculates that [kw] could possibly be related to [ts] if [ts] occurred only before front vowels. This is not the case in Yuchi today, at least. The segment [ts] can occur before all vowels in nonderived environments. In addition [kw] is found in Yuchi with no phonologically derived relationship to [ts]. Haas also suggested the possibility that the Yuchi [e] could have been derived from an [ẽ] in the proto-stem instead of [i]. Haas is assuming that lowering the soft palate for the nasal would lower the vowel as well. This is a

reasonable assumption, especially in Yuchi where nasalization regularly lowers the front vowels ([i] lowers to [ĩ], and [e] lowers to [ɛ]. However, positing a nasal vowel in the proto-language would necessitate a reason for Yuchi to have lost the nasal vowel today, made harder by the fact that Yuchi has contrastive nasal vowels. Without corresponding regular changes to posit lowering, loss of nasality, and of [kw] changing to [ts], the possibility of relationship between these words does not exist.

38. "The Proto-Gulf Word for Water (with Notes on Siouan-Yuchi)," 71–79, and "The Proto-Gulf Word for Land (with a Note on Proto-Siouan)," 238–40. Haas apparently uses Günter Wagner's Yuchi forms here. Her own field notes on Yuchi reveal that she did not analyze the language as having fully voiced stops, as are given in the forms here. Her work on Yuchi can be found in "Brief Field Notes on Yuchi Collected in 1940," manuscript in the Mary R. Haas Collection, American Philosophical Society Library, Philadelphia, Pennsylvania.

39. Mary R. Haas, "Athabaskan, Tlingit, Yuchi, and Siouan," in *XXXV Congreso Internacional de Americanistas, Mexico, 1962* (Mexico City: Universidad de Madrid, 1964), 495.

40. One such set shows regularity in three forms between stem-initial Proto-Athabaskan /*tš/ and Yuchi /s'/. However, her word for 'female' *s'e* is actually the active third person pronominal prefix referring to a male in women's speech. Haas must have copied the form in error from her field notes, where she correctly distinguished the form from *se-*, the active third person female pronominal prefix. This would reduce the resemblances between /*tš/ and /s'/ to two and skew the other data.

41. Haas gives the Yuchi word for 'smash' as -*kasa* and credits it to Wagner. However, Wagner, "Sketch of Yuchi," 329, gives -*stenō* as 'smash/bust' and -*kasa* as 'crush.' The Yuchi words for 'cut' are *l'i* 'cut/scratch,' *pha* 'cut open.'

42. Haas, "Athabaskan, Tlingit, Yuchi, and Siouan," 495.

43. James Crawford, "Timucua and Yuchi: Two Language Isolates of the Southeast," in *The Languages of Native America: Historical and Comparative Assessment*, ed. Lyle Campbell and Marianne Mithun (Austin: University of Texas Press, 1979), 327–54.

44. This was reported by Lewis Ballard in "More on Yuchi Pronouns," *International Journal of American Linguistics* 44 (1978): 103–21. Ballard, who worked intensively on Yuchi in the 1970s, also shared these beliefs. Wallace Chafe presented arguments for the Siouan-Iroquoian-Caddoan proposal in "Siouan, Iroquoian, and Caddoan," in *Current Trends in Linguistics 10: Linguistics in North America*, ed. Thomas Sebeok (The Hague: Mouton, 1973), 1198–99.

45. "The Comparative Dictionary of the Siouan Languages" is still in preparation by Richard T. Carter, A. Wesley Jones, and Robert L. Rankin. Rankin's Yuchi data comes from Wagner 1933; Ballard 1978; Lewis Ballard, "Aspects of Yuchi Morphophonology," 163–87; and Ballard's unpublished manuscript "A Yuchi-English, English-Yuchi Lexicon."

46. Robert Rankin, "An Ancient Siouan-Catawban and Yuchi Noun Classification System," paper presented at the Siouan and Caddoan Conference, Billings, Montana, June 1996; "Grammatical Evidence for Genetic Relationship and the Macro-Siouan Problem," PAMAPLA: *Papers from the 21st Annual Meeting of the Atlantic Provinces Linguistic Association/Actes du Colloque Annuel de l'Association de Linguistique des Provinces Atlantiques*, ed. Marie-Lucie Tarpent (Halifax NS: The Association, 1986), 20–46.

47. I have analyzed the 'human' morpheme as voiceless unaspirated *ko*-, and the 'face' morpheme as voiceless unaspirated *ta*-; thus, closer to the PSC forms but not changing the problems with the analysis.

48. A good overview of lexical affixation is found in Marianne Mithun, *The Languages of Native North America* (New York: Cambridge University Press, 1999), 48–56. Mithun hypothesized that lexical affixes begin life as a noun root compounded to a noun stem, in "Lexical Affixes and Morphological Typology," in *Essays on Language Function and Language Type: Dedicated to Talmy Givon*, ed. Joan Bybee, John Haiman, and Sandra Thompson (Philadelphia: J. Benjamins Publishing Company, 1997), 357–71. I argued in "Lexical Affixation in Euchee" (paper presented at the annual meetings of the Society for the Study of the Indigenous Languages of the Americas, San Francisco, California, 4 January 2001) that Yuchi provides clear evidence of this. The Yuchi right root in noun-noun compounds is in the process of becoming more prefixlike. Some are still able to be independent noun roots, while at the other extreme some must be attached to a noun and have generalized, classificatory meaning.

49. The Miwok and Indo-European similarities are pointed out in Catherine Callaghan, "An 'Indo-European' Type Paradigm in Proto Eastern Miwok," in *American Indian and Indoeuropean Studies: Papers in Honor of Madison S. Beeler*, ed. Kathryn Klar, Margaret Langdon, and Shirley Silver (The Hague: Mouton, 1980), 31–42. The problems with using pronominal forms in comparative work are well documented; especially significant here are Meillet, *Linguistique historique et linguistique général*; Nichols, "The Comparative Method as Heuristic"; and Lyle Campbell, "Amerind Personal Pronouns: A Second Opinion," *Language* 73 (1997): 339–51.

50. William Elmendorf, "Yukian-Siouian Lexical Similarities," *International Journal of American Linguistics* 29 (1963): 300–309.

51. William Elmendorf, "Item and Set Comparison in Yuchi, Siouan, and Yukian," *International Journal of American Linguistics* 30 (1964): 328–40. Elemendorf's data are *s'ẽ* 'bite, bite off' and *sa-tẽ* 'scrape/shave' (336). The hyphen is Elmendorf's faulty analysis. Neither segment is a recognizable morpheme by itself; the form should have been considered as a whole. The negative is given as *læ-* or *na-* (330), but the forms are *næ=* and *hæ=* , and where Wagner used *ᴛn* sequence to indicate a glottalized /'n/, Elmendorf compares the words with Yukian and Siouan words beginning with /t/. In addition, he apparently picked up the form *kasa* from Haas and uses it as the Yuchi word for 'cut' with no note of the semantic shift (339).

52. James Crawford, "Timucua and Yuchi." The Yuchi words compared to Atakapa and Tunica are provided on pages 344–45.

53. Blair Rudes, "Sound Changes Separating Siouan-Yuchi from Iroquoian-Caddoan," *International Journal of American Linguistics* 40 (1974): 117–19, includes Yuchi in his reconstruction of phonological rules that separated Siouan and Iroquoian-Caddoan, assuming Sapir's Siouan-Yuchi relationship. He uses Proto-Siouan forms from Wolff, "Comparative Siouan I–II," and Huber Matthews, "Some Notes on the Proto-Siouan Continuants," *International Journal of American Linguistics* 36 (1970): 98–109, which he gives as Proto-Siouan-Yuchi although neither used Yuchi in their reconstructions. He includes one verb from Yuchi in his example of the second person paradigm in Proto-Siouan-Yuchi. A reader not familiar with the history of Yuchi classification would assume the relationship to be confirmed.

54. A full review of the Siouan-Iroquoian-Caddoan-[Yuchi] hypothesis can be accessed in Campbell *American Indian Languages*, 262–69 and Chafe, "Siouan, Iroquoian, and Caddoan."

2. Enigmatic Origins
On the Yuchi of the Contact Era

~

In the fall of 1567 Spanish explorer Captain Juan Pardo received testimony from an Indian in the town of Satapo along the Little Tennessee River in what is now eastern Tennessee regarding a widespread plot to ambush Pardo's soldiers as they traveled toward the principal town of Coosa (Cosa), located in present-day northwestern Georgia.[1] According to this informant, in addition to the chief of Coosa, who seems to have been the principal architect of the plot, and the chief of Satapo itself, three other chiefs were also involved, including the chiefs of the towns of Olameco, Casqui, and Uchi (also rendered as Huchi). While this ambush was ultimately never implemented because of the hasty Spanish retreat eastward across the Appalachian summit, this documentary reference appears to have been simultaneously the first written mention of the Yuchi people during the European contact era and the last such reference for a space of nearly a century and a half. The next time the Yuchi appear in European records is during the first decades of the eighteenth century, when they were noted in relationship to both the Cherokee territory of the Appalachian highlands and the Lower Creek territory of the lower Piedmont–upper Coastal Plain region of Georgia and immediate portions of Alabama and South Carolina. As Brett Riggs explores in his chapter in this volume, although geographic locations become increasingly certain for Yuchi towns during and immediately after this period (and particularly so by midcentury), there is no clear and unequivocal indication that any of these early eighteenth-century Yuchi communities were necessarily situated within or near their original pre-European homeland, and indeed in several cases (such as the lower Chattahoochee River following the 1715 Yamasee War), there is clear evidence to the contrary, namely that the Yuchis were by that time recent immigrants from more distant lands.[2] Moreover, recent scholarship regarding the broader social and economic context surrounding the repercussions of European exploration and colonization during the sixteenth and seventeenth centuries in the interior southeastern United States suggests that transformation and relocation (sometimes radical) was more the rule than the exception, making it even less likely that the better documented Yuchi of the early eighteenth century had somehow weathered this traumatic era completely intact and unmoved from their sixteeenth-century homeland.[3]

For these reasons, the only likely hint that the documentary record has yet revealed about the original Yuchi homeland is in fact the preceding vague reference dating to the second Pardo expedition, which places the Yuchi chief in direct collaboration with a geographically extensive alliance of autonomous and semi-autonomous chiefs generally based in eastern Tennessee and northwestern Georgia during the late 1560s. Direct evidence from the Soto, Luna, and Pardo expeditions to this broader region between 1540 and 1560 provides only *negative* evidence for the Yuchi homeland, namely a narrow corridor within which the Yuchi name did *not* appear as such.[4] To this can be added the fact that the Yuchi were evidently well beyond the scope of direct European awareness until after 1700, despite the fact that indirect and occasionally direct references to a wide variety of named indigenous groups from a considerable geographic region filtered across the colonial frontier to Spanish, English, and French ports throughout this period. While this may simply have reflected their status and relative degree of autonomy in comparison to more visible groups nearer the colonial frontier, it may also have signified a more remote original location, one that only changed in the context of the turbulent colonial era, finally bringing the Yuchi to light only during the eighteenth century as refugees or migrants.

All this being said, it is important to note that any consideration of the pre-Columbian origins of the Yuchi must take into account the fact that the location of their original homeland may never be known precisely or with absolute certainty. Given that the Pardo expedition mentioned the Yuchi chief only indirectly, it may well be that no European ever set foot in the Yuchi homeland until the Yuchis dispersed to other areas. Nevertheless, recent advances in ethnohistorical and archaeological scholarship have placed modern scholars in a better position than ever to narrow down the range of possibilities for the Yuchi homeland and, regardless of this, to explore the broader social landscape within which the Yuchis likely found their pre-European roots as well as to investigate the sweeping changes that ultimately transformed the entire Southeast during the colonial era. In this way, the Yuchis can be better understood both as members of the broader world of indigenous chiefdoms in southeastern North America and as the product of a unique set of circumstances that led them to their eighteenth-century incorporation into the Creek confederacy and their persistence and survival to the present day.

At the time that the Yuchi chief was first documented by Juan Pardo among an allied group of important chiefs located in the Ridge and Valley district west of the Appalachian summit, the indigenous peoples of this interior portion of the Southeast are thought to have been routinely organized into a specific type of society that anthropologists refer to as a chiefdom.[5] Defined by a set of fundamental features including heirarchically ranked, multi-community political units with hereditary leadership based on kin-group affiliation, these chiefdoms represented the characteristic organizational dimension of the widespread Mississippian culture, within which the Yuchis and their ancestors likely participated prior to European contact. While it is not my goal in this essay to elaborate on the archaeological or ethnohistorical details of "typical" Mississippian chiefdoms in the region likely to have been home to the Yuchi during the sixteenth century, it is nonetheless important to note that recent reconstructions of the social geography of the Mississippian world provide some instructive insights into the typical demographic and geographic size of such polities as well as the extent to which smaller, local chiefdoms were commonly integrated into larger, regional structures sometimes called "paramount chiefdoms."[6]

One such instance is Coosa paramountcy, which has been reconstructed using a combination of early Spanish sources and archaeological data to have included an expansive range of named local chiefdoms extending across the Ridge and Valley district from as far south as northeastern Alabama all the way to northeastern Tennessee.[7] For the purposes of this chapter what is most notable about the proposed constituents of this overarching paramount chiefdom is that they match almost one-for-one the list of conspiring chiefs given in the Pardo documents. With the sole exception of Uchi/Huchi, all the remaining chiefs mentioned by Pardo's informant almost certainly represent the administrative centers of local chiefdoms within the northern half of the Coosa paramountcy, each of which apparently corresponds to a local cluster of late prehistoric archaeological sites. These include the Coosa chiefdom itself along the Coosawattee River, the Tasqui (Casqui) chiefdom along the Hiwassee River, the Satapo (Citico) chiefdom along the Little Tennessee River, and the Chiaha (Olamico) chiefdom along the French Broad River. Based on this interpretation, the most logical inference is that Uchi/Huchi was simply another corresponding chiefly administrative center for a local chiefdom (and its corresponding archaeological site cluster), either within or otherwise allied to the rest of these subordinate units of the Coosa paramountcy.

Given its notable mention in the Pardo account alongside other adjacent local administrative centers, Uchi/Huchi would most likely have been adjacent to or relatively near one or more of the archaeological site clusters named within the Coosa paramountcy (though presumably beyond a sparsely inhabited "buffer-zone" normally found around and between such riverine chiefdoms). Beyond this, the fact that none of the sixteenth-century Spanish expeditions into this region ever actually visited a town or chiefdom called Uchi/Huchi, combined with its complete absence from any other mention during the succeeding one and a half centuries, may imply that it was situated in a more remote location (i.e., northerly or westerly) with respect to the European colonial centers to the south and east. Indeed, Uchi/Huchi might well have been located only slightly northwest of the primary route taken by Soto, Luna, and Pardo, as was another poorly documented local chiefdom known as Napochin (its inhabitants also referred to as the Napochies), apparently located along the Tennessee River near present-day Chattanooga.[8] Had it not been for the remarkable Spanish-Coosa military expedition against this breakaway province during the Luna expedition in 1560, its name and affiliation with the Coosa paramountcy might well have been lost to history, since it too was never directly visited by any Spanish expedition.

The inhabitants of Uchi/Huchi may therefore simply have been a poorly documented local chiefdom within the Coosa paramountcy, like Napochin, perhaps originally located along the upper reaches of the Tennessee River drainage, just west or northwest of the Chiaha or Satapo chiefdoms. Alternatively, however, they may instead have been a separate people, allied but not subordinate to Coosa, and thus perhaps originally both more geographically extensive and more populous than might otherwise be expected. Their appearance within the list of allied chiefs reported at Satapo may actually have been as an autonomous and more remote group, perhaps even constituting one element of an adjacent but separate paramountcy, likely to the north. In this formulation the chief of Uchi/Huchi might have been situated farther upriver above the Tennessee River proper, perhaps along the Clinch or even Powell River drainages toward the modern Norris Basin. Recent analysis of archaeological data from this broader region indicates that there was indeed a substantial cluster of Late Mississippi period sites in the Norris Basin, probably corresponding to a discrete local chiefdom along the northern margin of the broader Dallas Phase culture characteristic of the Ridge and

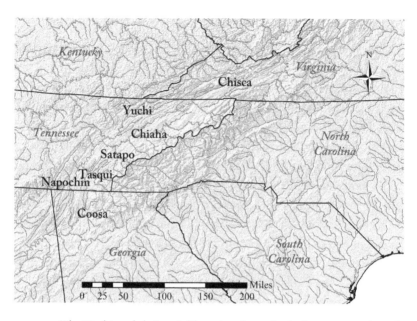

MAP 1. The Yuchi and their neighbors in a hypothetical reconstruction of regional social geography around the time of the Juan Pardo Expedition (1566–1568). Map by Brett Riggs and John E. Worth.

Valley region in eastern Tennessee.[9] Two other smaller Dallas Phase chiefdoms were located upriver in southwestern Virginia along the Clinch and Powell Rivers and might even have constituted allied or subordinate chiefdoms, which together with the Norris Basin chiefdom could have formed a smaller compound chiefdom roughly on a par with Coosa (if spatially and demographically smaller).

Map 1 provides a hypothetical overview of the reconstructed social geography of this broader region. As is evident from this scenario, this would place the possible Yuchi homeland along the northwestern fringe of the broader Dallas archaeological culture, a boundary also apparently shared by the similarly enigmatic Chisca to the east in southwestern Virginia.[10] Perhaps not coincidentally, both these groups would have comprised outliers to the geographically extensive Coosa paramountcy, which extended from the core of the Dallas Phase region southward into the northwestern margins of the Lamar archaeological culture area. Coosa itself sprawled across much of the Ridge and Valley geophysical province from Tennessee through Georgia into Alabama, and in this reconstruction, the Chisca and Yuchi polities were just distant enough to be autonomous, yet close enough to play at least some role in the broader history of the Coosa paramountcy. Synthesis of present evidence suggests that the Chisca abandoned their Virginia homeland in the first quarter of the seventeenth century, possibly as an indirect response to the Iroquois Wars farther north, and at present it is only possible to suggest that some or all of the Yuchi may have shared a similar fate, potentially dispersing toward the end of the seventeenth century in response to the same forces that seem to have affected much of the trans-Appalachian interior during the initial decades of the Indian slave trade.[11] During the first decades of the eighteenth century the Yuchi coalescence within the emerging Creek confederacy may therefore be seen as one more splinter in the broader colonial "shatter zone" of the Eastern Woodlands of North America.[12] Though apparently insulated from the effect of initial European exploration and contact due in part to their remote location, the Yuchi, like their Coosa co-conspirators in the anti-Spanish plot of 1568, ultimately left their homeland and banded together with other groups in an effort to survive the turbulent centuries of the colonial era. That they succeeded so dramatically when so many others failed is a testament to their resilience, and the story of that journey forms an important chapter in the survival of the southeastern Indians to the present day.

Notes

1. Juan de la Bandera, Relacion que dio el capitan Juan Pardo en el fuerte de Santa Elena de la entrada que hizo tierra adentro de la Florida, June 1, 1569, Archivo General de Indias, Santo Domingo 224, Ramo 1, no. 8; transcribed and translated by Paul S. Hoffman in an appendix to Charles Hudson, *The Juan Pardo Expeditions: Exploration of the Carolinas and Tennessee, 1566–1568* (Washington DC: Smithsonian Institution Press, 1990), 223–24, 270–71.

2. See John E. Worth, "The Lower Creeks: Origins and Early History," in *Indians of the Greater Southeast*, ed. Bonnie G. McEwan (Gainesville : University Press of Florida, 2000), 285–86.

3. See, for example, Marvin T. Smith, *Archaeology of Aboriginal Culture Change in the Interior Southeast: Depopulation during the Early Historic Period* (Gainesville: University Presses of Florida, 1987); Charles Hudson and Carmen Chaves Tesser, eds., *The Forgotten Centuries: Indians and Europeans in the American South, 1521–1704* (Athens : University of Georgia Press, 1994); Robbie Ethridge and Charles Hudson, eds., *The Transformation of the Southeastern Indians, 1540–1760* (Jackson, University Press of Mississippi, 2002).

4. Modern scholarly reconstructions of the routes of these three early expeditions can be found in Charles Hudson, *Knights of Spain, Warriors of the Sun: Hernando De Soto and the South's Ancient Chiefdoms* (Athens: University of Georgia Press, 1997); Charles Hudson, Marvin T. Smith, Chester DePratter, and Emilia Kelley, "The Tristan de Luna Expedition, 1559–1561" *Southeastern Archaeology* 8 (1989):31–45; and Hudson, *Pardo Expeditions.*

5. The anthropological concept of the chiefdom has evolved considerably since its early usage by Elman R. Service, *Primitive Social Organization: An Evolutionary Perspective* (New York: Random House, 1962); for the southeastern United States see, for example, John F. Scarry, ed., *Political Structure and Change in the Prehistoric Southeastern United States* (Gainesville: University Press of Florida, 1996).

6. A paramountcy forms one variant of a broader category of what I have termed "compound chiefdoms," in recognition of the observed diversity in regional polities made up of several discrete local chiefdoms linked by an overarching sociopolitical structure; see John E. Worth, "An Ethnohistorical Synthesis of Southeastern Chiefdoms: How Does Coosa Compare?" paper presented in the symposium "Coosa: Twenty Years Later" at the 60th annual meeting of the Southeastern Archaeological Conference, Charlotte, North Carolina, 12–15 November 2003.

7. Charles Hudson, Marvin Smith, David Hally, Richard Polhemus, and Chester DePratter, "Coosa: A Chiefdom in the Sixteenth-Century Southeastern United States," *American Antiquity* 50 (1985): 723–37. See also Marvin Smith, *Coosa: The Rise and Fall of a Southeastern Mississippian Chiefdom* (Gainesville: University Press of Florida, 2000).

8. For a detailed overview of this expedition, see Charles Hudson, "A Spanish-Coosa Alliance in Sixteenth-Century North Georgia," *Georgia Historical Quarterly* 72 (1988): 599–626. Recent independent documentary confirmation of both the name Napochin and the Spanish-Coosa expedition is discussed in Worth, "An Ethnohistorical Synthesis."

9. Maureen S. Meyers, "Leadership at the Edge," in *Leadership and Polity in Mississippian Society*, ed. Brian M. Butler and Paul D. Welch, 156–77

Center for Archaeological Investigations, Occasional Paper no. 33 (Carbondale: Southern Illinois University, 2006).

10. For an overview of Chisca origins and history, see entry in Patricia Galloway, Marvin D. Jeter, Gregory A. Waselkov, John E. Worth, and Ives Goddard, "Small Tribes of the Western Southeast," in *Handbook of North American Indians*, vol. 14: *Southeast*, ed. Raymond D. Fogelson, (Washington DC: Smithsonian Institution, 2004), 174–90.

11. The Chisca flight to Spanish Florida is discussed in John E. Worth, "Spanish Missions and the Persistence of Chiefly Power," in Ethridge and Hudson, *The Transformation of the Southeastern Indians*, 39–64; see also John E. Worth, *The Timucuan Chiefdoms of Spanish Florida*, vol. 2: *Resistance and Destruction* (Gainesville: University Press of Florida, 1998), 18–21, 34–35. A recent analysis of primarily English sources relative to the Indian slave trade appears in Alan Gallay, *The Indian Slave Trade: The Rise of the English Empire in the American South, 1670–1717* (New Haven CT: Yale University Press, 2002); see also Eric Bowne, *The Westo Indians: Slave Traders of the Early Colonial South* (Tuscaloosa: University of Alabama Press, 2005).

12. Robbie Ethridge, "Creating the Shatter Zone: The Indian Slave Trade and the Collapse of the Mississippian Chiefdoms," in *Light on the Path: The Anthropology and History of the Southeastern Indians*, ed. Thomas J. Pluckhahn and Robbie Ethridge (Tuscaloosa: University of Alabama Press, 2006).

3. Reconsidering Chestowee
The 1713 Raid in Regional Perspective

~

One of the first substantive narrative accounts of a Yuchi community in the southeastern interior was documented in the South Carolina Board of Indian Trade's May 1714 inquest into the Cherokee
attack on the Yuchi town of Chestowee.[1] Although Chestowee was
far distant from Charles Town, the raid concerned the board because
the Yuchis and Cherokees were both English allies, and it appeared
that licensed Carolina traders incited the attack and upset a critical
balance in the backcountry.[2] Testimony in the case reveals that the
raiders sacked the town, killed many of the defenders, and enslaved
the remainder to pay off accumulated trading debts. The commissioners investigated the role of traders Alexander Long and Eleazer Wiggan in the affair and concluded to free all the Yuchi prisoners, ban Long and Wiggan from the Indian trade, and recommended
their further prosecution by the colony.[3]

The Board of Trade account of the Chestowee affair is significant
as a documentary point of departure for discussions of colonial era
Yuchi history. Earlier ethnohistoric treatments interpreted Chestowee
as the last vestige of a late Mississippian Yuchi chiefdom in eastern
Tennessee that was expunged by Cherokee conquest.[4] More recent
analyses situate the Chestowee affair as part of a mounting trend
of trader abuses that helped spark the catastrophic Yamasee War

of 1715.[5] This chapter reexamines the geopolitical contexts of the Chestowee incident and situates the massacre as an episode characteristic of the chaotic "shatter zone" that engulfed eastern North America in the late seventeenth and early eighteenth centuries.[6]

The Board of Trade Account

Testimony in the Chestowee hearings was convoluted, but the key depositions reveal a well-planned conspiracy to "cut off" the Yuchis. Deponents at the hearings indicated "that 2 or 3 Year agoe there was a difference between Mr. [Alexander] Long and one or two People of Chestowe about debts," and Long declared that "he was abused by some Euchees and his hair torn off 2 or 3 Year agoe."[7] Witnesses noted that Long swore "he would be revenged on the People of Chestowe," that "he would have some of the Euchees' Heads on a Pole," and that "the Euchee should be cut off before green Corne Time." Long and fellow trader Eleazer Wiggan conspired with Cherokee leaders Flint and Caesar to exact revenge on Chestowee, and promised the Cherokees "a brave Parcel of Slaves if Chestowe were cut off," a particular enticement to pay off Cherokee trading debts.[8] Long apparently sought sanction for his conspiracy from South Carolina's governor, Charles Craven, in letters carried to Charles Town by Flint and Caesar in May 1713, and told the Cherokees to expect the governor's orders to cut off Chestowee. In response, Craven sent an "Order to Capt. [Robert] Card to treat the Euchees civily." Long and his co-conspirators, who may have included many of the Carolina traders among the Cherokees, delayed the delivery of Craven's letter "behind the Mountains" and presented a false document represented as the governor's orders to cut off Chestowee. Trader and explorer Price Hughes secured a promise from Cherokee leaders "not to molest the Euchee till the Agent [Thomas Nairne] came." Hughes was apparently aware that the governor's orders had been detained, and he journeyed to fetch the directive to the Cherokee leaders. In the meantime Long exhorted his Cherokee co-conspirators to carry out the attack on Chestowee before explicit orders to the contrary arrived. An expedition led by "the War Captain of

Euchase, Flint, and Caesar, and one or two more att the Middle Settlements contrived the cutting off of the Euchees and kept itt very
private till they came near the Town then painted with a Design
to fall on them."[9] The group excluded the Cherokee Lower Towns
from "their Design because they shoold not come in with them for
a Share" of the slaves and loot. Long supplied the raiders with "a
Quantity of Powder and Bulletts for Caesar and Flint to cut them
off." The raiders fell suddenly upon Chestowee, and after a desper-
ate fight, "the Euchees killed their own People in the War House
to prevent their falling into the Hands of the Cherikees."[10] The enslaved Euchee survivors were given over to traders Long, Wiggan,
Clea, Dillon, Douglas, Richardson, and others to pay off trading
debts.[11] After the attack on Chestowee the traders urged the Cherokees to "cut off the other Euchees att the Savano Town too, or elce
there would be no Travailing," implying that Yuchi vengeance was
expected against Cherokees and traders alike.[12]

Official collusion in the affair is intimated by Clea's statement
that he had received a 7 October 1713 letter from Peter St. Julien
stating "that the Governor seemed pleased with the Euchees being
cut off and that he knew no Reason why the Prisoners should not be
Slaves."[13] Despite Craven's purported post hoc approval, the board
ordered the traders "that the Euche People detained . . . shall with
all convenient Speed be delivered to their own People and that they
[the traders] shall receive no farther Satisfaction from the Euchees
for them." The board also "Ordered that Mr. Alexa. Long and Mr.
Elea. Wigon have their Licenses taken from them and that their
Bonds be prossecuted and that the President doe desire the Governor to order them to be prossecuted att the Sessions."

Previous Interpretations of the Raid on Chestowee

Early interpretations of the Chestowee affair framed the episode within constructions of an "ethnographic present" of pre-contact and early contact era southeastern native landscapes, or simply as a footnote
in Cherokee history.[14] Frederick Hodge noted both the Yuchi town at
Chestowee and the cartographically documented Cherokee town of

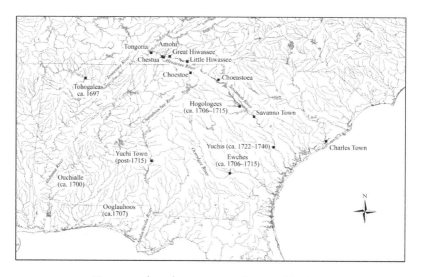

MAP 2. Towns and settlement areas discussed in this chapter. Chestua (Tennessee), Choestoe (Georgia), and Choeastoea (South Carolina) are indicated; these are orthographic variants of the Cherokee locative *Tsi sdu yi* (Rabbit Place). Other variants include Chestowee, Chestuee, and Choastea. Map by the author.

Chestuee, situated in the lower Hiwassee River Valley of eastern Tennessee, but did not specifically link the two settlements (map 2).[15] John Swanton conflated the Yuchi Chestowee with the Cherokee Chestuee of the lower Hiwassee River Valley, citing representations on slightly later English maps.[16] He also strenuously (but erroneously) asserted Yuchi-Chisca synonymy and interpreted the Yuchi settlement at Chestowee as the last vestige of Chisca occupation in the trans-Appalachian region.[17] Swanton further argued for equating the Yuchis with the Westos-Recrihecrians and Tomahitans of early English accounts to create narrative continuity through the seventeenth century.[18]

Swanton's authoritative assertion of Yuchi-Chisca synonymy became ingrained in subsequent literature as an orthodoxy that placed the Yuchis (as putative Chiscas) in the southern Appalachians in late prehistory. This equation is perpetuated in current literature as the central point of reference for Yuchi identity in the early contact period, despite John Worth's demonstration of exclusive Yuchi and Chisca identities evident in mid-sixteenth-century Spanish accounts.[19]

Joseph Bauxar revisited the Chestowee account in devising an ethnohistorical framework for the archaeological investigations in the Chickamauga Basin area of eastern Tennessee.[20] He argued that Chestowee was located along the lower Hiwassee but should be differentiated from the Overhill Cherokee settlement of Chestuee depicted on slightly later English maps.[21] Bauxar elected instead to associate Chestowee with "Tongoria" (var. of Taogaria, the Illinois term for Yuchi), a settlement near the mouth of the Hiwassee River indicated by the 1717 Vermale and 1718 de l'Isle French maps.[22] He viewed this association as consistent with a Cherokee tradition recorded in the early nineteenth century by Cherokee assistant chief Charles Hicks:

> So far as our traditioners gives any account of the extension of the settlements made by our ancestors, we are induced to believe them to be as correct as could be expected at this distant period, by which we are informed that the Highwassee old towns and Ches to eh, were the lowest settlements that composed the whole nation, who had emigrated from Big Tellico; and the first account given by traditioners was that the Uchees became their nearest neighbors who settled on the south side opposite to the mouth of Highwassee River.[23]

Inexplicably, Bauxar dismissed the existence of the Cherokee Chestuee town ("Ches to eh" in the Hicks account) in the early eighteenth century and explained the incidence of "Chestoee" or "Chestoa" in 1721, 1725, and 1733 English map depictions as persistent vestiges of the former Yuchi town. Bauxar also discussed the "probability that the apparently nearby settlement of Euphase mentioned in the proceedings is Hiwassee Old Town," an Overhill Cherokee town situated at Hiwassee River Mile 42.

Thomas Lewis and Madeline Kneberg integrated Bauxar's perspectives on Chestowee and the Yuchi occupation of the lower Hiwassee River Valley into *Hiwassee Island*, a landmark 1946 study of eastern Tennessee prehistory.[24] Citing Hicks's 1826 account as a primary basis for reconstructing the occupancy of multiple ethnic groups in the Chickamauga Basin area, Lewis and Kneberg projected

47

Creek and Yuchi affinities onto the prehistoric archaeological record to account for perceived synchronic variation (subsequent research has proven this variation essentially diachronic). Like Swanton, Lewis and Kneberg interpreted Chestowee as the last vestige of a long Chisca-Yuchi presence in eastern Tennessee and assigned Yuchi affinity to the late prehistoric Mouse Creeks archaeological focus.[25] They placed Chestowee at the Mouse Creek site (40Mn3) near the mouth of North Mouse Creek (rather than the more obvious South Chestua Creek, where the 1721 Barnwell-Hammerton map locates "Chestoee"). Extensive excavations at the Mouse Creek site yielded no European trade materials referable to the 1713 time horizon, but Lewis and Kneberg suggested that the destruction of Chestowee antedated substantial trade involvement.[26] By contrast, however, their work at the nearby Ocoee site, the contemporaneous Overhill Cherokee town of Amohee, recovered abundant early eighteenth-century trade goods, an indication that the area was well supplied by English traders at the time of the Chestowee incident. The absence of an early eighteenth-century component at the Mouse Creek site negates the purported linkage to the Yuchi community at Chestowee, and Lewis and Kneberg's failure to isolate early eighteenth-century components associated with either Chestowee or Tongoria compromises their well-known application of the direct historical approach to the Mouse Creeks focus.[27]

Such interpretations of Chestowee as the *in situ* remnant of a late prehistoric Yuchi occupation in the lower Hiwassee River Valley (and, conversely, of the lower Hiwassee River Valley as the prehistoric Yuchi homeland) were predicated on a series of interdependent arguments that no longer appear valid. Swanton's conflation of the Yuchis and Chiscas is refuted by co-occurrence of both groups in early Spanish accounts (see Worth, this volume). Swanton's placement of the Chiscas in or near the lower Hiwassee River Valley based upon his reconstruction of the route of the De Soto entrada is upended by more recent route analyses by Charles Hudson and his collaborators, which situate the enigmatic province of Chisca in upper east Tennessee.[28] Lewis and Kneberg's attempt to apply the direct historical approach to link the Mouse Creeks focus of the archaeo-logical record to the Yuchis of the documentary record falters with-out archaeological evidence of the early eighteenth-century Yuchi occupation at Chestowee and fails in the absence of the Swanton's Chisca-Yuchi construct.

Chestowee: "Cutt off" in the Shatter Zone

How then should we interpret the incident at Chestowee, a Yuchi settlement with a Cherokee name, situated on the southwestern bor-der of Cherokee territory and documented by a single contempora-neous source? Anne Rogers suggests a more immediate and literal reading that considers Chestowee within the broader trends of the early eighteenth century: "The fact that the town of Chestowa is known to have been occupied by Yuchi does not necessarily mean that they also inhabited other sites in the area. . . . By the early eigh-teenth century, that extensive mobility which characterized most of the post-contact period was well developed, and the Yuchi at Chestowa could have been recent arrivals in the area."[29] The "ex-tensive mobility that characterized most of the post-contact period" was symptomatic of the highly disrupted and dynamic character of the southeastern native landscape at the turn of the eighteenth cen-tury. Robbie Ethridge and others have recently described this cha-otic landscape—wracked by the Indian slave trade and the imperial struggles of England, France, and Spain—as a "shatter zone" com-parable to those that developed in West Africa in the eighteenth and nineteenth centuries as a result of the trans-Atlantic slave trade.[30] Ethridge notes that this shatter zone was a

> large region of instability created by the inauguration of the capi-talist market system through the trade in Indian slaves in the sev-enteenth century. The shatter zone encompassed the eastern wood-lands of the North American continent, from the St. Lawrence river valley to the Lower Mississippi river valley. Rampant slaving, com-bined with population losses from European diseases, created a re-gion of political turmoil, cultural upheaval, dislocation, and social

transformation. Indians living within the shatter zone responded in various ways — migration, militarization, extinction, coalescence, amalgamation, and dependency.[31]

The shatter zone concept, which describes a chronic and pervasive state of "political turmoil, cultural upheaval, dislocation, and social transformation," provides a structure within which the Chestowee account and the scant antecedent record of Yuchi communities are rendered more comprehensible and more consistent with regional processes and events.

The general disordering and continual reconfigurations of the native landscape that characterized the shatter zone are reflected in the broad, asynchronous dispersal of Yuchi communities and high frequency of Yuchi community relocation in the two decades prior to the Chestowee incident. The brief Yuchi occupation at Chestowee appears congruent with that pattern. The relative brevity of the Chestowee occupation can be inferred from the lack of cartographic evidence for Yuchi settlements in the lower Hiwassee River Valley prior to the Chestowee affair, despite earlier representations of Yuchi settlements in the middle Tennessee Valley and Cherokee settlements in the upper Tennessee Valley (including the lower Hiwassee region). The 1717 Vermale and 1718 de l'Isle maps depict "Tongoria" at the mouth of the Hiwassee years after the raid on Chestowee obviated Yuchi settlement within or adjacent to Cherokee territory. Earlier cartographic depictions of Yuchi settlements include the 1697 Louvigny map, which locates "V. des Togales," (i.e., Tohologees or Yuchis) on the "R. des Kasquinampous" (Tennessee River) near the "V. des Tales," the "fort des Anglois," and "4 V. des Kasquinampous."[32] Sauvole, in recounting a 1701 exploration of the Tennessee River by Canadian *coureurs de bois*, situates this locality more precisely: "The first village they found belongs to the Chicassas [Chickasaws]: it is situated on the right as one goes upstream, about one hundred and forty leagues from the Mississippi. Next one meets the Taougalés [Tohologees or Yuchis], [and] the Tales. . . . The Cassotis [Koasati] and the Caskinonpas [Kaskinampos] are on an island."[33]

Coxe noted (based on 1698 observations) a similar multi-ethnic cluster, approximately "thirty or forty leagues above the Chicazas" where "this river forms four delicate islands, which have each a nation inhabiting them, viz, Tahogale, Kakigue, Cochali, and Tali."[34] These approximated distances (if gauged in late seventeenth-century French *lieues* of 2.02 statute miles) place Chickasaw settlements in the vicinity of Georgetown, Alabama, and the Tohoglogee (Yuchi), Tali, Koasati, and Kaskinampo settlements in the vicinity of Decatur, Alabama.[35] This cluster of settlements in the middle Tennessee Valley appears on the 1701 de l'Isle map and on an anonymous, undated English map in the Crown Collection, which also depicts "Tohogalegas" on the Savannah River above present-day Augusta and "Ewches" situated on the lower Ocmulgee River.[36] These maps indicate clusters of unnamed Cherokee towns on the Little Tennessee and Hiwassee rivers but depict no Yuchi settlements in the eastern Tennessee region. Other Yuchi settlement locations are indicated by Levasseur's 1700 journal, which lists "Outchialle" (i.e., Yuchi) among the nations residing in the Alabama River basin; the 1707 Lamhatty map, which depicts "Ogolaúghoo" (i.e., Hoglogee) near the Gulf Coast (perhaps in the Chipola or Yellow river basins); and the 1718 de l'Isle map, which places "les Tongorias" in the Ohio Valley.[37]

Narrative and cartographic records present three interrelated factors that conditioned apparent Yuchi settlement mobility and location. First, records dating as early as 1691 indicate Yuchi-English trading and military alliances and document consistent enmity on the part of Yuchis toward the French and their native allies.[38] Second, each location indicated for Yuchi communities in the 1697–1715 period appears to have been in proximity to or conjunction with other English-allied native communities or trading partners.[39] Third, the native slave trade with the English of South Carolina appears to have been a common economic strategy among these multi-ethnic community clusters and may have been the basis for the formation and reformations of such clusters.[40] A native informant told Levasseur of the "Outchialle" and neighboring groups on the Alabama

River "that the English were in those nations every day, and . . . the greatest traffic between the English and the savages is the trade of slaves which the nations take from their neighbors whom they war with continously, such that the men take the women and children away and sell them to the English, each person being traded for a gun."[41] Sauvole related that in the midst of the "Taougalés," "Tales," "Cassotis," and "Caskinonpas" "there is an Englishman established to trade in slaves, as they are among several other nations." Slightly later, the "Tohogalegas" on the Savannah River and "Ewches" on the Ocmulgee River positioned themselves among other native groups that were heavily involved in the Carolina slave trade.[42] At Chestowee (whether at Chestua, Tennessee, Choestoe, Georgia, or Choeastoa, South Carolina), the Yuchi community settled adjacent to the Cherokees, English trading partners who also participated in the slave trade, albeit later and to a lesser degree than groups such as the Chickasaws, Yamasees, and Westos.[43]

The periodic movement of Yuchi communities and their recombination with other English-allied slaving groups at the beginning of the eighteenth century reflects an adaptation to the rapidly changing, and increasingly dangerous, native landscape wrought by the slave trade — the shatter zone. As slavers decimated the ranks of Spanish-allied, French-allied, or nonaligned native groups in the course of Queen Anne's War, they repositioned themselves in different areas for continued advantage in the capture and sale of slaves (along with peltry and other items) to English traders. Coalition with and proximity to other English-aligned native communities probably provided mutual protection against reprisals from French or Spanish allies. Although conclusive narrative evidence of the extent and duration of the Yuchi role in the Indian slave trade system is lacking, the strategic repositioning of Yuchi settlements, and their consistent associations with "slaving societies," suggest that the Yuchis were active slavers who raided the Ohio country and French Louisiana.

The apparent movement of Yuchi communities into the eastern Tennessee Valley, the Savannah River Valley, and the Ocmulgee River Valley during Queen Anne's War (1702–13) may also have been part of an English-directed effort to bolster Carolina's frontiers while retaining ready access to the theaters of war in Louisiana, Florida, and the Illinois country.[44] Anticipation of a major French-Spanish offensive against Carolina in 1706 prompted the English to rally their native allies, and Yuchi settlements appear to have drawn into a closer arc around Carolina's frontiers about this time.[45] Placement of the strongly pro-English Yuchi community at Chestowee, which appears to have been a "guest" town that borrowed a preexisting Cherokee settlement location and name, may also have served to guard against French influence among the Cherokees, who remained peripheral to Queen Anne's War and whose English alignment was considered insecure. In 1713 Yuchi warriors captured a group of Frenchmen with their goods, who, it was supposed, "might have a Design to tamper with the Charikees."[46] The Yuchis of Chestowee may also have helped to guard the thinly settled Cherokee frontier on the lower Hiwassee River against "the French Indians" that "frequently molest Euphase Town." Chestowee was the westernmost settlement on the Cherokee frontier, an outlier that would have absorbed the brunt of raids from Louisiana or Illinois. Additionally, the Yuchis' closer proximity to Carolina from bases at Chestowee, Savanno Town, and the Ocmulgee promoted greater access to English trade and increased opportunities to participate in profitable English expeditions, such as the 1711 campaign against the Choctaws and the 1712 Tuscarora campaign.[47]

Unfortunately for the Yuchis of Chestowee and other groups, English alliance and co-residence with other English-aligned groups did not confer immunity from the Carolina slavers. The flow of slaves from wartime expeditions only whetted the avarice of some unscrupulous traders, who, as agent Thomas Nairne observed in 1709, were "inciting one Tribe of our friends to destroy others, merely to purchase the prisoners taken for slaves. Kidnapping and selling free people of such weak Towns as were unable to resent the Injury."[48] Nairne also noted that "those English traders, who live among them had gott a trick of setting them to surprize one another's towns, by that means to have the quicker sale of their goods for the prissoners taken." Such raids were probably facilitated by uncomfortable relations within coalitions of disparate native groups cobbled together by Carolina agents. Yuchi-Cherokee relations appear to have been especially uneasy. In 1712 James Douglas, a trader at the Cherokee town of Echoe, "heard some grumbling against the Euchees" and Eleazer Wiggan testified "that the Cherikees were dissatisfied for the Loss of some of their People" to the Yuchis, apparently a reference to kidnapping and enslavement of Cherokees. Benjamin Clea testified "that the Euches before the Disturbance killed one Cherikee."[49] Alexander Long, who resented the loss of his scalp to Yuchi warriors in 1711, seized upon Cherokee "dissatisfaction" to engineer his revenge upon Chestowee. Long applied a proven formula for "cutting off" and enslaving small towns, probably patterning his scheme after a 1707 incident in which "one James Child . . . raised the people of some of the Chereckie towns and led them to cutt off two or three small towns of our friends, pretending 'twas the Governor's order, they destroyed the towns" of Coosas and Tallapoosas and sold the captives.[50] When Long wrote to Governor Craven in 1713 to seek official sanction for the planned raid, he may have cited reports that "the Uche or Round Town People were going from their Settlement and itt was thought were goeing to the French" as justification for attacking the Yuchis.[51] Under the pretexts of Yuchi desertion from the English and rumored Yuchi attacks on their Cherokee hosts, and perhaps with official collusion, Long probably assumed that he could execute his plot with impunity. Instead, Long and his co-conspirators fell afoul the recently reinstated agent Thomas Nairne, who had increased enforcement of trade policies in an attempt to rein in the abusive traders who jeopardized Carolina's security by alienating the colony's native allies.[52]

Aftermath of the Chestowee Affair

Long's scheme achieved his immediate objectives; Chestowee was destroyed, and its inhabitants were either killed or enslaved to pay Yuchi and Cherokee trading debts. Long's burning desire for vengeance was presumably sated. The trader probably neither foresaw nor cared about the broader repercussions of his scheme, which reverberated through the Southeast for decades. The most immediate outcome of the Chestowee raid was extirpation of the Yuchis from the Tennessee Valley for most of the eighteenth century.[53] Driven from eastern Tennessee, the Chestowee survivors joined the Savanno Town Yuchis or the "Ewches" of Ocmulgee River, in close contact (and, presumably, alliance) with Lower Creeks, Yamasees, Apalachees, Savannas, and Pallachacolas, key combatants in the Yamasee War of 1715–18.[54] These settlements were rife with anxiety and unrest over increasingly abusive Carolina traders and spiraling trade debt. The Yuchis' experience at Chestowee informed mounting native distress about Carolina's loss of control over rogue traders and attested the very real threat of the Carolina slave trade cannibalizing its own allied slavers.[55] When rumors circulated "that the white men would come and fetch . . . the Yamassees in one night . . . take all the rest of them for slaves, and . . . send them all off the country," the Chestowee survivors could vouch for the plausibility of the rumor.[56] At the outbreak of the Yamasee War in April 1715, the Yuchis cast their lot with the militants and were in the forefront of attacks on Carolina. After initial successes the Yamasees and their allies suffered a series of military setbacks, and the militant settlements on the Savannah and Ocmulgee retreated to the Chattahoochee to escape the reprisals of the Carolinians.[57]

The Yamasee War deepened the Yuchis' dependent alliance with the Lower Creeks, especially connections with the town of Cussita.[58] This alliance strengthened the Yuchi position for avenging the Chestowee killings, and events in the Yamasee War enabled Yuchis to prosecute their revenge on the Cherokees with support from their Creek hosts. Early in the Yamasee War Carolina dispatched Eleazer Wiggan to woo the Cherokees into English alliance, specifically to fight the Yuchis, Yamasees, and Apalachees.[59] Later, when George Chicken conferred with Cherokee leaders about joining the fight against "ye Southward Indians" (i.e., Lower Creeks, Yamasees, Yuchis, Apalachees, and Savannas), the Conjuror of Tugaloo informed him that the Yamasees were "his ancient peapall and that he would not fitte ageanst them and as for ye Crickes [Creeks] they hade excepted [accepted] ye flag of trouce," but that the Cherokees would eagerly join the fight against "ye Sauonoses [Savannas] and yutsees [Yuchis] and apolachees [Apalachees]." In another meeting Chicken held out the lure of plunder and slaves for the Cherokees to join the war against "ye Southward Indians," they responded, "It was not plunder they wanted from them, but to go to war with them and cut them of[f], for it was but as yesterday as they were at war together & It was by ye perswasions of ye English they were ever at peace."[60] The pro-English war faction among the Cherokees committed the nation by killing eleven Lower Creek ambassadors at Tugaloo, thus embroiling the Cherokees in a conflict with the Lower Creeks (and their Yuchi constituents) that dragged far beyond the Yamasee War.[61] With Lower Creeks (and occasionally Tallapoosas, Coosas, and Abihkas) in the lead, Yuchi warriors participated in raids that cut off a number of Cherokee towns, including Naucoochee and Quannassee, and assailed key settlements such as Tugaloo and Estatoe, causing a general retrenchment and contraction of the Cherokee periphery.[62] The protracted Creek-Cherokee War spun into a supraregional conflict that consumed the Cherokees, Chickasaws, Catawbas, Creeks, Choctaws, and even the northern Iroquois in endless cycles of blood revenge that played out across much of eastern North America.

While the Chestowee attack certainly did not cause either the Yamasee War or the ensuing Creek-Cherokee War, the 1713 raid clearly informed and shaped these conflicts by delineating Yuchi-Cherokee opposition. Yuchi alliance with, and eventual incorporation into, the emergent Creek Nation grew from these conflicts that spanned an entire generation. This dependent alliance originally derived, in part, from Yuchis' need for a secure base from which to avenge Chestowee, and it came to define the Yuchis' place in the sociopolitical landscape of the Southeast that emerged in the aftermath of the Yamasee War.

Conclusions

The Board of Trade account of the Chestowee affair provides an important narrative window on a Yuchi community in the crucible of the southeastern shatter zone. Contrary to early interpretations of the account, the presence of the Yuchi community at Chestowee in 1713 cannot be construed as evidence of pre-contact or protohistoric Yuchi occupation in the Hiwassee River Valley. Conversely, neither does the account negate the hypothesis of protohistoric era Yuchi presence in eastern Tennessee; it simply does not speak to that point. Instead, the Chestowee account, in conjunction with narrative and cartographic evidence from the preceding decade, yields a view of the Yuchis as a small, yet militarily potent and highly mobile nation that adapted to the chaos of the late seventeenth and early eighteenth centuries by assuming roles as armed proxies, trading partners, and slavers for the English. This alternative reading of the Yuchis' role in the shatter zone runs counter to representations of the Yuchis as an embattled tribe on the run, forced from their ancient homeland and compelled to seek refuge on the margins of more powerful groups.

The Yuchis' probable engagement as active participants in the slave trading economy reflects one of the few strategies for survival available to small societies that were trapped in the maelstrom of the shatter zone. This strategy, marked by frequent relocations and shifting alliances, closely parallels that of the Westos and Chiscas, and the common adaptations and trajectories of these culturally distinct groups may have led Swanton to mistake their shared roles for shared identity.

The shatter zone presented its inhabitants with repugnant choices; groups such as the Yuchis, Westos, and Chiscas either became well equipped and militarily aggressive or suffered the fate of tens of thousands of Indians shipped off to toil away short lives on the sugar plantations of the West Indies. The Yuchis opted for survival as a small nation that cast a large and heavily armed shadow across the Southeast, but at Chestowee, that strategy failed, and one Yuchi community reaped the whirlwind when the Carolina Indian slave trade consumed some of its own.

Acknowledgments

The author gratefully acknowledges the contributions of a host of attentive readers who reviewed and commented on this paper, to wit: Steve Davis, Duane Esarey, Robbie Ethridge, Mary Beth Fitts, Michael Green, Lance Greene, Charles Hudson, Bill Jurgelski, Jon Marcoux, Gerald Schroedl, Vin Steponaitis, Lynn Sullivan, and John Worth. In addition I particularly appreciate Jason Jackson's care, patience, and tenacity in assembling this volume; I hope this offering furthers his goal to make Yuchi history more accessible to Yuchi people.

Notes

1. Minutes of the inquest are reproduced in William L. McDowell Jr., ed., *Journals of the Commissioners of the Indian Trade, September 20, 1710–August 29, 1718*, The Colonial Records of South Carolina, series 2, vol. 1 (Columbia: South Carolina Archives Department, 1955), 53–57 (hereafter cited as JCIT).

2. The location of Chestowee is not directly indicated by the trade board records or other contemporary documents, but various statements in the hearings suggest an eastern Tennessee location. Swanton and Bauxar equate the Yuchi Chestowee with the Overhill Cherokee Chestuee (*Tsi sdu yi*: Rabbit Place) and locate the settlement in the lower Hiwassee River Valley of eastern Tennessee (indicated as Chestoee on the 1721 Barnwell-Hammerton map). Other Cherokee places named Chestuee are Choestoe, in Union County, Georgia (near Blairsville) and Choestoea Creek near Westminster, South Carolina (see Map 2). See John R. Swanton, *The Early History of the Creek Indians and Their Neighbors*. Bureau of American Ethnology Bulletin 73. (1922; repr., Gainesville: University Press of Florida, 1998), 97; and J. Joseph Bauxar, "Ethnohistorical Reconstructions," in *The Prehistory of the Chickamauga Basin in Tennessee* by Thomas M. N. Lewis and Madeline D. Kneberg Lewis [ca. 1940], ed. Lynne P. Sullivan (Knoxville: University of Tennessee Press, 1995), 241–64.

3. JCIT, 56.

4. See John R. Swanton, "Identity of the Westo Indians," *American Anthropologist* 21 (1919): 213–16; Swanton, *Early History of the Creek Indians and their Neighbors*; Thomas M. N. Lewis and Madeline Kneberg, *Hiwassee Island: An Archaeological Account of Four Tennessee Indian Peoples*

(Knoxville: University of Tennessee Press, 1946); and J. Joseph Bauxar, "Yuchi Ethnoarchaeology: Parts II–V," *Ethnohistory* 4 (1957): 369–464.

5. For recent discussions of the Yamasee War and the contributing role of the Chestowee massacre, see Steven James Oatis, *A Colonial Complex: South Carolina's Changing Frontiers in the Era of the Yamasee War, 1680–1730* (Lincoln: University of Nebraska Press, 2004); William Ramsey, "'Something Cloudy in Their Looks': The Origins of the Yamasee War Reconsidered," *Journal of American History* 9 (2003): 44–75; and Alan Gallay, *The Indian Slave Trade: The Rise of the English Empire in the American South, 1670–1717* (New Haven CT: Yale University Press, 2002), 319–20.

6. For a discussion of the application of "shatter zone" theory in the southeastern United States, see Robbie Ethridge, "Creating the Shatter Zone: The Indian Slave Trade and the Collapse of the Mississippian Chiefdoms," in *Light on the Path: The Anthropology and History of the Southeastern Indians*, ed. Thomas J. Pluckhahn and Robbie Ethridge (Tuscaloosa: University of Alabama Press, 2006). In Robbie Ethridge and Sheri M. Shuck Hall, eds., *Mapping the Mississippian Shatter Zone* (Lincoln: University of Nebraska Press, 2009), contributing authors present case studies of the destabilizing effects of "shatter zone" conditions on native societies of the Southeast.

7. Alexander Long was a licensed trader among the Cherokees (ca. 1711–14), JCIT, 7, 53–57. Chicken (1716) relates that the "Cherry heague of Cusauwaithee" stated: "The reasons he gives that he has had from several of the war's first breaking out was one Alexander Long running away from Carolinay, came up here and told these people that the English was going to make war with them and that they did design to kill all their head warriors which was the reason he ran away." Long hid among the Cherokees throughout the Yamasee War but later returned to South Carolina and penned a tract on the Cherokees for the Society for the Propagation of the Gospel. See George Chicken, "Journal of the March of the Carolinians into the Cherokee Mountains," in *City of Charleston Year-book, 1894*, ed. Langdon Cheves (Charleston SC: Walker, Evans and Cogswell, 1895), and Alexander Longe, "A Small Postscript on the Ways and Manners of the Indians Called Cherokees," ed. David Corkran, *Southern Indian Studies* 21 (1969): 3–49.

8. Eleazer Wiggan, an early licensed trader among the Cherokees, "was also conserned in incouraging the Cherikees to cut off the Euchees" (JCIT, 55) and was censured by the board. He was restored to colonial favor during the Yamasee War, when he successfully carried out a mission to lure the Cherokees away from the uprising and into re-alliance with Carolina. In 1717 Wiggan was appointed principal factor in the Catawba trade (JCIT, 179).

"Flint, a Cherikee Indian living on Cussata River" (JCIT, 45), was one of the principals of the Chestowee affair. At the outset of the eighteenth century, the "Hohologees or Cussates River" denominated the Tennessee; the name derives from a cluster of Tohogalege (Yuchi), Koasati, and Tali towns situated on islands in northern Alabama. The term "Cussata River" probably extended up the Little Tennessee as far as the Cherokee Upper Towns in eastern Tennessee. Flint (Tawiskala) appears to have been a war leader from the Upper or Overhill Towns.

Caesar was a headman in the Cherokee Middle Towns (most likely Watogoa or Watauga), on the upper Little Tennessee River, and a former slave of John Stephens. He was fluent in English and acquainted with English customs and frequently served as translator and broker in Cherokee transactions with the Carolinians. For an account of Caesar's role as broker in 1715, see Chicken, "Journal of the March of the Carolinians into the Cherokee Mountains."

9. "Euchase" is probably a mistranscription of "Euphase," the only named Cherokee settlement implicated in the Chestowee affair. Euphase Town refers to a Cherokee settlement designated Hiwassee (*A hyu wha si*: Meadow Place). Great Hiwassee was located in the lower Hiwassee River Valley near Delano, Tennessee; Little Hiwassee was located on the upper Hiwassee River at Peachtree, North Carolina. In 1721 "Great Euphusee" had 202 inhabitants while "Little Euphusee" had 252 souls. Prior to the Yamasee War, Carolina traders were more thoroughly acquainted with Little Hiwassee.

In the aftermath of the raid on Chestowee,

> the Indians had been perswaded to desert Euphase Town. And being asked if any white Men had any Hand in perswading them to remove said that Mr. Long had been the Cause of it as the Indians told him. . . . Partridg being called said the People have left Euphase all but six Houses; that Mr. Long said that the Warriers were ould Women and that he was going down to the Governor and that he would have them cutt off as the Euchees had been.

Abandonment of Euphase Town probably reflects apprehension of Yuchi reprisals to avenge the role of the "War Captain of Euchase" and his followers in the attack. The town was largely abandoned after the visit of the board's agent, Thomas Nairne, who undoubtedly expressed the disapproval of the board and the colony over the attack on Chestowee and who probably ordered the detention of Long and Wiggan for the board hearing. Long was incensed when he attempted to "gather Meat and Oyle" and found that "the People have left Euphase all but six Houses." Long's procurement of meat and oil at Euphase indicates his residence within or near the town. Testimony "that one of the Euchees was att Long's House before the Town was cut off for Powder and that Long put Powder behind him and sett fier to itt and blew him up" indicates that the Euchees of Chestowee also traded at Long's establishment and implies that the Cherokee town of Euphase and the Yuchi town of Chestowe were located in relative proximity. The Overhill settlement of Great Hiwassee was located some eight miles from the Overhills Chestua; Choestoe, Georgia, is situated thirty miles from Little Hiwassee in the Valley Towns.

The respective populations of Great Hiwassee and Little Hiwassee are documented by the 1721 Varnod census, reproduced by Peter H. Wood, "The Changing Population of the Colonial South: An Overview by Race and Region, 1685–1790," in *Powhatan's Mantle: Indians in the Colonial Southeast*, ed. Peter H. Wood, Gregory A. Waselkov, and M. Thomas Hatley (Lincoln: University of Nebraska Press, 1989), 62.

10. This attack clearly occurred prior to October 1713 (JCIT, 56) and may have taken place "before green Corne Time" at the full moon of July or early August, the traditional time for the busk or Green Corn Ceremony.

11. Carolina traders Benjamin Clea, Robert Card, Garrett Dillon, John Chester, George Sheel, James Douglas, and Stephen Trumbull gave testimony in the Chestowee hearings. Most were involved in the Cherokee trade; in 1713 Dillon and Douglas appear to have been situated at Itsho (Echoy) in the Middle settlements (JCIT, 49).

12. The "Euchees att the Savano Town" refers to a community established on the southwestern side of the Savannah River in present-day Columbia County, Georgia, about 1706–7. Savano Town, a settlement established by the Savannah (Shawnee) nation after the expulsion of the Westos in 1683, became a major center of the South Carolina Indian trade in the late seventeenth and early eighteenth centuries. Most of the Savannahs "deserted" the Savannah River and the Carolina trade in 1707. For discussions of the Savannah exodus, see Verner W. Crane, *The Southern Frontier, 1670–1732* (1929; repr. Ann Arbor: University of Michigan Press, 1956), 148, and Gallay, *The Indian Slave Trade*, 210–12.

13. JCIT, 56.

14. The attack on Chestowee enters the historical literature with Logan's 1859 *A History of the Upper Country of South Carolina*, and may be reflected (although not by name) in Ramsey's 1853 account of the Cherokee extirpation of the Yuchis at "Uchee Old Fields" in eastern Tennessee. James G. M. Ramsey, *The Annals of Tennessee to the End of the Eighteenth Century* (Philadelphia: Lippincott, Grambo and Company, 1853).

15. Frederick Webb Hodge, ed. *Handbook of American Indians North of Mexico*, Bureau of American Ethnology Bulletin 30 (Washington DC: Government Printing Office, 1907–10), 190.

16. Swanton, *Early History of the Creek Indians and their Neighbors*, 297.

17. Swanton based the presumptive Yuchi-Chisca connection "on circumstantial evidence only, but that of the strongest. We have it ["the name Chisca"] first as of a people in the eastern mountains of Tennessee encountered by De Soto, Pardo, and Moyano, and we know that there was a Yuchi band there, occupying in later times a town called Tsistuyi [Chestowee], "Frog town," [sic] by the Cherokee, possibly a pun on Chisca, a town which the Cherokee destroyed about 1714." John R. Swanton, "Identity of the Westo Indians," *American Anthropologist* 21 (1919): 213–14.

Worth demonstrates the co-occurrence of discretely named Chiscas and Uchis in the Bandera document and traces a long (if sparse) history of the Chiscas distinct from that of the Yuchis. See "Chisca" in Patricia Galloway, Marvin D. Jeter, Gregory A. Waselkov, John E. Worth, and Ives Goddard, "Small Tribes of the Western Southeast," in *Handbook of North American Indians*, 14: *Southeast*, ed. Raymond D. Fogelson (Washington DC: Smithsonian Institution, 2004), 176–90; and John E. Worth, *The Timucuan Chiefdoms of Spanish Florida*, vol. 2: *Resistance and Destruction* (Gainesville: University Press of Florida, 1998), 208. See especially Worth's contribution to this volume.

18. Crane debated Swanton's equivalencies and argued convincingly for an Erie-Rickahecrian identity for the Westos; Bowne's recent research reinforces Crane's argument that the Westos were a recently emigrated band of Eries displaced by the Five Nations. See Verner W. Crane, "An Historical Note on the Westo Indians," *American Anthropologist* 20 (1918): 331–37, and Eric Bowne, *The Westo Indians: Slave Traders of the Early Colonial South* (Tuscaloosa: University of Alabama Press, 2005). The fabled Tomahitans of Abraham Wood's 1674 account of the travels of Needham and Arthur have been variously identified as Cherokee or Yuchi, but such associations are apparently negated by William Hatton's 1724 report of a raid on a trader's house at the Cherokee Lower town of Tugaloo by a party of "Tallepoosas," "Euchees," "Tooegellahs," "Cowealahi," and "Tomahitake." This account differentiates the "Euchees" from the "Tomahitake," or Tamahita, as distinct members of the emerging Creek Confederacy. See William Hatton to Gov. Nicholson, November 12, 1724, British Public Record Office, CO 5/359, fol. 266, abstracted in William L. Anderson and James A. Lewis, *A Guide to Cherokee Documents in Foreign Archives* (Metuchen NJ: Scarecrow Press, 1983). For a presentation

and interpretation of Wood's report, see R. P. Stephen Davis Jr., "The Travels of James Needham and Gabriel Arthur through Virginia, North Carolina, and Beyond, 1673–1674," *Southern Indian Studies* 39 (1990): 31–55.

19. For a recent example of the continued conflation of documentary evidence of Chiscas and Yuchis, see John H. Hann, *The Native American World Beyond Apalachee* (Gainesville: University Press of Florida, 2006).

20. Joseph Bauxar [aka Joseph Finkelstein], "Ethnohistorical Reconstructions," 241–64, and "Yuchi Ethnoarchaeology, Parts II–V," 369–464. Bauxar later clarified and refined his ethnohistoric reconstructions for the Yuchis and presented well-reasoned and persuasive arguments to counter Swanton's conflation of the Yuchis with Chiscas, Westos, Tomahitans, Tacogane, and Taharea. Nevertheless, he observed: "The assumption that the Chisca dwelling had a sub-surface floor is the strongest evidence that the Chisca may have been Yuchi," and "The sub-surface house floor is one of the diagnostic traits of the Mouse Creeks Focus and is basic to the identification of Mouse Creeks as Yuchi. What may be considered such a type of house has been noted for the Chisca, identified by Swanton as Yuchi."

21. The first cartographic depictions of Chestuee are included on the 1721 Barnwell-Hammerton map of the Southeast and the 1730 George Hunter map of the "Cherokee Nation and the Trader's Path from Charlestown via Congaree." For discussions of these maps, see William P. Cumming, *The Southeast in Early Maps* (Chapel Hill: University of North Carolina Press, 1998), 218–19, 228.

22. Ives Goddard and Jack B. Martin note: "The Shawnee name for the Yuchi is *tahokale* (pl. *tahokale·ki*) . . . this has no meaning as an Algonkin word and was presumably borrowed from Yuchi, perhaps from a town location. The Shawnee word was borrowed as Illinois taogaria." Ives Goddard and Jack B. Martin, "Synonymy," in Jason Baird Jackson, "Yuchi," in *Handbook of North American Indians*, vol. 14: *Southeast*, ed. Raymond D. Fogelson (Washington DC: Smithsonian Institution, 2004), 428

23. Charles R. Hicks, letter to John Ross, 1 March 1826, Payne Papers, Newberry Library, Chicago. Hicks's traditional history makes no mention of the attack on Chestowee, but John Norton relates a similar incident involving the Natchez, with the reported murder of Cherokee hosts by Natchez guests, and near annihilation of the Natchez in a townhouse, in which "The Natchez Chief and some of his followers put an end to their lives by their own hands" rather than be taken. Carl F. Klinck and James J. Talman, eds., *The Journal of Major John Norton, 1816* (Toronto: Champlain Society, 1970), 46–47. Ramsay reported a probable Cherokee tradition that:

"A small tribe of Uchees once occupied the country near the mouth of Hiwassee. Their warriors were exterminated in a battle with the Cherokee. Little else is known of them.

. . . [The Cherokee] met the entire tribe of the Uchees, at Uchee Old Fields, in what is now Rhea county, and exterminating all its warriors."
Ramsey, *The Annals of Tennessee*, 81, 84

24. Lewis and Kneberg, *Hiwassee Island*.

25. The Mouse Creeks focus, now termed the Mouse Creek phase (ca. AD 1400–1600), is a late Mississippian period configuration defined by components at the Mouse Creek, Rymer, and Ledford Island village sites in the lower Hiwassee River Valley. See Lynn P. Sullivan, "The Mouse Creek Phase Household," *Southeastern Archaeology* 6 (1987): 16–29, and Lynn P. Sullivan, "The Late Mississippian Village: Community and Society of the Mouse Creek Phase in Southeastern Tennessee," PhD diss., University of Wisconsin, Milwaukee, 1986.

26. Lewis and Kneberg's well-known Chestowee-Yuchi-Chisca-Mouse Creek construct was a classic house-of-cards argument based on a series of interdependent assumptions. They assumed (1) the validity of Swanton's Yuchi-Chisca equation; (2) the accuracy of Swanton's reconstruction of the route of the DeSoto entrada and placement of the Chisca in the Hiwassee River Valley; (3) that the region "had been continuously inhabited by Muskhogean peoples (assuming Muskhogean to be equated with Middle Mississippi culture) for a long period"; (4) that variability in the archaeological record was primarily synchronic, and therefore attributable to ethnic differences; (5) that Mouse Creeks focus sites dated to the historic era because some postholes yielded undecayed wood; and (6) that Overhill Cherokee constituted a very late, intrusive horizon in the lower Hiwassee River Valley. All of these assumptions have since proven invalid.

27. Sullivan has firmly situated the Mouse Creek site and other Mouse Creeks focus/phase components in the ca. AD 1400–1600 span (Lynn P. Sullivan, "Mississippian Household and Community Organization in Eastern Tennessee," in *Mississippian Communities and Households*, ed. J. Daniel Rogers and Bruce D. Smith, (Tuscaloosa: University of Alabama Press, 1995), 99–123. Neither have subsequent archaeological surveys in Chickamauga Reservoir and the lower Hiwassee River Valley identified archaeological components referable to the early eighteenth century Yuchi occupations at Chestowee or Tongoria. Archaeological components dating to the time of the attack on Chestowee have been identified at the Overhill Cherokee sites of Ocoee (Amohee, 40PK2)

and Hiwassee Old Town (40PK3) and in contexts of undetermined cultural af-filiation at Hiwassee Island (40MG31). See Marvin T. Smith, *An Archaeological Survey of Portions of the Chickamauga Reservoir, Tennessee 1987–1988*, submitted to Tennessee Valley Authority (Atlanta, GA: Garrow and Associates,1988); Joseph L. Benthall, *An Archaeological Reconnaissance of Portions of the Hiwassee and Ocoee Rivers in Polk, Bradley, and McMinn counties, Tennessee, 1985–1986* (Nashville: Tennessee Department of Environment and Conservation, Division of Archaeology, 1995).

28. Charles Hudson, *Knights of Spain, Warriors of the Sun: Hernando De Soto and the South's Ancient Chiefdoms* (Athens: University of Georgia Press, 1997); Charles Hudson, Marvin Smith, David Hally, Richard Polhemus, and Chester DePratter, "Coosa: A Chiefdom in the Sixteenth-Century Southeastern United States," *American Antiquity* 50 (1985): 723–37; and Charles Hudson, Chester B. DePratter, and Marvin T. Smith, "Hernando de Soto's Expedition through the Southern United States," in *First Encounters: Spanish Explorations in the Caribbean and the United States, 1492–1570*, ed. Jerald Milanich and Susan Milbrath (Gainesville: University of Florida Press, 1989), 77–98. In the present volume John Worth suggests that the Chiscas were located in southwestern Virginia at the time of initial Spanish contact. See also John E. Worth, Chisca entry, in Galloway et al., "Small Tribes of the Western Southeast," 174–90.

29. Anne Frasier Rogers, "Ethnohistory, Archaeology and the Yuchi," *Early Georgia* 7 (1979): 27–42, at 36. Rogers alludes to the central flaw in the application of the direct historical approach to the Mouse Creeks focus—the lack of documentary linkage to specific archaeological sites. Although Lewis and Kneberg contended that the Mouse Creek site was referable to Chestowee, they found no materials or site attributes related to early eighteenth-century components at Chestowee or Tongoria as beginning reference points for their argument, and thereby violated Julian Steward's original dictum that "the direct historical approach involves the elementary logic of working from the known to the unknown." See Julian H. Steward, "The Direct Historical Approach to Archaeology," *American Antiquity*, 7 (1942): 337–43.

30. Robbie Ethridge, "Introduction," in *Mapping the Mississippian Shatter Zone*, ed. Robbie Ethridge and Sheri M. Shuck Hall (Lincoln: University of Nebraska Press, 2009), and Robbie Ethridge, "Creating the Shatter Zone: The Indian Slave Trade and the Collapse of the Mississippian Chiefdoms," in *Light on the Path: The Anthropology and History of the Southeastern Indians*, ed. Thomas J. Pluckhahn and Robbie Ethridge (Tuscaloosa: University of Alabama Press, 2006). The application of the shatter zone concept in the Southeast

was featured in the symposium "The Social History of the Southeastern Indians: The Seventeenth-Century Indian Slave Trade and the Creation of a Shatter Zone" at the 59th Annual Southeastern Archaeological Conference, Biloxi, Mississippi, 2002, with papers including Maureen S. Meyers, "Adapting to the Shatter Zone," Marvin D. Jeter, "Shatter Zone Shock Waves Along the Lower Mississippi," and John E. Worth, "Reign of Terror: The Indian Slave Trade and the Devastation of Spanish Florida, 1659–1715."

31. Robbie Ethridge, "Shatter Zone: The Early Colonial Slave Trade and Its Consequences for the Natives of the Eastern Woodlands," paper presented at the Annual Conference of American Society for Ethnohistory, Riverside, California, 2003.

32. Louis de la Porte Louvigny, *Carte de Fleuve Missisipi*, Depot de la Marine, Paris, B.D.H. C-4-4-10 (ca. 1697), catalogued in Woodbury Lowery, *A Descriptive List of Maps of the Spanish Possessions within the Present Limits of the United States, 1502–1820*, ed. Philip Lee Phillips (Washington DC: Government Printing Office, 1912).

33. M. Sauvole, Suite de ce qui s'est passé dans le Fort de Biloxy, 4 Aoust 1701, Archives Nationales, Colonies, C13 A1:f. 315–22 (transcript in Library of Congress).

34. Daniel Coxe, "A Description of the English Province of Carolana, 1705," in *Historical Collections of Louisiana*, part II, ed. B. F. French (Philadelphia PA; n.p., 1850).

35. Neither Savoule nor Coxe is explicit about the length of the league in these descriptions. The seventeenth-century French *lieue* equals 2.02 statute miles; the eighteenth-century *lieue de poste* translates as 2.42 statute miles; and the *lieue marine* equals 2.76 statute miles. If Savoule and Coxe referenced *lieues de poste* (and if they both referenced the same units), the Chickasaw settlement would be farther upstream near Decatur, Alabama, and the Tohogalogee, Koasati, Tali, and Kaskinampo towns would be located upstream from Guntersville, Alabama.

36. A. B. Hulbert, *Crown Collection*, Series III, Plates 13–16, British Public Record Office, CO 700, Carolina no. 3 (London), in *Nairne's Muskhogean Journals*, ed. Alexander Moore (Jackson: University Press of Mississippi, 1988). Moore notes that the map is typically credited to Richard Beresford and that the basic information derives from Nairne's 1708 expedition. A more readily available version and discussion of this map is presented in Cumming, *The Southeast in Early Maps*, 206. Cumming assigns a date of circa 1715 to this map, based on assumptions that annotations of "since ye war" refer to the Yamasee War, but these more likely refer to Queen Anne's war. Map features

and annotations generally reflect a sociopolitical landscape that predates the 1715 Yamasee War. The map also indicates Bath, North Carolina (founded in 1705) and Fort Louis/Fort Mobile (1702–11) but does not depict New Bern (1710), Edenton (1712), or Fort Condé (1711).

37. Vernon James Knight Jr. and Sheree L. Adams, "A Voyage to the Mobile and Tomeh in 1700, with Notes on the Interior of Alabama," *Ethnohistory* 28 (1981): 179–94. Lamhatty, a Towassa Indian who traveled from the Gulf Coast to Virginia ca. 1706–8, drew a map of his route with annotations dictated to and recorded by Robert Beverly. For discussion of Lamhatty and his map, see David I. Bushnell Jr., "The Account of Lamhatty," *American Anthropologist* 10 (1908): 568–74, and Gregory Waselkov, "Indian Maps of the Colonial Southeast," in *Powhatan's Mantle: Indians in the Colonial Southeast*, ed. Peter H. Wood, Gregory A. Waselkov, and M. Thomas Hatley (Lincoln: University of Nebraska Press, 1989), 292–343. Guillaume de l'Isle, *Carte de la Louisiane et du Cours du Mississippi*, 1718, reproduced in Cumming, *The Southeast in Early Maps*, plate 47.

38. Crane cites a 1691 act by the colony of South Carolina that indicates "Attohokolegys" involved in the English trade. See Verner W. Crane, "An Historical Note on the Westo Indians," 331–37. De la Harpe noted in 1703 that "four Chicachas brought the news that five Frenchmen had been killed by the Taogarios, a nation established on the river of the Casquinambo . . . that this stroke had been executed at the solicitation of the English carrying on the trade that had been established with that nation." Bernard de La Harpe, *Journal Historique de l'Etablissement des Français à la Louisiane* (Nouvelle-Orléans: A.-L. Boimare, 1831).

39. Yuchi associates during the late seventeenth and early eighteenth centuries include the Koasati, Alabamu, Tallapoosas, and particularly the Savannahs. Consistent association with the Savannahs (Shawnees) is reflected use of the Shawnee term *tahogale* in reference to Yuchis, the Yuchi use of the Shawnee language in conversing with early French explorers in the Mississippi Valley, and Bartram's confusion of the "Savanucca" tongue as the Yuchi language.

40. The Yuchis' early locations in the middle Tennessee, Coosa-Tallapoosa, and Gulf areas may reflect an adaptation to Carolina's proprietary rules that ostensibly barred slaving within a 200-mile to 500-mile buffer around Charles Town. For discussions of the Carolina slave trade, see Gallay, *The Indian Slave Trade*, and John E. Worth, "Reign of Terror: The Indian Slave Trade and the Devastation of Spanish Florida, 1659–1715," paper presented in the symposium "The Social History of the Southeastern Indians: The Seventeenth-Century Indian Slave Trade and the Creation of a Shatter Zone" at the 59th Annual Southeastern Archaeological Conference, Biloxi, Mississippi, 2002.

41. See Knight and Adams, "A Voyage to the Mobile and Tomeh in 1700," 181–82.

42. On the Savannah, the Tohogaleas were situated near the Savannahs (Shawnees), Apalachicolas, and Apalachee refugees. "Ewches" located on the Ocmulgee lived near Chehaw (a Yamasee settlement), Atasi, Oconee, Ocmulgee, Coweeta, and other "Lower Creek" towns as well as a remnant of the Westos. See John E. Worth, "The Lower Creeks: Origins and Early History," in *Indians of the Greater Southeast*, ed. Bonnie G. McEwan (Gainesville: University Press of Florida, 2000), 285–86.

43. Ethridge, "Creating the Shatter Zone," 208–9, proposes the term "militaristic slaving society" to denote those groups that became heavily armed, highly militarized, and aggressive in adaptation to the commercial slave trade. She contends that for such groups, this adaptation "became one of the structural principles of life around which most everything else revolved."

44. As early as 1703 the South Carolina House of Commons authorized "one or two Sensibile men" to "perwade ye Talabooses if possible to Remove to the Cussitaw River." Agent Thomas Nairne actively encouraged the Yazoos, Natchez, Tasses, Talapoosas, Chickasaws, and other confirmed English allies to relocate to Cussate (Tennessee) River and proposed to establish trading factories and small forts to defend traders. See A. S. Salley (ed.), *Journals of the Commons House of Assembly of South Carolina for 1703* (Columbia SC: State Printing Company, 1934), 32, and Thomas Nairne to the Earl of Sunderland, July 10, 1709, in *Calendar of State Papers, Colonial Series, American and West Indies*, vol. 24. (London: Longmans HMSO, 1922), 421.

45. For discussions of the disastrous 1706 French-Spanish expedition against Charles Town, see Mark F. Boyd, *Here They Once Stood: The Tragic End of the Apalachee Missions* (Gainesville: University Press Florida, 1951), and Crane, *The Southern Frontier.*

46. JCIT, 45.

47. Gallay, *The Indian Slave Trade,* provides descriptions of the 1711 Choctaw expedition and the 1711–13 Tuscarora expedition as state-sponsored slaving forays. The Barnwell expedition against the Tuscaroras included fifteen "Hog Logees"; Yuchi participation in the subsequent Moore expedition is undocumented.

48. Thomas Nairne to Earl of Sunderland, 28 July 1708, in *Calendar of State Papers, Colonial Series, American and West Indies*, vol. 24. (London: Longmans HMSO, 1922), 662.

49. JCIT, 53.

50. Thomas Nairne to Earl of Sunderland, 28 July 1708.

51. At the 14 May 1713 session of the Board of Commissioners, "two Letters from the Cherikees by Alexa. Longe to the Honourable the Governour" (delivered by Cherokees Flint and Caesar) were read aloud and copies were forwarded to Nairne (JCIT, 45). Possible Yuchi "desertion" to the French (JCIT, 25) provided ample justification for the English and their allies to war on the tribe. The defection of some of the Savannahs to Virginia and Pennsylvania in 1707 prompted Carolina to lose their native proxies to pursue and attack the "deserters," simply to punish the Savannahs and resettle them in Carolina; see Gallay, *The Indian Slave Trade*, 210–12.

52. Thomas Nairne, a Scots trader and planter, served as the board's Indian agent from 1707 until June 1708, when he was arrested on trumped-up treason charges after accusing Governor Nathaniel Johnson of collusion in illegal Indian slave trading. Nairne, exonerated of the treason charges and reinstated as agent in 1711, struggled to enforce trade regulations and reform but was embroiled in escalating factionalism and political strife among traders. It is unclear whether Long and his cohort were members of the faction opposed to Nairne. For additional background on Nairne's role in this period, see Moore, *Nairne's Muskhogean Journals*.

53. James Mooney reported that Rattling Gourd, a western Cherokee informant, recalled scattered Yuchi families residing among the Cherokees of southeastern Tennessee and northwestern Georgia prior to the 1838 removal; see *Nineteenth Annual Report of the Bureau of American Ethnology, 1897–98*, part I (Washington DC: Government Printing Office, 1900, 385). Mooney speculated that they had "drifted north from the Creek country before a boundary had been fixed between the tribes"; Swanton opined that these Yuchis were the descendants of the Chestowee survivors who had remained among the Cherokees. In view of the decades of Yuchi-Cherokee enmity that followed the attack on Chestowee, Mooney's suggestion appears more plausible. During the American Revolution and subsequent Chickamauga conflict, close alliance between Creeks and Chickamauga faction Cherokees promoted frequent hosting and intersettlement around the Chickamauga towns, providing an opportunity for allied Yuchi families to relocate in the Cherokee Nation. During the Redstick War (1813–14) Lower Creek refugees, perhaps including Yuchis, sought sanctuary among the Cherokees and continued to reside in the Cherokee Nation. Hundreds of resident Creek families, including Yuchi households, emigrated with the Cherokee Nation in the forced removal of 1838–39.

54. The 1715 census indicates that the Yuchis numbered 400 souls who resided in two towns situated "180 miles WNW of Charles Town"; see "An Exact Account of ye Number and Strength of all the Indian Nations that

were subject to the Government of South Carolina, and solely traded with them in ye beginning of ye year 1715," in *A Chapter in the Early History of South Carolina*, ed. William J. Rivers (Charleston SC: Walker, Evans and Cogswell, 1874), 94.

55. William Ramsey discusses trade debt and the enslavement of English trading partners to pay those debts as factors contributing to the outbreak of the Yamasee War. Ramsey contends that Carolina's diplomatic failures to stem trade abuses, along with native anxiety over the 1715 Indian census (perceived to be a preamble to wholesale Indian enslavement), sparked the Yamasee conflict. Ramsey, "'Something Cloudy in Their Looks,'" 44–75. For discussions of the deteriorating trade situation as a contributing factor in the Yamasee War, see Richard L. Haan, "The 'Trade Do's Not Flourish as Formerly': The Ecological Origins of the Yamassee War of 1715," *Ethnohistory* 28 (1981): 341–58.

56. The rumored impending enslavement of the Yamasees was reported in a letter from the Yamasee Huspah King, taken from the body of a warrior slain on the battlefield. For a description of the letter and its role in the outbreak of the war, see Ramsey, "'Something Cloudy in Their Looks,'" 54.

57. For a discussion of the relocation of the Lower Creeks and other Yamasee War combatants to the Chattahoochee River Valley, see Worth, "The Lower Creeks: Origins and Early History,"285–86.

58. Piker, this volume, discusses the Yuchis' dependent alliance with the Lower Creeks and notes the long relationship between Cussita and the Yuchi town.

59. Wiggan's rehabilitation as an emissary to the Cherokees is indicated in a 16 July 1715 letter report from George Rodd to Joseph Boone and Richard Beresford, reproduced as "Letter from a Gentleman in Charles Town to the Carolina Agents in London," *City of Charleston Year-book, 1894*, ed. Langdon Cheves (Charleston SC: Walker, Evans and Cogswell, 1895) 319–23. Rodd noted: "Eleazer Wiggin & another Indian Trader have undertaken with two Indians more to go to the Cheroquese with design to persuade them to be for Us and fall upon the Euchess, Apalatchess & Yamassees."

60. Chicken, "Journal of the March of the Carolinians into the Cherokee Mountains," 342.

61. For discussions of the Creek-Cherokee wars of 1716–27 and 1743–53, see Oatis, *A Colonial Complex*, and David H. Corkran, *The Creek Frontier, 1540–1783* (Norman: University of Oklahoma Press, 1967).

62. In 1717 agent William Hatton observed, "The Creeks came upon a Town call'd Nogoutchee and Destroyed it, carreing off a abundance of slaves and kill'd most of the Rest of the inhabitance"; see Rena Vassar, "Some Short

Remarkes on the Indian Trade in the Charikees and in Management thereof since the Year 1717," *Ethnohistory* 8 (1961): 401–3. The "cutting off" of Quanassee by the Coosas is recorded in "Journal of Colonel George Chicken's mission from Charleston, S.C., to the Cherokees, 1726," in *Travels in the American Colonies*, ed. Newton D. Mereness (New York: Macmillan, 1916), 95–172.

DANIEL T. ELLIOTT

4. Yuchi in the Lower Savannah River Valley
Historical Context and
Archaeological Confirmation

~

As revealed in other contributions to this volume, along with other recent ethnographic, ethnohistorical, linguistic, and archaeological work, the complexity of Yuchi social and cultural history, especially before the removal era, is daunting. In some ways, previous scholarship is as much a hindrance as a help, as provisional speculations and proposals to be tested further have instead come to be taken as facts that have then misled later students. Unraveling the tangled ball of yarn of that is Yuchi history before and after contact with Europeans, however, is beyond the scope of this essay. What is offered here is a description and interpretation of one archaeologically known village site that is positively linked with the Yuchi. I hope this study will help advance future work seeking to identify the archaeological correlates of this important Native American people.

The Archaeology and History of Yuchi Settlement
in the Savannah River Region

The precise date of the arrival of the Yuchi in the Savannah River valley is undocumented. The Westo were settled in a large village in the central Savannah River region in 1674 when they were visited by Henry Woodward. This approximate vicinity was later occupied by the Yuchi. Although the Westo were once considered to be synonymous

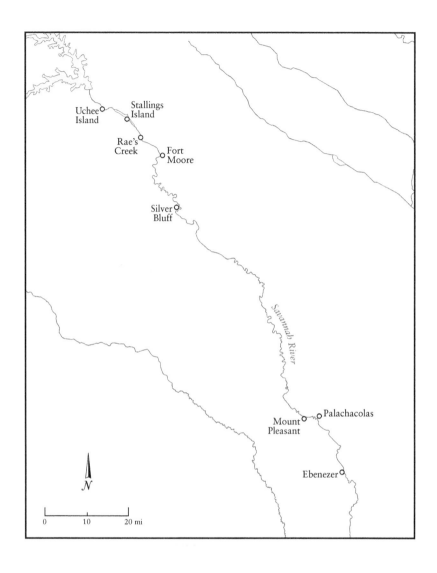

MAP 3. Location of Mount Pleasant Yuchi Town and related settlements in the Savannah River Valley.

with the Yuchi, more recent research clearly indicates they were a different people. Most of the Westos on the Savannah River were extinguished by 1683.[1] About four hundred Yuchis moved to the Savannah River valley after breaking their affiliation with the Cherokee Nation in eastern Tennessee around 1710. From present-day Tennessee they moved to an area of the lower Piedmont, several miles upstream from Fort Moore (Augusta).[2] This Yuchi town was located at the confluence of Uchee Creek and the Savannah River in Columbia County, Georgia (map 3). A large island in the Savannah River, known either as Germany or as Uchee Island, is located near the Savannah River and Uchee Creek confluence. Some archaeological reconnaissance, systematic shovel test survey, and small-scale excavations were conducted in this vicinity.[3] Historic Native American burials and material goods were discovered at Stallings Island site and the Rae's Creek site, which are both located several miles downstream from Uchee Island.[4] Several sites may be associated with eighteenth-century Yuchi, although determining a definitive association is not possible with current data.

A Yuchi settlement was established in the early eighteenth century at Silver Bluff in the upper coastal plain, several miles below Fort Moore, shortly after the Yamasee War. Silver Bluff, which is located overlooking the Savannah River in Aiken County, South Carolina, probably contained a large Yuchi village, although archaeological confirmation of this settlement is scant. Archaeological research at Silver Bluff identified one area that is possibly associated with the Yuchi occupation. Sometime after the Yuchi moved to the Silver Bluff area, the area was settled by George Galphin, who established a thriving trading post.[5]

Approximately five miles below Mount Pleasant, Georgia, was Palachacolas, or Stokes Bluff, in Hampton County, South Carolina. Palachacolas represents the southernmost known Yuchi settlement in the Savannah River valley. Although, as the place name suggests, this locale was primarily associated with the Apalachacolas who lived there prior to the Yamasee War, it was occupied by the Yuchis in 1736. After the Apalachacolas abandoned the site, it was the site of a South Carolina Ranger fort (Fort Prince George).[6]

Archaeological confirmation of the Yuchi settlement at Stokes Bluff (or even for the Apalachacolas, for that matter) is problematic. Archaeological study of the site is a mixed bag of collector information, archaeological reconnaissance, and a limited amount of intensive shovel test survey. Avocational archaeologist Roland Steiner visited the site in the late 1890s and sent a small collection of pottery and beads to anthropologists at the Smithsonian Institution.[7] Historic Indian burials and a dwelling at Palachacolas were reported to the Smithsonian Institution by Marmaduke Floyd, a local historian. Floyd made five or more visits to the Palachacolas site in 1936 and 1937, where he observed several burials, house floors, ceramics, and beads eroding from the bluff.[8] Floyd described his observations in a surviving letter sent to John R. Swanton:

> For the past thirty years I have heard of the burials being exposed by the erosion of the bluff at Pallachocolas but my first visit there was in the spring of 1936. I have made five visits to the place since then and one or two partly exposed burials have been reported to me or seen by me since then on each visit. The house floors I saw last summer have fallen into the river. A much larger one is now visible which may remain in sight for several years. From now on I shall visit the place often and keep a record of whatever I can see without disturbing anything except surface potsherds and whatever is exposed by the elements. The collection of sherds is becoming astonishing.[9]

Archaeologist Joseph Caldwell later made a visit to the site, which he briefly described.[10] Despite subsequent visits to the site, professional archaeologists have failed to yield significant historic Indian materials, and it is likely that most of that component has eroded into the river or was otherwise destroyed.

On a bluff overlooking the Savannah River in Effingham County, Georgia, sat the Yuchi village at Mount Pleasant. Mount Pleasant was home to approximately one hundred Yuchis and the town was described by Baron Georg Friedrich von Reck, when he attended a Green Corn Ceremony at the town site in July 1736.[11] This town later served as a Georgia Ranger fort, where the forces included Yuchi foot soldiers. The location of this town on a trade route is probably no coincidence.[12] Mount Pleasant was strategically located along a well-established trade path, which is a trait shared by several other Yuchi towns. The Yuchi village at Mount Pleasant was discovered archaeologically in 1989.[13] This town site is the focus of the remainder of this chapter.

The History of the Mount Pleasant Yuchi Community

In 1728 the authorities in Charles Town encouraged the Yuchis to settle at "Savannah Town or the Pallachocolas," which had been abandoned by the Apalachicolas during the Yamasee War.[14] During 1728 the area on the west bank of the Savannah River was still part of South Carolina, since Georgia had not yet formed. Those who settled at Palachacolas may be the same people who later became the Mount Pleasant Yuchi. The Yuchi migration from Palachacolas to Mount Pleasant may have been triggered by the establishment of a garrison of South Carolina Rangers at the former settlement.[15] Yuchis may have selected a more comfortable settlement nearby on the west bank of the Savannah River and a few miles upstream from the Ranger fort at Mount Pleasant.

The Yuchi Town that later was to be called Mount Pleasant was the southernmost of all Yuchi settlements in eastern Georgia. It was located on the lower Savannah River, five miles upstream from Palachacolas and thirty miles from the German settlement of New Ebenezer. A Yuchi settlement does not appear on pre-1730s historical maps, but the settlement later known as Mount Pleasant is shown on several maps made after that date.[16] Baron Von Reck, a member of the Ebenezer colony of Germans who settled downstream from Mount Pleasant, visited "the busk, or annual Indian festivity" at Yuchi Town from 28 to 30 July 1736. The word *busk*, derived from the Creek word *poskitv* (*poskita*) and referring to the fasting associated with the southeastern Indian version of the Green Corn Ceremony, was widely used by non-native people as a name for this ceremony. Von Reck noted that this feast was celebrated "every year when the corn is ripe, at the end of July or the beginning of August." While

FIGURE 2. "War Dance." What is probably a Yuchi War Dance ceremonial, pictured on the colonial frontier of Georgia in 1736 by Philip Georg Friedrich von Reck or someone in his retinue. NKS 565 4° (Von Reck's drawings), 29 recto. The Royal Library, Copenhagen, Denmark.

For discussion of this image and the collection from which it comes, see Hvidt, *Von Reck's Voyage*, 118–19, and Jackson, "A Yuchi War Dance in 1736." The image is online at http://www.kb.dk/permalink/2006/ manus/22/eng/29+recto/?var=.

observing the Yuchi at Mount Pleasant in July 1736, Von Reck or one of his servants made a series of water color sketches.[17] As a result we can study these vivid contemporary images of the Yuchi who were living at the Mount Pleasant village site (fig. 2).

Mount Pleasant was located where a major trail that led from Charleston to the Lower Creek Nation crossed the Savannah River. Soon after Georgia was established the Ranger commander Captain John Cuthbert, stationed at Mount Pleasant, was paid to cut a path from Augusta to Mount Pleasant.[18] General James Oglethorpe was so impressed with the strategic location of Mount Pleasant, when he passed through on his way to treat with the Creek Nation in 1739, as to authorize that a Ranger garrison be established there.

Additional "Rangers and Companys of Indians" were established by March 1740.[19] Captain Thomas Wiggins served as commander of the Company of Indian Foot and as the Ranger commander at Mount Pleasant. Captain Wiggins and his four hundred Native American infantrymen (likely including many Yuchi warriors) burned Fort Picolata in Spanish Florida during King George's War.[20]

Within ten years of Von Reck's account of Yuchi Town, the settlement was severely reduced and possibly abandoned. Frequent petty conflicts had transpired between the Yuchis along the middle Savannah River and the German settlers at Ebenezer and New Windsor. In 1746 Reverend Boltzius, leader of the Ebenezer Salzburger settlement, made a formal request on the townspeople's behalf for the Yuchi land beyond Ebenezer Creek in order to make the area secure from the "Robberies of the Indians."[21] The Salzburgers and others perceived the acquisition of the Yuchi lands as necessary for the enlargement of New Ebenezer.[22] The Georgia Trustees instructed Trustee President William Stephens to find out whether the Yuchis were disposed "to settle in any other place," and to determine what they expected in presents, "in Return for their quitting it to the Trustees." The Trustees were determined to procure the land from the Yuchis "by gentle means and by Treaty," and Stephens was instructed to proceed. By January 1748 the Trustees lamented that they had received no word from Stephens about the acquisition of lands "lying a little above Ebenezer"—a message that was repeated in 1749 and 1750.[23] The royal government issued a series of land grants in the Mount Pleasant vicinity during the 1750s, but legal title to the Mount Pleasant lands was not officially released by the Yuchi until the 1763 treaty at Augusta. While historical documents mention "vagrant Creeks" living in the vicinity of Mount Pleasant, it is likely that the majority of the Yuchis had abandoned the area by the late 1740s. As late as May 1757, however, William Moore, a resident of Mount Pleasant, commanded a militia troop of forty Indian gunmen.[24]

A 1715 census of the Hogologe band of Yuchis, who lived near the fall line on the Savannah River, noted that they were living in two towns and had a total population of four hundred. This census was taken before Mount Pleasant was settled. A 1725 census of the Creek Nation specifically listed the following population for the Yuchi: 180 men, 200 women, and 150 children. The Yuchi were the largest single Creek-affiliated tribe in the 1725 census.[25] Approximately one hundred other Yuchis were settled at Mount Pleasant by the 1730s.[26] Lower Creeks also were living at Mount Pleasant as a minority population; nineteen Creeks were mentioned there in 1738. Although Yuchis may have continued to reside in the vicinity of Mount Pleasant into the 1750s, their formal town was likely defunct by the mid-1740s. William Stephens recorded in his journal on 7 February 1741 that Mount Pleasant "was once the Habitation of a Tribe of Euchees, who deserted it a few Years since, chusing to settle farther up; but a few of them frequent it still, with some Vagrant Creeks among them, occasionally; and one Thomas Wiggin, an Indian Trader, keeps Stores there."[27] A span of occupation from about 1720 to 1750 is posited for the Mount Pleasant Yuchi settlement.

Only three Yuchis are specifically linked by name, or by their sketched representation, to the Mount Pleasant village. These three were in positions of power. The remaining people, who numbered just under one hundred, remain anonymous. Kipahalgwa was, in Von Reck's words, "Der oberste Kriegs Hauptmann der Uchi Indianischen Nation," supreme commander of the Yuchi Nation, and may have lived at Mount Pleasant. Since Kipahalgwa's portrait was produced by Von Reck in 1736 during his visit to Mount Pleasant, a close association with the town is implied. Senkaitschi was the king or "miko" of the Yuchi. The king and his wife, who is not specifically identified, probably resided at Mount Pleasant. Von Reck's description suggests that they were subservient to Kipahalgwa.[28]

Several non-Yuchis lived at Mount Pleasant, and they played important roles in the politics of the town. Two of the Ranger commanders, Thomas Wiggins and John Barnard, deserve particular mention. Captain Thomas Wiggins was the first commander of the Ranger troop at Mount Pleasant and the Indian Company of Foot, which was formed in 1739.[29] He was also a trader who dealt among the Yuchi and Creek. Wiggins was associated with Mount Pleasant by 1738. He is likely related to an earlier Indian trader named Eleazer Wiggan, who was associated with the Yuchi and Cherokee in Tennessee and who had his trading license temporarily revoked as a result of inciting the Cherokee against the Yuchi in 1714 (see preceding chapter). Eleazer Wiggan's service as an interpreter for the Cherokee continued into the 1730s.[30]

Captain John Barnard was the Ranger commander at Mount Pleasant after Captain Thomas Wiggins's death. Barnard, originally from Scotland, was the nephew of a Scottish nobleman. He married Jane Bradley and fathered two sons, Timothy and William. He possessed an Indian slave, as indicated in his will dated 1748 and probated in 1757. John's son, Timothy Barnard, was a Scottish trader, who lived with a Yuchi wife and eleven children at Yuchi Town on the Chattahoochee River and later resided on the Flint River.[31] One of Timothy Barnard's sons, Timpoochee (John), was an important leader of the Yuchi in the era of Creek removal in the 1830s. While John Barnard of Mount Pleasant was not a Yuchi, he established a strong, multi-generational connection between the Barnard family and the Yuchi tribe.

Other European inhabitants of Mount Pleasant during the 1730s to 1750s include the following surnames: Barnett, Cuthbert, Forest, Gilmore, Goldwire, Ladson, Moore, Randall, Spencer, and Willey.[32] In addition there were several dozen Rangers stationed at Mount Pleasant who remain anonymous. Thirteen people were enumerated at Mount Pleasant as "assistants" in a 1743 trader census.[33] These assistants may have included some members of the Yuchi tribe.

The people who lived at Mount Pleasant represent a broad spectrum of cultures, but the largest demographic group was the Yuchis. While the region around Mount Pleasant was quickly settled as plantations by the 1760s, "one hundred acres round and adjoining the Place where the Garrison was formerly kept," which includes most of the Yuchi town site, was reserved "for his Majesty's use."[34]

The Archaeology of the Mount Pleasant Community

In 1989 and 1990 archaeological explorations began to locate the settlement of Mount Pleasant.[35] Mount Pleasant is located on a high bluff immediately adjacent to the Savannah River but not near any significant stream confluence. The land opposite Mount Pleasant is a vast river swamp, which extends for several miles. The Mount Pleasant site extends for more than 360 meters (1,181 feet) along the Savannah River bluff, but it occupies a distance less than 200 meters (656 feet) away from the bluff. The outline of the site is irregular in plan and takes advantage of the topography of high dissected bluff margins close to the Savannah River channel (map 4). This type of elongated settlement pattern along major river fronts is commonly associated with eighteenth-century Native American villages in the southeastern United States. Baron Von Reck noted in 1736 that Creek towns and dwellings were "usually situated on a river. . . . The houses are scattered here and there without order, and the plantations are nearby."[36] His major point of reference for this description was the Mount Pleasant settlement.

The physical plan of the Yuchi component at Mount Pleasant is not entirely known. The northern boundary of the site was not fully determined because it extended beyond the study area. Yuchi pottery was found for at least 360 meters (1,181 feet) along the bluff but was not found more than 125 meters (410 feet) inland from the bluff. The settlement is irregular in shape and is strongly correlated with the shape of the bluff formation, which dominates the site. The town does not appear to be particularly planned in its layout, although the Lamar Institute research team based this conclusion on preliminary survey shovel test information.[37]

One problem with the archaeological data from Mount Pleasant is its multi-ethnic composition. The eighteenth-century artifacts from Mount Pleasant include objects used by the Yuchis, Euro-American deerskin traders, and Georgia Rangers, and it is difficult to separate these various components of the site since they were essentially contemporaneous. The Yuchis at Mount Pleasant had ready access to European trade goods, as clearly reflected in the archaeological

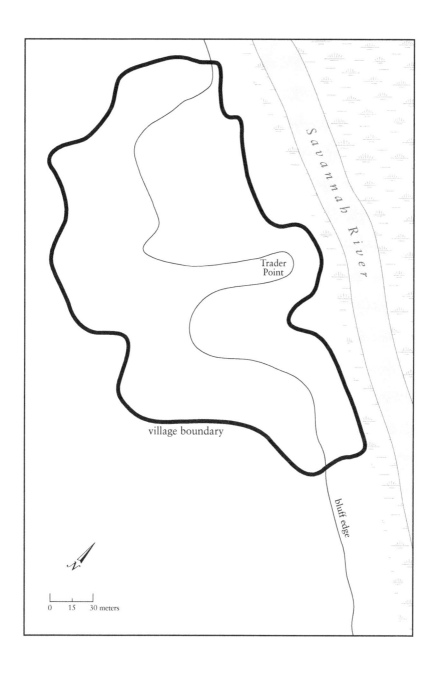

Trader
Point

village boundary

Savannah River

bluff edge

0   15   30 meters

MAP 4. Yuchi Mount Pleasant village plan.

83

record. The Yuchi artifacts cover most of the archaeological site, while refuse associated with the Europeans is more localized. The greatest concentration of artifacts came from an area designated Trader Point, which consisted of accumulated debris from all the ethnic groups represented on the site. The survey data reflect a general Yuchi pattern of artifact discard characterized by a variety of aboriginal pottery, ball clay tobacco pipe fragments, small pieces of dark green spirit bottle glass, and few metal items. A small sample of 22 tobacco pipe stems from the survey gave a date of 1723, while the test unit excavations at Trader Point produced a date of 1744.84, based on a sample of 205 pipe stems. This suggests that most of the village was abandoned before Trader Point, which corroborates the historical account of 1740.[38]

Pottery was the main diagnostic artifact of the Yuchi at Mount Pleasant. Foster (this volume) argues that currently available Yuchi and Lower Creek ceramic assemblages from the Chattahoochee and Flint River watersheds are insufficient for distinguishing a Yuchi component. Lower Creek assemblages in the lower Savannah River watershed are undescribed, so any statements as to the differentiation between Yuchi and Lower Creek wares in the Savannah River region are premature. Ceramics from the Mount Pleasant site have the potential to address this topic, but larger samples are needed (as well as a better understanding of their depositional context within the site). Also, comparable pottery samples from a documented Lower Creek site in the region dating from the period 1720–50 need to be gathered.

The diagnostic traits of Yuchi pottery may be reflected in frequencies of occurrence of various decorative motifs rather than in variations in the motifs themselves, such as the low incidence of brushing on the Mount Pleasant assemblage. Statistical variations in paste and tempering agents also may help to distinguish Yuchi from other Lower Creek ceramics, such as the higher frequency of shell tempering compared to the Chattahoochee Valley collections. Admittedly, some of these ceramic differences may be chronological rather than ethnic markers, but these are questions that can be addressed

FIGURE 3. Yuchi pottery sherds from Trader Point at Mount Pleasant.
Photo by the author.

in future investigations in the region. The Mount Pleasant village is
a prime candidate for this type of study.

The collection of Yuchi pottery from Mount Pleasant is fairly
small (n = 791) and consists primarily of relatively small sherds with
mostly plain (86%) and brushed (7%) surface treatments. Twenty-
one incised specimens were also recovered. About one-third of the
aboriginal pottery from Mount Pleasant was shell tempered, including examples that are plain, incised, brushed, punctated, and cord
marked and wares featuring rims with pinched appliqué strips below the lip. Examples of decorated pottery from Mount Pleasant
are shown in figure 3.

The primary aboriginal pottery at Mount Pleasant was an unglazed
low-fired earthenware pottery, generally brown to dark gray with
thin walls, often burnished or smoothed, and well executed. Small
jars and medium-sized bowls were found in nearly equal amounts.
Vessel diameter estimates were made for three vessels: one jar, 30
cm (11.8 inches), and two bowls, each measuring 28 cm (11 inches).
Both sand/grit and shell were used as tempering agents, but shell

tempering was slightly less common than grit. Temper and decorative motif appear to be uncorrelated, although brushing was less common on shell-tempered paste.[39]

Pottery decorative motifs include incising, punctate, pinching, notching, and other specialized rim application. Incised examples include the use of zoned, parallel, medium, and fine incised lines forming chevrons and almost no curvilinear designs. Incising was used to decorate vessel exteriors below the rim on jars and bowls and on the interior of a few bowls. No complete patterns were identified from the excavated sample. Incising occurred on nearly equal amounts of shell- and grit-tempered pottery. Punctated sherds consisted of examples with rows of small multiple punctations, including river cane punctates and smaller round punctates. Punctation was sometimes used in conjunction with incising and was used to decorate rim and vessel exteriors of jars and bowls. Narrow pinched or notched appliqué rim strips were slightly more common on jars than bowls. Occasionally narrow, notched-appliqué strips on the shoulder of carinated bowls were observed. Folded pinched rims in the classic Lamar style were present but uncommon. Some of the notching is almost squarish and well executed and has a generally delicate appearance. Handles and adornments were rare. Occasionally plain loop handles were applied to bowls, as seen on one plain shell-tempered bowl.[40]

The Yuchi pottery at Mount Pleasant was overwhelmingly undecorated (85.6% of the assemblage). Brushed pottery, a common design element in the Chattahoochee Valley settlements, is in the minority at Mount Pleasant, making up less than 7 percent of the wares. Incision, punctation, cord marking, and specialized rim treatments made up less than 10 percent of the assemblage. A summary of the pottery by decoration is provided in table 4. A minimum vessel estimate was conducted for the pottery assemblage recovered from the Trader Point unit excavations. Twenty-six distinct vessels were identified, and twenty-two of these yielded evidence of vessel shape. These were equally divided between jars and bowls, eleven examples of each.[41]

TABLE 4. Summary of aboriginal pottery,
Mount Pleasant, Georgia

Decoration	Trader Point Count	Point Percent	Village Count	Percent	Total Count	Percent
Plain	568	86.3	261	90.3	829	87.5
Brushed	38	5.8	3	1.0	41	4.3
Folded punched rim	19	2.9	15	5.2	34	3.6
Incised	19	2.9	9	3.1	28	3.0
Punctate	8	1.2	1	0.3	9	1.0
Cord marked	6	0.9	0	0.0	6	0.6
Total	658	100.0	289	100.0	947	100.0

Trader Point yielded fourteen types of European glass trade beads. Glass beads were not found over most of the site. All of the beads were common eighteenth-century types, including eight drawn cane types and six wire wound types. A tinkler cone, made from thin sheet brass cut from trade kettles, was among the artifacts recovered. This was likely a personal clothing adornment. Other clothing artifacts, including buckles, buttons, and straight pins were found in the excavations at Trader Point, but these cannot be directly linked with the Yuchi.[42]

The Yuchi were skilled hunters who often provided their German neighbors at New Ebenezer with fresh meat, as reflected in the faunal material culture remains and the historical record.[43] Food remains from Trader Point at Mount Pleasant include deer, cattle, raccoon, chicken, pig, fish, and many other wild species. The zoo-archaeological sample from Mount Pleasant (summarized in table 5), while limited to the Trader Point portion of the site, provides some insight into the hunting and fishing practiced by the Yuchi.[44]

An important aspect of Yuchi material culture practices at Mount Pleasant was the modification of European artifacts for aboriginal purposes. This behavior is best reflected in the use of glass for chipped stone tools. Dark green spirit bottle glass sherds and clear leaded goblet stems were knapped by the Yuchi at Mount Pleasant. Spirit bottle glass was used to make scraper tools and used as drinking cups. The remaining evidence of glass tool production was

TABLE 5. Species list from two seasons of test excavations
at Trader Point Excavations, 9EF169

Common Name	Minimum Number of Individuals [MNI]
White-tailed deer	4
Cattle	4
Raccoon	3
Chicken	3
Pig	3
Channel catfish	2
Unidentified mammal	present
Opposum	1
Eastern gray squirrel	1
Fox squirrel	1
Domestic cat	1
Even-toed hoofed mammal	present
Unidentified bird	present
Swans, ducks, geese	present
Wood duck	1
Turkey	1
Box and water turtles	1
Unidentified fish	present
White catfish	1
Brown bullhead	1
Largemouth Bass	1
American oyster	1
Freshwater mussel	present

uncovered in the form of debitage. Although chert debitage was widespread on the site, none of it was clearly associated with the Yuchi component, and it is more likely associated with the prehistoric components. No small triangular points, which have usually been found on eighteenth-century Creek and Cherokee sites, were found at Mount Pleasant.[45]

Twenty-three features were identified in the excavations, but most of these are not directly attributable to the Yuchi component and are more likely linked to the Ranger outpost. Yuchi pottery was common in these features, numbering more than one hundred sherds. The presence of these sherds in a Ranger context may indicate that

Yuchi women were cooking for the Rangers. Most of the sherds from feature contexts were shell-tempered plain, followed by sand- and grit-tempered plain.[46]

Feature 20 was the only pit clearly associated with the Yuchi component. This large pit contained two large, undecorated pottery vessel sherds and a large portion of a ball clay tobacco pipe in the upper fill, and a cluster of metal and stone artifacts that had formerly been the contents of a small pouch in the lower fill. The pouch contained a small brass buckle, heavily used gunflints, gunflint preforms, crudely fashioned lead balls, lead scrap, a wrought nail, and a small quartz pebble hammerstone. These clues attest that this pouch contained accoutrements for a flintlock gun. The pouch was found near the base of the pit. In retrospect, Feature 20 may have been a looted Yuchi burial, but no trace of human bone was observed in the fill.[47]

The artifacts from Mount Pleasant were grouped into functional categories, and the resulting artifact pattern is shown in table 6.[48] When these data were compared with Stanley South's Frontier Pattern, as revised, the Trader Point assemblage falls within the range of kitchen, clothing, arms, and activity groups, but the Trader Point assemblage is outside the range for architecture, tobacco, personal, and furniture groups. South's Frontier Pattern was based on data from four eighteenth-century frontier sites in eastern North America, which included Spaldings Store, Florida; Fort Ligonier, Pennsylvania; Fort Prince George, South Carolina; and Brunswick Town, North Carolina. The lower representation in the personal and furniture groups is easily explained by the small sample size from Trader Point. Tobacco artifacts become increasingly uncommon with increasing distance from the Atlantic Ocean, which probably reflects difficulties with transporting these relatively fragile items overland. The low incidence of architecture artifacts at Trader Point is more enigmatic, although a similar dearth of these items is characteristic of early colonial sites throughout coastal Georgia. The lower frequency of architecture artifacts and the higher than normal frequency of tobacco artifacts are less easily explained, however, and should be topics of future study.

TABLE 6. Artifact pattern at Mount Pleasant

| | Mount Pleasant | | | | South's | |
| | Trader Pt. | | Survey (Site-wide) | | Revised Frontier Pattern | |
Group	Count	Percent	Count	Percent	Range Percent	Mean Percent
Kitchen	987	43	185	72	35.5–43.8	40.7
Architecture	676	30	20	8	41.6–43.0	42.4
Clothing	58	3	3	1	0.3–1.6	0.9
Tobacco	370	16	39	15	1.3–14.0	7.9
Personal	6	0	0	0	0.1	0.1
Arms	81	4	3	1	1.4–8.9	5.0
Furniture	0	0	0	0	0.1–1.3	0.6
Activities	92	4	7	3	0.5–5.4	2.4
TOTAL	2,270		257			

Conclusion

Who were the Mount Pleasant Yuchis? Were they a pristine group of Yuchis, or did they include refugee factions from decimated and splintered southeastern groups? We know from twentieth-century ethnohistorical research among Yuchis living in Oklahoma that members of the tribe retain distinctive cultural elements of ceremonies, language, myths, and traditions.[49] While the group is classified by the U.S. government as a branch of the Muscogee (Creek) Nation, many anthropologists and almost all Yuchis would argue that they form a distinct culture and that their shifting, on-again, off-again alliance with the Creeks was a practical political decision made by varied Yuchi groups during the eighteenth and nineteenth centuries for their survival in the context of the complexities and conflicts of the colonial and early American periods. One way that their cultural autonomy can be documented is through historical and archaeological research. Native American groups were highly mobile during the eighteenth century. Historical documentation places several tribes in the lower Savannah River region during the early part of that century, including the Apalachicolas, Chickasaws, Creeks, Shawnees, and Yamacraws. Did the Native American population at Mount Pleasant include peoples associated with these groups?

Can the ethnic identity of the Yuchis at Mount Pleasant be established through archaeological pursuits? I am optimistic that archaeology holds the key to understanding and defining the Yuchis at Mount Pleasant. Early indications of ethnic affiliation from the limited sample of material culture that has been retrieved may be reflected by ceramic analysis and by artifact pattern analysis. The challenge with the Mount Pleasant data is untangling the Yuchi component from the Euro-American trader/ranger component, and the minor (but historically documented) Lower Creek presence. This task would be facilitated if a comparable dataset of Lower Creek material culture from the lower Savannah River region were located and rigorously described.

In conclusion, several alternate *hypotheses* concerning the Mount Pleasant site are offered for further study. Given the history of research on Yuchi identity, it is crucial to stress these are matters to be investigated, not findings.

1. Mount Pleasant had an earlier (non-Yuchi) Native American occupation, possibly Apalachicolas, which predates 1730.
2. Among the Native American groups at Mount Pleasant during the period 1720s–50s were minor contingents of tribes other than Yuchi and their material culture is mixed with the Yuchi materials.
3. The Yuchi occupation at Mount Pleasant consisted of an ethnically distinct group of Yuchis and this occupation was tightly restricted in time to the period 1720–60.

These questions cannot be answered with existing data, but future research at Mount Pleasant, joined with additional documentary work, should help address these issues. The Mount Pleasant site provides an exceptional laboratory for the study of Yuchi social and cultural history. More specifically, it also promises to provide hard facts about their experience in the lower Savannah River valley in the eighteenth century.

Acknowledgments

Special thanks are due to many people who aided in the discovery of the Mount Pleasant Yuchi village. Richard C. Kessler was most gracious in providing access, accommodations, and financial support of the Lamar Institute's work at the site for two seasons. Thanks go to Dennis Blanton, who in early 1985 helped to plant the seed of inquiry. Thanks go to R. Jerald Ledbetter, Lisa D. O'Steen, Marvin T. Smith, Mark Williams, and Karen G. Wood for their scholarly contributions. I thank Richard, Martha, Mark, and Laura Kessler for their collective sweat equity in the discovery of this important archaeological site. And I thank the late Al Roland for his aid, as a Yuchi tribal member, in promoting Yuchi awareness. Last, heartfelt thanks go to my colleague and helpmeet Rita Folse Elliott, who endured the freezing rain and sleet to share in the Yuchi discovery.

Notes

1. John R. Swanton, "Identity of the Westo Indians," *American Anthropologist* 21 (1919): 213–16; John R. Swanton, *The Indians of the Southeastern United States* (Washington DC: Smithsonian Institution Press, 1984), 213; Verner W. Crane, *The Southern Frontier 1670–1732* (New York: Norton, 1981), 19–20; Chad O. Braley, *Historic Indian Archaeology of Georgia's Coastal Plain* (Athens: University of Georgia Press, 1995), 9; Eric E. Bowne, *The Westo Indians: Slave Traders of the Early Colonial South* (Tuscaloosa: University of Alabama Press, 2005).

2. John R. Swanton, *Early History of the Creek Indians and Their Neighbors*, Bureau of American Ethnology Bulletin 73 (Washington DC: Government Printing Office, 1922), 288; Louis DeVorsey Jr., *DeBrahm's Report of the General Survey in the Southern District of North America* (Columbia: University of South Carolina Press, 1971), 20; Daniel Sturgess, *Georgia*. Map collection, Office of Surveyor General (Atlanta, GA: Department of Archives and History, 1818).

3. For discussions of the Yuchi settlement on Uchee Island in Columbia County, see Richard L. Smith, "The Archaic Period in the Central Savannah River Area: A Study of Cultural Continuity and Innovation," PhD diss. draft, University of North Carolina (Manuscript on file, Lamar Institute, Box Springs GA, 1974); Daniel T. Elliott, *The Clark Hill River Basin Survey*, Lamar Institute Publication Series Report 26, and Savannah River Archaeological Research Papers 7, and Occasional Papers of the Savannah River Archaeological Research Program (Watkinsville GA: Lamar Institute, and New Ellenton SC: University of South Carolina, 1995); George D. Price and Rita F. Elliott,

Intensive Archaeological Survey of the Riverwood Plantation/Big Three Golf Club Columbia County, Georgia (Ellerslie GA, 1999); Swanton, *Indians of the Southeastern United States*, Bureau of American Ethnology Bulletin 137 (Washington DC: Smithsonian Institution Press, 1946), 214.

4. For a discussion of the historic Indian settlement at Rae's Creek, see Ray Crook, *Rae's Creek: A Multicomponent Archaeological Site at the Fall Line along the Savannah River*. (Atlanta: Georgia State University, 1990); for a discussion of the possible Yuchi presence on Stallings Island, see Wilfred T. Neill, "An Historic Indian Burial from Columbia County, Georgia," *Southern Indian Studies* 7 (1955): 3–9.

5. Wilfred T. Neill, "The Galphin Trading Post Site at Silver Bluff, South Carolina," *Florida Anthropologist* 21 (1968): 42–54. Recent archaeological study of Galphin's post has revealed many aspects of life in this frontier outpost. See David C. Crass, Bruce Penner, Tammy R. Forehand, Lois Potter, and Larry Potter, "A Man of Great Liberality: Recent Research at George Galphin's Silver Bluff," *South Carolina Antiquities* 27 (1996):53–62, and Tammy R. Forehand, Mark D. Groover, David C. Crass, and Robert Moon, "Bridging the Gap between Archaeologists and the Public: Excavations at Silver Bluff Plantation, the George Galphin Site," *Early Georgia* 32, no. 1(2004): 51–73. For discussion of Silver Bluff, Galphin, and the Yuchi, see also Joshua Piker's contribution to this volume.

6. Kristin Hvidt, ed., *Von Reck's Voyage: Drawings and Journal of Philip Georg Friedrich von Reck* (Savannah GA: Beehive Press, 1980), 44–50; Swanton, *Indians of the Southeastern United States*, 212–15.

7. Joseph R. Caldwell, "Palachacolas Town, Hampton County, South Carolina," *Journal of the Washington Academy of Sciences* 10 (1948): 321–24.

8. Marmaduke Floyd, letter to John R. Swanton, 2 July 1937. Georgia Historical Society, Floyd Manuscript Collection 1308, folder 64 (Savannah, Georgia, 1937), 1.

9. Floyd, letter to Swanton, 2 July 1937, 1. I can note that a sample of artifacts from this site in Hampton County, South Carolina, is held by the National Museum of Natural History, Smithsonian Institution. The collection includes complete pottery vessels, glass trade beads, and other items. I briefly examined the collection in the early 1990s. Some of the material was collected in the 1890s by Roland A. Steiner, who donated it to the Smithsonian. Additional material from the site, collected by Marmaduke Floyd, may be contained at SCIAA in Columbia, South Carolina, but I have not examined it.

10. Caldwell, "Palachacolas Town," 321–24. Caldwell may have grown curious about this site after examining a small collection in the Smithsonian

Institution gathered by archaeologist Roland Steiner in the late 1800s, as indicated in the preceding note. Caldwell's visit to Palachacolas Town with Marmaduke Floyd in the late 1930s was quite brief; many sites in the region were the subject of active excavations as part of the New Deal archaeology, and professional interest in the Palachacolas Town site quickly waned. Several archaeologists revisited the site in the 1970s and 1980s, but by then the site was largely destroyed. Evidence of the historic Indian village at the bluff was ephemeral at best. A large prehistoric village site was identified nearby, however; it was being actively looted in the 1980s and has since been acquired for preservation. For the most part, the Yuchi settlement at Palachacolas is inadequately delineated or described and its historical significance is poorly understood.

11. Hvidt, *Von Reck's Voyage.*

12. John Goff, *Placenames of Georgia: Essays of John H. Goff,* ed. Francis Lee Utley and Marion R. Hemperley (Athens: University of Georgia Press, 1977).

13. Daniel T. Elliott and Rita F. Elliott, *Mount Pleasant: An Eighteenth-Century Yuchi Indian Town, British Trader Outpost, and Military Garrison in Georgia,* Lamar Institute Publication Series Report 10 (Watkinsville GA: Lamar Institute, 1990); Daniel T. Elliott and Rita F. Elliott, "The Yuchi Village at Mount Pleasant," paper presented at the Annual Meeting of the Society for American Archaeology, Nashville, 1997; Daniel T. Elliott, *The Lost City Survey: Archaeological Reconnaissance of Nine Eighteenth Century Settlements in Chatham and Effingham Counties, Georgia,* Lamar Institute Publication Series Report 19 (Watkinsville GA, 1990); Daniel T. Elliott, *Ye Pleasant Mount: 1989 and 1990 Excavations,* Lamar Institute Publication Series Report 11 (Watkinsville GA: Lamar Institute, 1991); Daniel T. Elliott, "Lost and Found: Eighteenth-Century Towns in the Savannah River Region," *Early Georgia* 19 (1991): 61–92; and see three contributions within Elliott, *Ye Pleasant Mount:* Marvin T. Smith, "Appendix I: Glass Beads from Mount Pleasant," 120–27; Karen G. Wood, "Appendix II: Zooarchaeological Analysis of the Mount Pleasant Site, Effingham County, Georgia," 127–51; and Lisa D. O'Steen, "Appendix III: Zooarchaeological Analysis of the Mt. Pleasant Site, 9Ef169," 152–64.

14. J. H. Easterby, ed., *The Journal of the Commons House of Assembly,* The Colonial Records of South Carolina, series 1, 10 vols. (Columbia: South Carolina Archives Department, 1951–86), 1:142.

15. Larry E. Ivers, *Colonial Forts of South Carolina 1670–1775* (Columbia: University of South Carolina Press, 1970), 50.

16. See John Barnwell Map, 1715; John Herbert Map, 1725; and Wilhelm G. DeBrahm, A Map of South Carolina and a Part of Georgia, 1757, all in Map Collection, South Carolina Department of Archives and History, Columbia.

17. Hvidt, *Von Reck's Voyages*. For a discussion of a Yuchi Green Corn Ceremony in its contemporary form, see Jason Baird Jackson, *Yuchi Ceremonial Life: Performance, Meaning and Tradition in a Contemporary American Indian Community* (Lincoln : University of Nebraska Press, 2003); for the term *busk*, see 304, n. 3.

18. Allan D. Candler et al., comps., *The Colonial Records of the State of Georgia*, 33:92, 35:401. These records are transcripts of letters, reports, and other documents sent to London by colonial officials and archived by the British Public Records Office. Volumes 1–26 are published and widely available (vols. 1–19 and 21–26, Atlanta: Franklin Printing, 1904–16; vol. 20, Athens: University of Georgia Press, 1974). Volumes 27–39 are bound typescripts available at the University of Georgia Library, Georgia Room, Athens, or at the Georgia Department of Archives, Morrow. The series is available on microfilm at the University of Georgia (vols. 1–19, 21–26, 27–39).

19. Candler et al., *Colonial Records of the State of Georgia*, 30:218.

20. Candler et al., *Colonial Records of the State of Georgia*, 35:235, 241, 245, 273. For additional discussion of Thomas Wiggin and the Yuchi, see also Joshua Piker's contribution to this volume.

21. Candler et al., *Colonial Records of the State of Georgia*, 31:73.

22. George F. Jones, *The Salzburger Saga: Religious Exiles and Other Germans along the Savannah* (Athens: University of Georgia Press, 1984), 91; De-Vorsey, *DeBrahm's Report of the General Survey in the Southern District of North America*, 67.

23. Candler et al., *Colonial Records of the State of Georgia*, 31:73, 82, 250, 349, 386.

24. Candler et al., *Colonial Records of the State of Georgia*, 7:549; Chapman J. Milling, *Red Carolinians* (Chapel Hill: University of North Carolina Press, 1940), 186. Relations between the Lower Creeks and Yuchis were good during the 1730s, but in the mid-1740s this relationship soured when a group of Creeks, instigated by the French, attacked a group of Yuchi in South Carolina. The Silver Bluff Yuchis had moved west by 1751 to live among the Lower Creeks after war erupted between the Cherokee and Yuchi. Swanton, *Indians of the Southeastern United States*, 214.

25. Milling, *Red Carolinians*, 182.

26. Georgia Historical Society, *Collections of the Georgia Historical Society*, vol. 2 (Savannah: Printed for the Society, 1842), 71.

27. Milling, *Red Carolinians*, 186; Candler et al., *Colonial Records of the State of Georgia*, 4:86; Benjamin Hawkins, *A Sketch of the Creek Country*, in

The Collected Works of Benjamin Hawkins, 1796–1810, ed. H. Thomas Foster (Tuscaloosa: University of Alabama Press, 2003), 61–67. Hawkins estimated the total number of Yuchi gunmen at 250 in 1798 and 1799, but by that time the Savannah River settlements had long been abandoned and this figure likely represents Yuchi elsewhere in Georgia, on the Flint and Chattahoochee rivers.

28. Hvidt, *Von Reck's Voyage*, 114–15, 120–21, 128–29.

29. K. G. Davies, ed., *Documents of the American Revolution, 1770–1783*, Colonial Office Series, 21 vols. (Shannon, Ireland: 1972–81). Note: Documents selected from Colonial Office records in the Public Record Office, *Calendar of State Papers Colonial, America and West Indies, Volume 45: 1739*, British Public Record Office, CO 5/654, fol. 250.

30. Easterby, *Journal of the Commons House of Assembly*, 1:447; William L. McDowell Jr., ed., *Documents Relating to Indian Affairs, May 23, 1750–Aug. 7, 1754*, The Colonial Records of South Carolina, series 2, vol. 2 (Columbia: South Carolina Archives Department, 1958), 175; South Carolina Department of Archives and History, *Journal of the Commons House of Assembly, 1739–1750* (Columbia: South Carolina Archives Department, 1755); William L. McDowell Jr., ed., *Journals of the Commissioners of the Indian Trade: 1710–1718*, The Colonial Records of South Carolina, series 2, vol. 1 (Columbia: South Carolina Archives Department, 1955).

31. Louise F. Hays, *The Unpublished Letters of Timothy Barnard, 1784–1820*, (Atlanta GA: Works Progress Administration, 1939), 323, 337; Hawkins, *A Sketch of the Creek Country*, 66–67.

32. Marion Hemperley, *English Crown Grants in St. Mathews Parish in Georgia 1755–1775* (Atlanta GA: State Printing Office, 1974); Pat Bryant, ed., *Entry Claims for Georgia Landholders, 1733–1755* (Atlanta: State Printing Office, 1975); S. E. Lucas Jr., *Records of Effingham County, Georgia Containing Annals of Georgia Volume II and Effingham County Legal Records from the Georgia Genealogical Magazine* (Easley SC: Southern Historical Press, 1983), 1–65.

33. Georgia Historical Society, *Collections of the Georgia Historical Society* 2:123.

34. Candler et al., *Colonial Records of the State of Georgia*, 7:828–29. Several other important Yuchi settlements are known by historical and archaeological research and these provide additional context for the Mount Pleasant town. The Yuchi on the Hiwassee River in Tennessee were known as the "Round Town People," and their principal village was Chestoi, which was located at the confluence of the Hiwassee and Tennessee rivers. The Yuchi lived among the Cherokee during the late 1600s and very early 1700s until warfare

with the Cherokee forced them to relocated southward. One suspected Yuchi town at Mouse Creek on the Hiwassee River system was almost completely excavated and mapped by New Deal archaeologists, as recently reported. Revisits to the Mouse Creek site and other similar sites near the Hiwassee and Tennessee river confluence by the cultural resource management firm of Garrow and Associates are detailed in a summary report. For additional information on the Mouse Creek Yuchi sites, see Daniel T. Elliott, Marvin T. Smith, and Guy Weaver, *Chickamauga Reservoir Archaeological Site Inventory: Results of Survey from 1987 to 1993*, 2 vols., submitted to Tennessee Valley Authority (Atlanta, GA: Garrow and Associates, 1993), and Lynn P. Sullivan, ed., *The Prehistory of the Chickamauga Basin in Tennessee*, 2 vols. (Knoxville: University of Tennessee Press, 1995).

A Yuchi town (generally known as Yuchi Town) described by William Bartram was located on a high terrace near the confluence of Uchee Creek and the Chattahoochee River. This town was occupied until forced removal of its inhabitants by the U.S. Army in 1838. The Chattahoochee River town site, presently located on Fort Benning, is considered by many to be the "mother town" of the Yuchi of some antiquity, although recent research at the site by archaeologist Chad Braley and his colleagues indicates that the Yuchi association with this site is a relatively recent event. Archaeological excavations at this town provide details about the layout of the village, but these interpretations are hampered by the presence of an earlier Blackmon phase village as well as extensive looting of burials on the site. These adverse factors combined to reduce the interpretive value of the "mother" Yuchi town in characterizing its Yuchi people. For additional information on this Yuchi town, see Thomas Foster's contribution to this volume as well as David Chase, "An Historic Indian Town Site in Russell County, Alabama," *Coweta Memorial Association Papers*, 2 (1960): 1–19; W. Dean Wood, *Damage Assessment Report, Yuchi Town Archaeological Site (1Ru63), Fort Benning Military Reservation, Russell County, Alabama* (Fort Benning GA, 1992); Chad O. Braley, *Archaeological Data Recovery at Yuchi Town, 1Ru63, Fort Benning, Alabama* (Savannah GA, 1991); Chad O. Braley, *Yuchi Town (1Ru63) Revisited: Analysis of the 1958–1962 Excavations* (Athens GA: Southeastern Archeological Services, 1998); Chad O. Braley, Frank Schnell Jr., and David Chase, *The Yuchi Town Site, 1RU63, A Summary of the 1958–1962 Excavations* (Tallahassee FL, 1994); Russell M. Weisman, *An Archaeological Study of the Yuchi Town Site (1Ru63), Fort Benning Military Reservation, Russell County, Alabama* (Fort Benning GA, 2000); and Michael L. Hargrave, Charles R. McGimsey, III, M. J. Wagner, L. A. Newson, L. Ruggiero, E. Breitburg, and L. Norr, *The Yuchi*

Town Site (1Ru63), Russell County, Alabama: An Assessment of the Impacts of Looting USACERL Special Report 98/48 (Ft. Benning GA, 1998). For these reports see Georgia Archaeological Site File, University of Georgia, Athens.

35. Elliott and Elliott, *Mount Pleasant*, 1–58; Elliott, *Ye Pleasant Mount*, 1–170.

36. Hvidt, *Von Reck's Voyage*, 49–50.

37. Elliott, *Ye Pleasant Mount*, 26.

38. Elliott, *Ye Pleasant Mount*, 98.

39. Elliott, *Ye Pleasant Mount*, 103; Elliott and Elliott, "The Yuchi Village at Mount Pleasant," 10.

40. Elliott, *Ye Pleasant Mount*, 45–53.

41. Elliott, *Ye Pleasant Mount*, 45–53.

42. Smith, "Appendix I: Glass Beads from Mount Pleasant"; Hvidt, *Von Reck's Voyage*, 47, 39–40. Von Reck noted that the Yuchi were "satisfied with the little that they have, even if it consists only of a gun, kettle and mirror." He also mentions that a man while hunting carries "only his gun, mirror, shot pouch and sometimes a bottle of brandy." During May 1736 Von Reck described an exchange of presents with the Yuchi that took place at Frederica on St. Simons Island, Georgia. Yuchis gave prepared deer skins to the Georgians. James Oglethorpe presented "muskets, red and blue cloth, powder, lead, colors, knives, and small whetstones" for the men; and "linen and woollen cloth, ear-rings, pots, coral, &c" for the women. Von Reck's description of the Yuchi at Frederica contained many detailed references to Yuchi dress, including "faces painted—red and blue-black [made from charcoal dust]; corals around their necks; rings in their ears; brightly colored feathers; wearing little white feathers on their heads; plumes [through] their ears; hair tied with a red band or ribbon; short blanket [breechcloth]; deer skin wrap; woollen sheep quilt [trade blankets]; white woolen leggings; deerskin shoes with laces"; and men who "continually smoke tobacco."

43. Hvidt, *Von Reck's Voyage*, 44.

44. O'Steen, "Appendix III: Zooarchaeological Analysis of the Mt. Pleasant Site," tables 1–3; Wood, "Appendix II: Zooarchaeological Analysis of the Mount Pleasant Site," table 2. Although the sample of recovered faunal remains from Mount Pleasant was relatively small, O'Steen and Wood worked hard to maximize the information recovered from the sample. Our current understanding of Yuchi diet remains sketchy at best, but their efforts demonstrate the archaeological site's potential for addressing these questions.

45. Elliott, *Ye Pleasant Mount*; Daniel T. Elliott, "Flake Tools or Fake Tools? Bottle Glass Uses among the Lower Creeks," paper presented at the Society

for American Archaeology Annual Meeting, Chicago IL, 24–28 March 1999.

46. Elliott, *Ye Pleasant Mount*; Elliott, "Flake Tools or Fake Tools?"

47. Elliott, *Ye Pleasant Mount*; Elliott, "Flake Tools or Fake Tools?"

48. Stanley A. South, *Method and Theory in Historical Archaeology* (New York: Academic Press, 1977), 141–45; Thomas R. Wheaton, Amy Friedlander, and Patrick H. Garrow, *Yaughan and Curriboo Plantations: Studies in Afro-American Archaeology* (Marietta GA: Soil Systems, 1983).

49. In Oklahoma the modern Yuchi maintain three town settlements, each with an associated town square–centered ceremonial ground site at which community events, especially ceremonies like the annual Green Corn Ceremony, are held. The form and significance of these sites, which have been partially documented in ethnographic studies, should provide a useful source of guidance to future archaeologists seeking to interpret Yuchi and potentially Yuchi town sites. In addition to work by Frank Speck (ca. 1904–9), Jason Baird Jackson (1993–present), and other recent students, there are accounts (ca. 1965–75) of the Polecat (aka Kellyville) Ceremonial Ground by William L. Ballard and Norman Feder. See William L. Ballard, *The Yuchi Green Corn Ceremonial: Form and Meaning* (Los Angeles: American Indian Studies Center, 1978), and Norman Feder's description given as an appendix titled "The 1965 Yuchi Green Corn Dance at Kellyville, Oklahoma" in James H. Howard's monograph *The Southeastern Ceremonial Complex and Its Interpretation*, Memoir 6 (Columbia: Missouri Archeological Society, 1968), 165–69. Yuchi traditions have changed since they were documented by Von Reck in 1736, but the opportunity to examine vestiges of this tradition in the archaeological and historical record exists. If a plaza or town square at Mount Pleasant can be defined through additional archaeological study, then a comparison with the modern Yuchi town squares would be most helpful for examining continuity of culture.

5. The Yuchi Indians along the Chattahoochee and Flint Rivers (1715–1836)
A Synthesis

~

The purpose of this chapter is to initiate a synthesis of the ethnohistoric and archaeological evidence for Yuchi Indian settlement along the Chattahoochee and Flint rivers. Given space constraints and the provisional state of research, this essay provides only a brief summary of that synthesis. I discuss the archaeological evidence at sites that are likely to represent the material remains of the Yuchi Indians during the eighteenth century. I also discuss problems and biases within that data. Since no synthesis of Yuchi archaeology exists, I discuss the evidence for their settlement history in the Lower Chattahoochee and Flint River valleys. Although a synthesis of Lower Creek sites has been published, that analysis was limited to those sites that were clearly identified with Muscogee or Hitchiti peoples.[1] It did not include the Yuchi sites because archaeologists have not clearly identified the differences between the material cultures of these Native peoples. That was one of the goals of the synthesis.

The study of the Yuchi Indian history on the Chattahoochee and Flint rivers is both exciting and frustrating. There has been a significant amount of archaeological research on Yuchi sites; however, little of it has been published.[2] Two exceptions are a book chapter by John Worth and my book-length synthesis describing the nearby Muscogee and Hitchiti sites.[3] Worth dealt mostly with the pre–Yamasee War period when the Yuchi were not settled along the Chattahoochee and Flint rivers. In the monograph, I synthesized available data on all known archaeological sites that were identified from archaeological and historical sources to be Lower Creek occupations. That book is both a synthesis of the material culture of the Lower Creek Indians and a study of the cultural diversity within the Lawson Field phase. The Lawson Field phase is an archaeological unit that is identified through a set of archaeological data such as artifacts and structural elements. Although Yuchi sites are part of the Lawson Field phase, I left Yuchi sites out of the discussion of Lawson Field archaeology in that book because archaeologists are not confident about which archaeological components at the major Yuchi site were actually Yuchi and not associated with the previous occupants of the site, the Hitchiti. Thus my book does not deal adequately with the Yuchi of the Lawson Field phase. The inability to distinguish cultural groups is a significant problem within the archaeology of the Lower Creek Indians and allied tribes.[4] Some of the groups who made up the Lower Creek Indians had drastically different languages and culture histories, yet we cannot distinguish them archaeologically.[5]

Archaeologists have traditionally lumped all Native American sites along the Chattahoochee River that were occupied between 1715 and 1836 as the Lawson Field archaeological phase. If we are going to pursue the study of the Yuchi Indians (or any other southeastern Indian groups) over time, we need to analyze their archaeological components at the town level instead of making the interpretation of archaeological data fit the models.[6] This study takes such an approach by isolating only those archaeological and historic data that can be associated with Yuchi Town. While there is significant evidence for an earlier archaeological component at sites that are associated with the Yuchi, I am not including those non-Yuchi data in this chapter.

The majority of the archaeological research dealing with the Yuchi along the Chattahoochee and Flint River watersheds has been the result of legally mandated cultural resource management (CRM) work conducted when sites were threatened with destruction because of construction. My review of the archaeological evidence of the Yuchi Indians in this part of the country is based solely on reports describing such work and other unpublished research reports. As is common for CRM archaeology, those reports are not peer reviewed in the traditional sense. They are reviewed by the State Historic Preservation Offices (in this case, Georgia and Alabama) and by the client who commissioned the project for compliance with particular laws. I mention this because I want to point out the potential bias of this data for non-archaeologist readers and to highlight the early stage of our understanding of Yuchi settlement along the Chattahoochee and Flint River valleys. The only significant sources for Yuchi sites along the Flint River are a master's thesis and a conference paper by Worth.[7]

As discussed elsewhere in this volume, Yuchi Indians probably aligned with and settled among the Lower Creek Indian towns on the Chattahoochee during the immigration associated with the Yamasee War (circa 1715). Members of the Yuchi people were located and listed in twelve colonial censuses taken between 1716 and 1832, and they seem to have remained in the same general location from about 1715 until the Red Stick War (circa 1813). After the Red Stick War they seem to have split up and moved in with various Upper Creek towns in what is now central Alabama. The fact that they stayed in the same location for such a long period when Muscogee and Hitchiti towns were usually abandoned after a few years may reflect the Yuchis' political position among the Lower Creek towns (Hahn and Piker, this volume).[8] While they were allowed to settle among the Lower Creek Indians on the Chattahoochee early in the eighteenth century, they may not have had the political clout to claim new land except for far on the periphery.

In the late eighteenth century, when we have the most detailed descriptions of Yuchi Town's location, it is located immediately south of Uchee Creek (in present-day Russell County, Alabama) at the confluence of that creek and the Chattahoochee River on the river's western bank (map 5). David Taitt visited the town and described it as "about

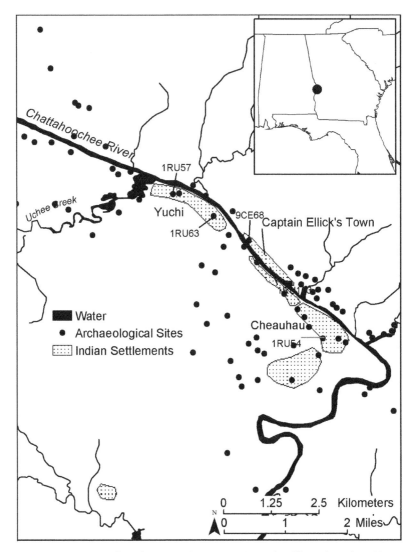

MAP 5. Location of Yuchi Town (1715–1836) on the Chattahoochee River in what is today the state of Alabama. Map by the author.

three miles up the Chatahutchie river" from Cheauhau.[9] Benjamin Hawkins, in 1796, said the town was "on the right bank of Chat-to-ho-che, ten and a half miles below Cow-e-tu-tal-lau-has-see. . . . Above the town and bordering on it, Uchee creek, eighty-five feet wide, joins the river."[10] Cowetuh Talluahassee was located at the archaeological site named 1RU11, and Cheauhau was located at 1RU54, so Yuchis of the late eighteenth century were located approximately at 1RU63 and 1RU57. These archaeological site names are a standard nomenclature and refer to a discrete and definable boundary of artifacts that have been identified on the surface or below the surface. A single site may be the result of the activity of a single person that resulted in artifact remains, or it may be the result of many people's activity accumulated over time. Thus a "town" may be represented by multiple sites. The nomenclature is a Smithsonian system in which the first number refers to the order of states, the letters refer to the county within which the site was found, and the last set of numbers is the sequential order of the sites in which they were found. Thus 1RU63 was the sixty-third site found in Russell County, Alabama.

We do not yet know exactly when the Yuchi settled on the Chattahoochee River. However, Spanish documents indicate that their migration was correlated with other migrations from the Ocmulgee and Savannah watersheds around 1715 in response to the Yamasee War. It must be remembered that even for the Creek towns, this migration was gradual and that for a few years there were duplicate towns on the Chattahoochee and Ocmulgee watersheds. Between 1712 and 1713 the Yuchi were described as trading with the French.[11] The first mention of them on the Chattahoochee River was by the Spanish. This is consistent with Joshua Piker's research showing that the Yuchi were aligned with various groups during the seventeenth and eighteenth centuries (see Piker, this volume). In 1716 Diego Peña visited the Yuchi on the Chattahoochee River. He was traveling north and passed from Apalachicola to Hitchiti to Ocmulgee to Uche to Tasquique to Casista to Caveta.[12] If these towns were then situated as they were seventy years later in the last quarter of the eighteenth century, then Yuchi settlement was in approximately same area as is measured by the location of these towns relative to one another. This location, however, is general. We cannot tell from these data on which side of the river they were settled.

In 1720 John Barnwell reported that the Yuchis had two villages among the Lower Creeks. If there were Creek settlements split between the Ocmulgee and Chattahoochee rivers, then it is at least consistent with only one Yuchi town on the Chattahoochee River in 1720. In 1737 John Wesley, an early traveler to Georgia, described the Yuchi as having "only one small town left (near 200 miles from Savannah) and about 40 fighting men. The Creeks have been many times on the point of cutting them off."[13]

In 1751, in the *Journals of the Commissioners of the Indian Trade* in the Colonial Records of South Carolina, a communication from Governor Glen to the president of the Council of Georgia recorded that the "Euchees . . . did in like Manner till lately live in this Province at Silver Bluff, But being a Tribe belonging to the Lower Creek, they were called Home, when they broke out War with the Cherokee."[14] So in 1751 a group of Yuchis moved from Silver Bluff to the Lower Creek region, which at that time was on the Chattahoochee. We also learn from that passage that Governor Glen considered the Yuchi part of the Creek Indians. The Thomas Bosomworth journal of 1752 indicates that Yuchi Town was between Cussita and Apalachicola in the 1750s.[15] Cussita and Apalachicola in the 1750s were adjacent to the Chattahoochee near modern-day Columbus, Georgia. In the late eighteenth century the Indian agent Benjamin Hawkins confirmed this settlement history. He recorded in his *Sketch of the Creek Country* that the Yuchis "were formerly settled in small villages at Ponpon, Saltketchers (Sol-ke-chuh), Silver Bluff, and O-ge-chee (How-ge-chu)." They then moved sometime after 1729 down to the location where Hawkins knew them at the confluence of Uchee Creek and the Chattahoochee.[16]

Thus from the Spanish observations through Hawkins's detailed descriptions in the late eighteenth and early nineteenth centuries, there is consistency among the ethnohistoric references. Some Yuchis were settled along the Chattahoochee River by 1716, and others may have joined those people over the next few years. Their emigrations focused on the area south of the current Uchee Creek, around sites 1RU63 and 1RU57 in Alabama. There is no ethnohistoric reason to believe that the Yuchi formed any towns other than this Uchee Creek location during the first half of the eighteenth century.

History of Excavations at Yuchi Town

The site 1RU63 has been identified as representing Yuchi Town and has attracted extensive investigation by authorized and unauthorized excavators.[17] The University of Alabama and Wesley Hurt conducted a survey in the 1940s that identified a site near the 1RU63 site, but Hurt classified it as a Woodland period site without a Creek Indian component.[18] The most extensive investigations in the region of Yuchi Town were by Harold Huscher of the Smithsonian Institution and David Chase, an amateur archaeologist working at Fort Benning.[19] Most of the results from Huscher's investigations, still have not been analyzed. The funding for the River Basin Surveys initiative by the Smithsonian's Bureau of American Ethnology was cut off, and Huscher had to stop working on these archaeological materials.[20] There are approximately one hundred cubic feet of boxes of artifacts at the Smithsonian that have not been analyzed.

However, Chad Braley and Southeastern Archaeological Services analyzed the David Chase section of the excavations.[21] Based on the late eighteenth-century descriptions, we can locate the town relatively accurately as encompassing the area that is currently defined as sites 1RU63 and 1RU57. The site 1RU57, while just as valid as a candidate for representing Yuchi Town as is 1RU63, has not received as much study. This is because the density of artifacts is lower at 1RU57.[22] The case of Yuchi Town points out the importance of combining both archaeological and historic information. We know from observation as recorded in Hawkins's highly respected ethnohistorical account that the town spanned from some distance south *up to* Uchee Creek. This means that 1RU57 probably represents some portion of Yuchi Town and is *ethnohistorically* a better candidate for the archaeological representative of the town. Braley instead interpreted this inconsistency in favor of the archaeological data over the ethnohistorical data.[23] I would argue that given the ambiguities of the archaeological components at 1RU63, and the fact that most researchers are confident in Hawkins's accuracy, we should err on the side of the historical record.[24]

Chase identified the location of a concentration of surface artifacts at 1RU63 near the location that Hawkins described. He also found 1RU57 but did not think the density of artifacts at that site was consistent with the archaeological remains of Yuchi Town. He put in excavation units at 1RU63 based on positive probes for burials and on the surface artifact density observed earlier. They excavated approximately 200 square meters of 1RU63.[25] If the town spanned up to Uchee Creek, then the town was approximately 403,900 square meters (about 100 acres). The Smithsonian and Chase excavations would then represent a non-random sample of approximately 5/100,000 of the site. The sample is biased toward burials and artifact concentrations at the town because of the methods used by the investigators.

Apart from attempts to define the boundary of the site, those excavation units still form the majority of what we know about 1RU63 to this day. Since the excavators never finished the reporting for the site, the current landowners and Dean Wood, Dan Elliot, Chad Braley, and others began a series of studies in the 1990s that were intended to summarize those excavations as effectively as possible given available funds, artifacts, and time.[26] The owner of the Yuchi Town site is the Fort Benning Military Reservation, a United States Army base. The artifacts and documents from the Chase excavation and all subsequent research at the site are curated and managed by the army's Division of Environmental Services. The current archaeologist for Fort Benning is Dr. Christopher Hamilton. The Department of Anthropology at the National Museum of Natural History, Smithsonian Institution, curates the artifacts that were excavated by Huscher, along with the associated fieldnotes.

Frank Schnell Jr. of the Columbus Museum in Columbus, Georgia, was hired by Fort Benning in the early 1980s in order to define the site boundaries for nomination to the National Register of Historic Places. Earlier Schnell had helped with the Smithsonian excavations. He recorded that he found predominantly seventeenth-century artifacts. If the historical documentation about the Yuchi settlement on the Chattahoochee discussed earlier is accurate, then the seventeenth-century artifacts are not Yuchi. His methods included systematic shovel testing because he was not concerned with identifying stratigraphic context but was contracted only to define the boundary of 1RU63.[27]

Three years later Martin Dickenson and Lucy Wayne conducted shovel testing at portions of 1RU63 but found no definitive results regarding the occupants of the town.[28] Southeastern Archaeological Services and Rob Benson shovel tested the northern end of Yuchi Town at 1RU57 in the 1995.[29] They found artifacts that were consistent with an eighteenth-century Creek Indian occupation and with Hawkins's description of the location of the town.

Braley conducted two studies in the mid-1990s to summarize the Smithsonian excavations. He briefly described the Chase section of the Smithsonian excavations and then reexcavated the Smithsonian excavation units in order to define them better. Braley's 1998 report argues that there are two archaeological components and that the site was occupied almost continuously from the mid-seventeenth century through the early nineteenth century. Since Yuchi Indians did not settle on the Chattahoochee until around 1715, the pre-1715 occupants at site 1RU63 were not Yuchi Indians.[30]

Russell Weisman and Jim Ambrosino shovel tested portions of 1RU63 and found artifacts that were consistent with a pre-Yuchi and an eighteenth-century Creek occupation at the site.[31] They hypothesized that the pre-Yuchi component represented Ocmulgee Indians. While I would argue that there are not enough data to support the conclusion that the pre-1715 inhabitants were Ocmulgee Indians, it *is* reasonable to conclude that they were *not* Yuchi.

The next major investigation was by Michael Hargrave of the U.S. Army Corps of Engineers Construction Engineers Research Station in Champaign, Illinois, and an interdisciplinary team. Hargrave and the Corps of Engineers were contracted by Fort Benning to characterize and quantify unauthorized looting of 1RU63.[32] While they did excavate 76 square meters, the placement of excavation units was determined by looting activity. Since the location of looter holes is not necessarily correlated with the organizational layout of the town, this sample may approximate a random sample of sections of the town. They excavated approximately 1/100,000 of the area of the town and found artifacts consistent with a pre-Yuchi occupation. Pre-Yuchi occupation refers to use of the land bounded by 1RU63 by Native American people before the Yuchi were known to have migrated to the Chattahoochee Valley. If the Yuchi settled at 1RU63 after the 1720s, then whoever was living there before 1720 was not Yuchi and the artifact remains from those people are not Yuchi. Those pre-Yuchi inhabitants of 1RU63 were likely Hitchiti people.

Weisman and others took advantage of plowing and forestry management at sections of the site in order to collect artifacts from the surface. According to their report they did piece plot the location of individual artifacts, but those spatial data were not used or reported.[33] Consequently the surface-collected artifacts are useful primarily in determining presence or absence of artifacts at the site. Last, I worked with a crew from Panamerican Consultants, Inc., and investigated looting activity at a site at the far northern end of Yuchi Town. While some evidence of Creek occupation was found, there was very little. Excavations at this site, 1RU132, demonstrated that Yuchi Town probably did not spread far up Uchee Creek.[34]

What is important to note from this summary is that (1) the most extensive excavations have not been completely analyzed, (2) they represent a non-random sample of the town, (3) they represent approximately 6/100,000 of the town's area, (4) practically all other investigations used methods that are most reliably useful for determining the boundary of the site, not internal archaeological stratigraphy or context, and (5) occupation of the area is probably multiethnic (non-Yuchi and Yuchi).

This last point is important because we are just beginning to understand the variation of the archaeological signature of the people who have been called the Creek Indians.[35] We know that the Native people who were settled along the Chattahoochee in the eighteenth century were a multi-ethnic group. Indeed the Yuchi spoke (and still speak) a radically different language than the rest of the Muscogee people who lived in neighboring towns. Yet to this day, we cannot distinguish them based on their archaeological remains.

We are only beginning to be able to distinguish between these different Indian cultures archaeologically. Recent research shows that our previous understanding of Lower Creek Indian material culture is not as clear as we thought.[36] So it is important that we distinguish between those non-Yuchi and Yuchi cultural remains at 1RU63 and 1RU57 before drawing conclusions about the Yuchi. In the next section I discuss the archaeological evidence for the Yuchi at these sites.

Site-Specific Evidence

Since we do not know the archaeological signature or specific material culture of the Yuchi people along the Lower Chattahoochee River, our conclusions about the Yuchi at 1RU63 and 1RU57 are based on the assumption that archaeological remains found at those sites dating to the time period when we believe that Yuchis were living there (1715–1836) were Yuchi. The Huscher and Chase excavations were the only investigations with enough precision to distinguish artifact context and stratigraphy. Though it does not necessarily have to, the shovel testing and surface investigations at these sites have been analyzed in a way that creates bias in the results.[37] Braley noted the discrepancy between rim sherd analysis, which is a less biased metric of vessel frequency, and sherd counts, which are biased toward artifact context and "brokenness."[38] Since we cannot discern the cause of the variation observed in the shovel testing or surface collections, particularly lumping sherd counts, I do not consider those results here.

Huscher and Chase excavated evidence of structures and burials. Schnell, Joseph Mahan, and student volunteers from the Columbus College in Columbus, Georgia, helped with some of the excavations. A burial in excavation unit 1 contained the remains of a child, a shell gorget, and European trade goods. Braley claims that this is a Yuchi burial but does not state his justification for that conclusion. The artifacts' association with the burial is ambiguous.[39] Clay-lined pits in excavation unit 2 were investigated by Huscher. The function of these pits is unknown, but they may be "cellars" such as were found in structures elsewhere in the Lower Creek territory.[40]

Since Huscher excavated these units, the artifacts have not been analyzed. Excavation unit 3 contained a burial and was probably investigated because Chase found a burial with his probe. The burial contained a pot that is consistent with the seventeenth-century, pre-Yuchi period.[41] Artifacts consistent with the eighteenth century were found in the strata above the burial.

Chase excavated house remains after Huscher left to work on other River Basin Survey projects. The house was evidenced by daub. Daub is hardened clay that was used as wall filler. It is only found in association with structure walls. While the associated fieldnotes are missing, Braley reconstructed some of the excavation details from the artifact bags.[42] He concluded that all European trade goods were found from the layers "above" and postdating the structure. Based on artifact association, this structure was from the period before the time when the Yuchi were living in the region.

The largest excavation units were excavated by Huscher and have not been analyzed. Braley reconstructed some of the results from Huscher's fieldnotes, available on microfilm from the National Anthropological Archives at the Smithsonian Institution.[43] There are copies of these fieldnotes in the Department of Anthropology at the University of Tulsa and at the Columbus Museum in Columbus, Georgia. These notes indicate that at least one structure was identified and probably more than one. The structures are identified by linear alignments of posts and associated clay extraction pits and burials. Braley also reexcavated this excavation unit and remapped Huscher's features, excavated the post molds, and sifted what workers concluded was the backdirt pile from this excavation unit.[44]

Huscher excavated a number of features, including nine burials, pit features, postholes, and other structural remains such as daub concentrations. Some of the burial pits contained bundle burials and extensive trade goods. One of the trade items was part of a gun that was used between 1725 and 1770, according to an analysis by T. M. Hamilton in Huscher's notes.[45] While Braley's reexcavation documented artifacts from the postholes, the analysis of these artifacts lumped all of the artifact types from the entire site. Since the site has multiple components, the artifact analysis of the structural remains is useful only for indicating the presence of artifacts.[46] All we can say definitively is that there are burials with trade goods indicating that the burials date to the first half of the eighteenth century. We do not even know if these burials were associated with the structures.

The feature and structure concentration is consistent with eighteenth-century Muscogee and Hitchiti structures elsewhere on the Lower Chattahoochee River.[47] There are several possible interpretations of these structures. (1) The Yuchi Indians constructed their houses very similarly to those of their Muscogee and Hitchiti neighbors, and these structures were built by Yuchis. (2) These structures were built by non-Yuchi during the eighteenth century. (3) These structures were built by non-Yuchi during an earlier time period, such as the seventeenth century.

The first interpretation is consistent with the common interpretation that this site represents the archaeological remains of the Yuchi Indians. However, the only unambiguous archaeological evidence in support of that interpretation consists of the burials with trade goods that date to the eighteenth century. Nevertheless, we are not positive that they are Yuchi burials. The second interpretation is consistent with the hypothesis that Yuchi Town was located upstream from 1RU63 or at least upstream from Huscher's excavation unit 4. This seems unlikely because Hawkins described Yuchi Town spreading for a few miles south of Uchee Creek. However, in 1778 William Bartram passed through the town and described it as large (about one thousand people) and compact relative to other towns.[48] It would seem that if there were indeed one thousand people living in the vicinity of 1RU63, there would be unambiguous evidence of eighteenth-century occupation. Interpretation number three is possible only if the burials were not interred within the structures. The burials may be intrusive, and these structures may be from an earlier period.

The archaeological site called 1RU63 has been unanimously identified as the site of major Yuchi occupation during the eighteenth century. That identification seems to be based mostly on the general proximity to Hawkins's description and the density of artifacts at 1RU63 relative to 1RU57. I argue that we need to reassess our interpretation of the archaeological signature of Yuchi Town. We need to stop forcing it to fit a preconceived idea of what it should look like. Site 1RU57 is just as likely to represent Yuchi Town as 1RU63 but has not received as much attention because of lower artifact density. The former site has been investigated with shovel testing, which has shown it to contain a Lawson Field phase similar to other Muscogee and Hitchiti sites nearby. This assessment was made almost exclusively by the presence of the diagnostic Lawson Field ceramic type, Chattahoochee Brushed (Chattahoochee Roughened). Unfortunately, the conclusion is that we do not know much about the Yuchi based on archaeological data. We will probably learn more by looking at the single-component Yuchi towns, such as the "daughter" towns on the Flint River (discussed in the next section) and the Yuchi settlements on the Savannah River.[49]

Yuchi Communities in the Flint River Valley

According to our best estimate, the main Yuchi Town on the Chattahoochee River was settled continuously for about one hundred years. It was the only Yuchi town mentioned in the Chattahoochee area until the late eighteenth century, when migrants from the main Yuchi Town on the Chattahoochee established three daughter villages known to us by the Muscogee (Creek) language names Padjeeligau, Intuchculgau, and Toccogulegau (map 6).

Padjeeligau was one of three villages described as "belonging" to the main town. This relationship was one of a descendent, and the idea of towns maintaining relationships with a "mother" town is still in use today in Oklahoma.[50] A daughter village is a community that was formed by a subset of people who migrated from a "mother" town. Those individuals moved away from the Yuchi Town proper and formed a new community. The new community usually maintained alliance with the mother town and usually described themselves as being from the same "fire." This migratory pattern is an

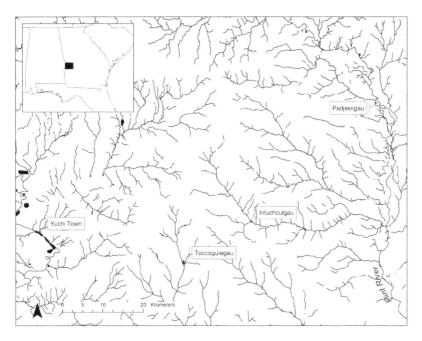

MAP 6. Location of the Yuchi daughter settlements on the Chattahoochee and Flint River watersheds (1715–1836).
Map by the author.

old one and was probably part of the normal settlement history of southeastern Indian towns.

Thomas Nairne described the process in 1708 in the following manner: "Suppose 1:2 to be a river, A: a populous flourishing Town on the river side, straightned for planting ground. Upon some disgust, or other reason 2 Leading men lead out Colonies of 30 or 40 famelies Each and sattle 2 New Villages B: C: Bechancing to florish and increase much, out of it by the same means arise D and E."[51] From Nairne's description we learn that towns split for a variety of reasons, sometimes because the population of the old town grew too large. Sometimes, a feud would cause a split. These towns were situated along rivers, and the daughter town would often move just across the river or down river. In the case of the Yuchi the daughter settlements moved to the next river valley, which was some 60 miles away. The fact that the Yuchi daughter settlements were placed so far from the mother town and not on the Chattahoochee River may be consistent with the earlier conclusion that the Yuchi were not politically powerful among the Lower Creek towns and were not able to expand their territorial claim on the Chattahoochee River.

The first evidence of a Yuchi daughter village was when David Taitt (1772) drew Padjeeligau on the Flint River on his map of the Indians of the southeastern United States.[52] Taitt's maps and journals are among the more reliable sources of locational data for this period and region. About twenty-five years later the Indian agent Benjamin Hawkins described the same town in approximately the same location as where Taitt drew it in 1772. It was situated on the west bank of the Flint River at the confluence with a creek of the same name as the town, Padjeeligau (Pigeon Roost).[53] He said the town had formerly been larger. Padjeeligau has been identified with two archaeological sites based on very cursory investigations; conclusions about it are tenuous. Worth in his master's thesis identified Padjeeligau with sites 9TR18 and 9TR23, but the sites have not been investigated beyond this initial survey.[54]

Intuchculgau and Toccogulegau were settled in the uplands between the major river valleys. Benjamin Hawkins described Intuchculgau in 1796 as being situated along the Opithlucco River (modern Buck Creek) and twenty-eight miles from that creek's confluence with the Flint River. There were fourteen families in the village and they had built a square ground around 1796. Towns built a square ground as a symbol of independence from their mother town. Toccogulegau was situated along Kitchofoone Creek farther to the west. Eight families were living there in 1796, but they had founded the village only two years earlier. Last, Yuchi Indians were settled in various towns throughout the Creek country. Timothy Barnard was a well-respected interpreter and trader who lived among the Yuchi Indians and married a Yuchi woman. He lived in various locations along the Flint River and fathered a number of children who were raised as Yuchi by their mother. One of these children, Timpoochee Barnard, is supposed to be buried at the historic Fort Mitchell site in Fort Mitchell, Alabama. There is a grave maker there with his name on it, though the identity of the body or even if there is a body buried there is unknown. In 1796 Hawkins said that Yuchi were also settled among the Shawnee in the Upper Creek Town of Sauvanogee.[55]

Conclusion

While there has been a fair amount of research in the region of Yuchi Town within the last few decades, it is important to understand the nature of that research and its limitations. I have reviewed archaeological and ethnohistoric evidence related to the Yuchi Indians in the Chattahoochee and Flint River watersheds. These data sources need to be used in combination with one another. Without historic references to the Yuchi being settled in the vicinity of 1RU57 and 1RU63, we would not be able to identify those sites archaeologically as containing an ethnically distinct group of people. I am not convinced that this is not an artifact of our metrics and our ability to distinguish between individual towns. Archaeologists have not attempted to distinguish between individual towns as much as they have attempted to identify Creek Indian sites.

With the intensive archaeological and historical investigations undertaken in the Lower Creek country in the last few decades, we are learning that the Creek-affiliated peoples were highly individualistic. Each town acted more independently than collectively. We are learning that each town adapted to a changing cultural, economic, and biophysical environment at its own rate in its own ways.[56]

The fact that we are unable to distinguish easily the archaeological remains of a culture that observers described as distinct is important. Bartram said that Yuchi of the late eighteenth century maintained their own traditions, and we know that the Yuchi today maintain their own beliefs and values. While they most certainly did maintain their own traditions in the eighteenth century, those traditions did not manifest themselves in a highly distinctive material culture drastically different from that of their surrounding Muscogee and Hitchiti neighbors.

I would like to close by making some recommendations about the sites' heritage management. Archaeological investigation and attention to the sites has brought public interest. Consequently, 1RU63 has been extensively looted. The owner, Fort Benning, is making a concerted effort to preserve the site. In addition, the site has been subjected to frequent shovel testing and surface collection that is beginning to be redundant. There is consistency between the surface and shovel testing.[57] There should not be any surface collection unless the artifacts are piece plotted, because it appears that the eighteenth-century component of the Yuchi settlement is very near the surface, so any intrasite data will only be found within the surface-collected artifacts. There should not be any more archaeological investigations at these valuable sites until the Huscher collection at the Smithsonian Institution is properly analyzed. Last, given the difficulty in distinguishing the Muscogee and Hitchiti components from the Yuchi components, it would seem worthwhile to compare pre-removal sites to post-removal sites in Oklahoma. Consistency in material culture has been demonstrated among Creek Indian sites.[58] By carefully isolating archaeological collections from sites with well-defined cultural and temporal contexts, we can begin to understand how the Yuchi related to the Muscogee and Hitchiti people. These particular cases will help to clarify the social and political organization of the southeastern Indians in general.

Acknowledgments

Thank you to Frank Schnell, Chris Hamilton, Dean Wood, Dan Elliot, John Worth, and Chad Braley for access to reports and to Lee Newsom for sharing data on her botanical research at Yuchi Town.

Notes

1. H. Thomas Foster II, *The Archaeology of the Lower Muskogee Indians, 1715–1836* (Tuscaloosa: University of Alabama Press, 2007).

2. Russell M. Weisman, *An Archaeological Study of the Yuchi Town Site (1RU63), Fort Benning Military Reservation, Russell County, Alabama* (Ellerslie GA: Southern Research, 2000), viii, 243.

3. John E. Worth, "The Lower Creeks: Origins and Early History," in *Indians of the Greater Southeast: Historical Archaeology and Ethnohistory*, ed. Bonnie G. McEwan (Gainesville: University Press of Florida, 2000), 265–98; Foster, *Archaeology of the Lower Muskogee Indians, 1715–1836*.

4. Foster, *The Archaeology of the Lower Muskogee Indians*; H. Thomas Foster II, "Evidence of Historic Creek Indian Migration from a Regional and Direct Historic Analysis of Ceramic Types," *Southeastern Archaeology* 23 (2004): 65–84.

5. Weisman, *Archaeological Study of the Yuchi Town Site*; Chad O. Braley, *Archaeological Data Recovery at Yuchi Town, 1RU63, Fort Benning, Alabama* (Athens GA: Southeastern Archaeological Services, 1991); Chad O. Braley, *Yuchi Town (1RU63) Revisited: Analysis of the 1958–1962 Excavations* (Athens GA: Southeastern Archaeological Services, 1998).

6. Brent Richards Weisman, *Excavations on the Franciscan Frontier: Archaeology at the Fig Springs Mission* (Gainesville: University Press of Florida, 1992); Braley, *Yuchi Town (1RU63) Revisited*.

7. John Worth, "Mississippian Occupation on the Middle Flint River," master's thesis, University of Georgia, 1988; John Worth, "The Eastern Creek Frontier: History and Archaeology of the Flint River Towns, ca. 1750–1826," paper presented at the Society for American Archaeology Meetings, Nashville TN, 4 April 1997.

8. H. Thomas Foster II, "Long Term Average Rate Maximization of Creek Indian Residential Mobility: A Test of the Marginal Value Theorem," PhD diss., Pennsylvania State University, 2001, 111–13.

9. Newton D. Mereness, ed., *Travels in the American Colonies* (New York: Macmillan, 1916), 546.

10. H. Thomas Foster II, ed., *The Collected Works of Benjamin Hawkins, 1796–1810* (Tuscaloosa: University of Alabama Press, 2003), 61s (s denotes *Sketch of the Creek Country*).

11. William L. McDowell Jr., ed., *Documents Relating to Indian Affairs May 21, 1750–August 7, 1754* (Columbia: South Carolina Department of Archives and History, 1992), 592.

12. Mark F. Boyd, "Diego Peña's Expedition to Apalachee and Apalachicolo in 1716: A Journal Translated and with an Introduction," *Florida Historical Quarterly*, 28 (1949): 1–27, 25.

13. Amos J. Wright, *Historic Indian Towns in Alabama, 1540–1838* (Tuscaloosa: University of Alabama Press, 2003), 172.

14. McDowell, *Documents Relating to Indian Affairs*, 170.

15. McDowell, *Documents Relating to Indian Affairs*, 280.

16. Foster, *The Collected Works of Benjamin Hawkins*, 61s.

17. Braley, *Archaeological Data Recovery at Yuchi Town, 1RU63*; Braley, *Yuchi Town (1RU63) Revisited*; Michael L. Hargrave, Charles R. McGimsey, Mark J. Wagner, Lee A. Newsom, Laura Ruggiero, Emanuel Breitburg, and

Lynette Norr, *The Yuchi Town Site (1RU63), Russell County, Alabama: An Assessment of the Impacts of Looting*, Special Report 98/48 (Champaign IL: Construction Engineering Research Lab [Army], 1998); Harold A. Huscher, microfilmed fieldnotes for Walter F. George Survey, River Basin Surveys, reels 1–7, (Washington DC, 1959); Robert Scott, ARPA [Archaeological Resourced Protection Act] *Damage Assessment of 1RU132, Russell County, Alabama* (Tuscaloosa AL, 2004).

18. Wesley R. Hurt, "An Archaeological Survey, Chattahoochee Valley, Alabama 1947," manuscript, Office of Archaeological Research, Tuscaloosa, Alabama, 1947; Wesley R. Hurt, "The Preliminary Archaeological Survey of the Chattahoochee Valley Area in Alabama," in *Archaeological Salvage in the Walter F. George Basin of the Chattahoochee River in Alabama*, ed. David L. DeJarnette (Tuscaloosa: University of Alabama Press, 1975), 47.

19. Braley, *Archaeological Data Recovery at Yuchi Town, 1RU63*; Braley, *Yuchi Town (1RU63) Revisited*.

20. Braley, *Yuchi Town (1RU63) Revisited*; Hurt, "An Archaeological Survey, Chattahoochee Valley, Alabama 1947."

21. Braley, *Yuchi Town (1RU63) Revisited*.

22. Weisman, *An Archaeological Study of the Yuchi Town Site*; David W. Chase, "An Historic Indian Town Site in Russell County Alabama," *Coweta Memorial Association Papers* (1960): 1–19.

23. Braley, *Yuchi Town (1RU63) Revisited*.

24. Foster, *Archaeology of the Lower Muskogee Indians*.

25. Braley, *Yuchi Town (1RU63) Revisited*.

26. Weisman, *An Archaeological Study of the Yuchi Town Site*; Braley, *Archaeological Data Recovery at Yuchi Town, 1RU63*; Braley, *Yuchi Town (1RU63) Revisited*; Hargrave et al., *The Yuchi Town Site (1RU63)*; Frank T. Schnell, *A Cultural Resources Investigation of Sites 1RU63 and 9CE66, Fort Benning, Alabama and Georgia* (Columbus GA: Columbus Museum, 1982).

27. Schnell, *Cultural Resources Investigation of Sites 1RU63 and 9CE66*.

28. Martin F. Dickinson and Lucy B. Wayne, *Chattahoochee River Valley Cultural Resource Study and Evaluation, Fort Benning Military Reservation, Russell County, Alabama and Chattahoochee County, Georgia* (Gainesville FL: Water and Air Research, Inc., 1985).

29. Robert W. Benson, *Cultural Resources Survey of Selected Timber Compartments on Fort Benning Chattahoochee County, Georgia*, (Athens GA: Southeastern Archaeological Services, 1996).

30. Braley, *Archaeological Data Recovery at Yuchi Town, 1RU63*; Braley, *Yuchi Town (1RU63) Revisited*.

31. Russell M. Weisman and Meghan LaGraff Ambrosino, *Phase I Archaeological Survey within Fort Benning, Compartments Z-2 and Z-3, Russell County, Alabama, Volumes 1 and 2* (Tuscaloosa AL, 1997).

32. Hargrave et al., *The Yuchi Town Site (1RU63)*.

33. Weisman, *An Archaeological Study of the Yuchi Town Site*.

34. Scott, ARPA *Damage Assessment of 1RU132*.

35. Foster, *Archaeology of the Lower Muskogee Indians*; Braley, *Yuchi Town (1RU63) Revisited*; Worth, "The Eastern Creek Frontier"; Chad O. Braley, *Historic Indian Period Archaeology of the Georgia Coastal Plain*, Georgia Archaeological Research Design Paper no. 10, University of Georgia Laboratory of Archaeology Series Report no. 34 (Athens: Southeastern Archaeological Services, 1995).

36. Foster, "Evidence of Historic Creek Indian Migration."

37. Foster, "Evidence of Historic Creek Indian Migration"; Clive R. Orton and P. A. Tyers, "Counting Broken Objects: The Statistics of Ceramic Assemblages," *Proceedings of the British Academy* 77 (1992): 163–84; Clive R. Orton and P. A. Tyers, "Statistical Analysis of Ceramic Assemblages," *Archeologia e Calcolatori,* 1 (1990): 81–110; Clive Orton, *Sampling in Archaeology* (New York: Cambridge University Press, 2000).

38. Braley, *Yuchi Town (1RU63) Revisited*, 81; Orton and Tyers, "Counting Broken Objects"; Orton and Tyers, "Statistical Analysis of Ceramic Assemblages"; Orton, *Sampling in Archaeology*.

39. Braley, *Yuchi Town (1ru63) Revisited*.

40. Daniel T. Elliott, Karen G. Wood, Rita Folse Elliott, and W. Dean Wood, *Up on the Upatoi: Cultural Resources Survey and Testing of Compartments K-6 and K-7, Fort Benning Military Reservation, Georgia*, (Ellerslie GA: Southern Research, 1996); Jerald Ledbetter, Robbie Ethridge, Mary Theresa Bonhage-Freund, William G. Moffat, Lisa D. O'Steen, and John Worth, *Archaeological Investigations at Buzzard Roost 9TR41, 9TR54, and 9TR106 Taylor County, Georgia* (Athens GA, 2002).

41. Braley, *Yuchi Town (1RU63) Revisited*.

42. Braley, *Yuchi Town (1RU63) Revisited*.

43. Huscher, microfilmed fieldnotes, Walter F. George Survey, reels 1–7.

44. Braley, *Yuchi Town (1RU63) Revisited*.

45. T. M. Hamilton, *Early Indian Trade Guns: 1625–1775* (Lawton OK: Institute of the Great Plains, 1968); Huscher, microfilmed fieldnotes, Walter F. George Survey, reels 1–7.

46. See Braley, *Yuchi Town (1RU63) Revisited*, 81–95, table 11.

47. Foster, *Archaeology of the Lower Muskogee Indians*.

48. Francis Harper, ed., *The Travels of William Bartram* (Athens: University of Georgia Press, 1998).

49. For discussion of the Yuchi communities in the Savannah River Valley, see especially the chapters by Elliot, Piker, and Warren in this volume.

50. Jason Baird Jackson, *Yuchi Ceremonial Life: Performance, Meaning, and Tradition in a Contemporary American Indian Community* (Lincoln: University of Nebraska Press, 2003), 42–43, 78.

51. Alexander Moore, ed., *Nairne's Muskhogean Journals: The 1708 Expedition to the Mississippi River* (Jackson: University Press of Mississippi, 1988), 92.

52. Mereness, *Travels in the American Colonies.*

53. Foster, *Collected Works of Benjamin Hawkins.*

54. Worth, "Mississippian Occupation on the Middle Flint River."

55. Foster, *Collected Works of Benjamin Hawkins.* For discussion of Yuchi living among the Shawnee in Upper Creek Country, see Warren's chapter in this volume.

56. Foster, *Archaeology of the Lower Muskogee Indians*; Robbie Franklyn Ethridge, *The Creek Country: The Creek Indians and their World, 1796–1816* (Chapel Hill: University of North Carolina Press, 2003); Steven Hahn, *The Invention of the Creek Nation, 1670–1763* (Lincoln: University of Nebraska Press, 2004); Joshua A. Piker, *Okfuskee: A Creek Indian Town in Colonial America* (Cambridge MA: Harvard University Press, 2004).

57. Weisman, *An Archaeological Study of the Yuchi Town Site*; Schnell, *Cultural Resources Investigation of Sites 1RU63 and 9CE66.*

58. David J. Wenner Jr., *Preliminary Appraisal of the Archaeological Resources of the Eufaula Reservoir (Onapa and Canadian Reservoir Areas)* (Norman: Department of Anthropology, University of Oklahoma, 1948); George I. Quimby and Alexander Spoehr, "Historic Creek Pottery from Oklahoma," *American Antiquity* 3 (1950): 249–51; Marshall Gettys, "Historical Archaeology in Oklahoma," *Oklahoma Anthropological Bulletin* 44 (1995): 1–84.

6. "They Look upon the Yuchis as Their Vassals"
An Early History of Yuchi-Creek Political Relations

~

Standard historical sources provide good evidence that the historical Yuchi tribe has continuously been part of the political system of the Creek Confederacy since the 18th century. . . . A core of the Yuchi ethnic group, based on the evidence reviewed, is in some ways, socially and culturally distinct from other members of the Creek Nation, but does not form a separate, politically autonomous tribe. The MCN [Muscogee Creek Nation] is the continuation of the Creek Confederacy formed in the 17th and 18th centuries in the Southeast as a confederation of tribes of varying cultural and linguistic backgrounds. The Yuchi tribe has participated politically in the Creek Confederacy since that time. — U.S. DEPARTMENT OF THE INTERIOR, 1995

Since the early eighteenth century, interlopers into the American Deep South have regarded the Yuchis — as the Yuchis have generally regarded themselves — as a subgroup closely affiliated with, yet in many ways culturally distinct from the tribes who made up the Creek Confederacy. In spite of the evidence for Yuchi cultural distinctiveness, generations of colonial governors, Indian agents, ethnographic writers, and Bureau of Indian Affairs staffers, for the purposes administrative expediency, have viewed the Yuchis as part of the Creek Nation. As a consequence the Yuchis have historically found it difficult to identify themselves politically as something other than Creek. As it stands even now, the Yuchis "do not exist" in the eyes of the U.S. government, rendering them a "politically disadvantaged minority within the Creek Nation."[1]

Though scholars have compiled strong evidence for an ongoing, distinct Yuchi ethnic identity, little has yet been done to investigate the early history of their political relationship with the Creeks. If we are to understand the origins of that relationship, we must begin in the early eighteenth century, when the Yuchis made their first recorded appearance among the Creeks. A time of great transformation, the rise of the trade in deerskins and slaves, imperial warfare, and Creek political and territorial assertiveness provided the context for the emerging Yuchi-Creek relationship. Many simple questions concerning it have yet to be asked: How did the Yuchis and the Creeks conceive of their political relationship during the early to mid-eighteenth century? To what extent did the state of Yuchi and Creek political affairs govern their day-to-day intercourse? How did they get along? Did their political relationship change over time?

In answering these questions, a brief survey of the records suggests that the Yuchis' struggle to remain masters of their own destiny is nothing new. Since the early eighteenth century the Lower Creeks have generally regarded the Yuchis as their subordinates and have attempted to impose an asymmetrical relationship upon them that European observers likened to "vassalage." This perception, it seems, took root because of the Creeks' tendency to stake claims to Yuchi lands and to relegate the Yuchis to a subordinate role in politics. However, the Yuchis found ways to assert themselves politically when opportunities arose, the best of which came when they distanced themselves physically from the Creek Nation. Thus we see a rather complicated relationship emerge, one that oscillated between friendship and hostility and between political isolation and inclusion. Whether the Yuchis were forced or deliberately chose to remain outsiders remains inconclusive. But the fact remains that for the Yuchis, coping with what might be called Lower Creek hegemony was a consistent feature of life in the early eighteenth century.

The title of this essay takes inspiration from a comment issued in July 1750 by William Stephens, president of Georgia Assistants, in a letter to Georgia Secretary Benjamin Martyn. At issue was Yuchi land along the Savannah River above the town of Ebenezer, which the local Salzburg inhabitants were pressuring the Georgia government to annex. Stephens's letter suggested that the Georgia government had little to fear from the "few Indians called Euchees" still living there, as most of that nation had already abandoned the area. The Georgia Assistants, though, did fear drawing the wrath of the Creeks. Negotiating with the Yuchis for the Ebenezer lands, Stephens argued, "would induce the Creeks to make Pretentions to them [the Ebenezer lands] likewise." The reason, Stephens explained, was that the Creeks "look upon the Euchees as their vassals." Georgia officials opted to delay annexing the land officially, recommending that they quietly settle a few families there, as the likelihood of Creek interference "might create endless disputes and Expenses."[2]

It would be easy to dismiss Stephens's use of the term *vassals*, which appears occasionally in the words of British officials and was a favorite among Spanish authorities. As with many of the terms Europeans used to describe Native American institutions and social relationships — (*king, capital, emperor*) — the term *vassals* serves as much to obscure as it does to clarify the relationship that may have existed between Creeks and Yuchis. On the one hand, a vassal can be defined as "one who is completely subject to some influence," "a base person," or "a slave."[3] Such definitions evoke the idea of absolute power and feudal concepts of fealty and obedience that we know were not common among southern Indians, whose social relationships were far more egalitarian, particularly in the eighteenth century.

Still, there is something to the phrase that merits our consideration, as a vassal can also be defined as (in feudalism) "one holding lands from a superior on conditions of homage and obedience."[4] This idea is important because it connotes more generally the idea of reciprocal obligations between persons of different status. This concept was not unfamiliar to southern Indians, who used kinship terminology to assign individuals, towns, and nations to their proper place in many imagined hierarchies and to assign to all their proper social obligations to others. Therefore, the term *vassals* should not be shelved outright as a figment of the British imagination. It may indicate a pervasive—if contested—belief that the Yuchis owed some form of homage or obedience to the Creeks because they made their homes on Creek lands.

Yuchi association with the peoples who came to be known as Creek dates to the decade preceding the Yamasee War of 1715, when members of the Yuchi tribe began drifting south and east, away from their Appalachian homelands on the Tennessee River and into the orbit of the Creeks and their Carolina trade partners.[5] Documentary evidence suggests that migration did not involve a single act of relocation, but rather that it occurred in piecemeal fashion, some choosing to remain in their traditional homelands near the Overhill Cherokees as others drifted to the Savannah River and beyond. Our best evidence for this process comes from the records of the South Carolina Indian trade commissioners, who attest to a brief war of reprisal—orchestrated by a Carolina trader—between the Cherokees and the Yuchis living at a nearby town of Chestowee. The commission's minutes appear to distinguish between the Chestowee Yuchi community that the Cherokees had "cut off" in the spring of 1714 and "[the] other Euchees att [the] Savano town," which Carolina officials feared might be the Cherokees' next target.[6] One year later an anonymous map composed in 1715 places the "Ewches" on the Ocmulgee River in central Georgia, which the "Ochese Creek Indians" (mostly comprising towns later regarded as "Lower Creek") called home between 1691 and 1715. The Yuchi village's placement just downstream from the Creek towns of Ocmulgee and Chehaw attests to the development of ever-closer Yuchi involvement with the Creeks on the eve of the Yamasee War.[7]

We can only speculate as to the reasons why the Yuchis began gravitating toward Creek territory. For some, the fear of continued Cherokee reprisals may have constituted grounds for moving to a place they deemed safer. For many others, the lure of the Carolina trade would have been ample incentive. Yuchis living near Savana town (just upstream from present-day Augusta, Georgia) would have had frequent intercourse with a multitude of Indian neighbors, such as the Apalachees (who had recently relocated from Florida), the Savannahs, and other small tribes, which were deeply engaged in the trade for skins and slaves. Savana town, itself a center of trade, was in close proximity to the path connecting Charles Town to Ochese Creek and more westward Indian communities. This favorable position gave the Yuchis ready access to a commercial thoroughfare that would have allowed them to trade, travel, go to war, and become more closely acquainted with the English and with other Indian nations. As the trading path continued west from Savana town, it crossed the Ocmulgee River at the town of Ocmulgee, where the English had established a year-round trade outpost. As with their kinspeople living on the Savannah River, the Ocmulgee River Yuchis living downstream from the trading post would have had easy access to English traders and their wares.[8]

While it is possible to follow Yuchi movements into the Savannah and Ocmulgee River basins, documentary evidence provides few clues as to the nature or extent of the Yuchis' relationships with their new Indian neighbors or the English traders. That the Yuchis, like other Indian groups that traded with the Carolinians, had become caught in the web of English affairs prior to the Yamasee War seems undeniable. In the spring of 1713, for instance, the Yuchis apprehended an unspecified number of "French men and [their] goods," who many believed had been sent to trade and thus "tamper with" the Cherokees. Carolina officials were predictably pleased with the Yuchis' deed, which they viewed as "an Advantage to this [government]." The deed appears to have been advantageous as well for the Yuchis, who were to be given "satisfaction" for the detained Frenchmen, most likely in the form of trade goods.[9]

Given their proximity to the Carolina traders and their Indian allies, it would not be unreasonable to suggest that the Yuchis witnessed and experienced many of the same disturbing trends and events that prompted the Yamasees and their Creek allies to revolt against the English in 1715. As with these groups, the Yuchis must have been aware of Carolina's attempts to enlist (often reluctant) Indian warriors in their wars against the Spanish missions, against the Tuscaroras in North Carolina, and in wars of attrition against both French and Spanish outposts. As trading on "trust" or credit was widespread, it is difficult to think that the Yuchis would some-how have exempted themselves from the spiraling debt that kept war parties afield in search of slaves or from the threats of English trad-ers, who often resorted to physical abuse and enslavement to collect on Indian debts.[10] One can further surmise that, living amidst the Ochese Creek towns, the Yuchis would have been apprised of the meetings held at the Yamasee town of Pocotalico, where first blood against the English was drawn on Good Friday, 1715. It is even pos-sible that the Yuchis were among the "161 towns" that pledged to unite under the Coweta chief Brims to oust the Carolina traders and rekindle dormant relations with Spanish Florida.[11]

And while there is no positive evidence to suggest that the Yuch-is were among the combatants in the spring of 1715, Yuchi maneu-vers following the outbreak of hostilities suggest tacit or overt Yuchi assent to Creek and Yamasee actions and goals. As did many of the Indian groups allied with the Creeks, the Yuchis joined in the Creek exodus to the Chattahoochee River, a move completed in the spring of 1716. Diego Peña, a Spaniard who traveled to the newly estab-lished Chattahoochee River towns in 1716, found a mixed multitude of peoples living there, including Apalachees, Yamasees, and rem-nants of Florida Indian groups. Peña reported that the Yuchis were located centrally among Creeks, between Ocmulgee and Tasquique, but that they remained linguistically distinct, adding that "the vil-lage of Uchi has a speech different from the others, since there are for it not more than two or three interpreters."[12] When Diego Peña returned to the Chattahoochee River in the fall of 1717, he found the "chief of Uchis" (unnamed) acting in concert with other Creek chiefs, who were then eager to cultivate their resurgent relationship with the Spanish. At one point the Yuchi chief helped to escort Peña farther north along the Chattahoochee toward the Lower Creek villages. The chief later sent six of his warriors to confer with Chislacaliche, a Creek leader partial to the Spanish. During Peña's visit the Yuchi chief promised to send emissaries to St. Augustine for further diplomatic talks, just as many of his counterparts from Creek towns had done.[13]

That the Yuchis had situated themselves amidst the Lower Creek towns (for a second time, no less) should not be glossed over lightly. As I have argued elsewhere, the Lower Creeks in the early eighteenth century may have retained vestiges of a chiefdom-level political organization, with recognizable hierarchies among the various towns. In particular, the towns of Coweta and Cussita claimed wide-ranging political authority from the late 1670s. The Coweta "Emperor" Brims, who rose to power in the decade prior to the Yamasee War, exercised and perhaps even expanded this political influence by exploiting his connections with Carolina traders. The Lower Creeks, moreover, developed a keen sense of territorialism during the eighteenth century, partially inspired by their contact with land-hungry British colonists.[14]

Though forged in the context of British land grabs and treaty manipulations, Creek territorialism must be understood in culturally specific ways, meaning that territorialism has distinctly Native roots as well. William Cronon's description of territorialism among northern Algonquians is instructive in this regard. "Territorial rights," he argues, "were expressions of the entire group's collective right," hence the common assumption that Native peoples were communal in nature. But, Cronon adds, collective territorial rights "tended to be vested in the person of the sachem, the leader in whom the village's political identity at least symbolically inhered."[15] Similar assertions can be made about Creek towns, in which members of the founding lineage were often regarded as the "owners" and assumed positions of political authority on that basis. Joshua Piker's work on Okfuskee, for instance, illustrates that Creeks vested "ownership" of the town squares in the office of the *okeelysa*, who were members of the founding clan.[16] We may therefore imagine that any

HAHN

outsiders who wished to settle among the Lower Creeks first had to gain permission from the leaders of its various towns, and most especially the leaders of Coweta and Cussita. The parties in question, then, would have had to work out many details to establish an orderly relationship: where to build a town, which lands to cultivate, where to hunt, and the Yuchis' political status relative to the other Creek towns.

It is therefore tempting to imagine the conversations that must have occurred between Yuchi and Creek leaders before the Yuchis relocated their town on the Chattahoochee in 1715–16. No direct evidence for any such conversations exists, but we may extrapolate from extant sources that shed light on the kinds of agreements Native peoples made when outsiders came to live among established populations. Most telling is an agreement made in 1694 between Usanaca Andres, the Timucuan chief of the Florida mission village of San Luis, and a group of Chacato refugees, who sought refuge near San Luis to evade attacks by Lower Creeks. Usanaca Andres allowed the Chacatos to settle at the old fields of San Luis and granted them permission to harvest nuts and hunt deer. As it concerned these activities, the Timucua chief agreed to "make an unencumbered and free grant of them so that they may take them as their own and so that they may cultivate the lands as their own." However, Usanaca imposed a set of "qualifications and conditions" that circumscribed Chacato behavior in ways that were meant to remind the Chacatos of their subordinate status as the chief's guests. As it concerned bear hunting, for instance, the Timucua chief permitted the Chacatos to hunt only in conjunction with Timucua hunting parties, and he claimed the skins and the choicest cuts of meat for himself. The Timucuan chief also singled out the panther and white bird (*Pajaro blanco*) for similar restrictions, most likely for religious reasons; panther skins were to be given to the chief, and hunting the white bird was absolutely prohibited.[17]

Such agreements, while not "vassalage" in the strict sense, point to the notions of hierarchy implicit in southeastern Indian (if not all) systems of reciprocity.[18] Though eighteenth-century southeastern

Indian societies may have appeared egalitarian to outside observers on a material or perhaps political level, ritual and daily life involved myriad symbolic acts (both small and large) recognizing the asymmetrical relationships between towns, between clans, and between different Indian nations. In the eighteenth-century Southeast, where the coalescence of peoples from disparate tribes was commonplace, such acts can be viewed as the Indians' own way of symbolically recognizing the asymmetrical relationship between a "host" and a "guest," or to distinguish between founding and immigrant clans, as in the example mentioned of the Creek *okeelysa*. We must consider that the Creeks and Yuchis, who shared much the same worldview as their Timucuan and Chacato counterparts, could have made a similar arrangement. While it is likely that the Creeks granted the Yuchis considerable freedom in day-to-day affairs, the privilege of living on Creek lands must have come with some strings attached, involving at the very least symbolic recognition of the Creeks—or a particular Creek chief—as "owners" of the lands upon which the Yuchis settled. As the "ownership" of land endowed a ruling lineage with political authority, we may also infer that certain Creek leaders would have demanded Yuchi deference in matters relating to warfare, peacemaking, and diplomacy. Hence the Yuchis' compliance with Creek political goals during and just following the Yamasee War.

By the 1720s, however, Creek peoples found themselves grappling with related events that promoted high degree of political divisiveness on the Chattahoochee River and beyond. The English were primarily responsible for this, as they pressured Creek leaders—using the threats of military action and trade embargoes—to eliminate the Yamasees, who now lived in Florida and continued to conduct guerrilla warfare on Carolina's southern frontier. At the same time, Carolina officials urged the Creeks to make peace with the Cherokees, with whom they had been at war since 1716. As the various elements within the Creek Nation chose to act or not depending upon their particular relationships to the Yamasees and Cherokees, this divisiveness spurred political factionalism, from which the Yuchis were not immune. By the latter part of that decade the Yuchis chose to make a conspicuous stand against the Yamasees, which may have led to their alienation and exile from Creek country.[19]

Problems between the Yuchis and the Lower Creeks reached a critical stage in the early months of 1728, when Charlesworth Glover came to Creek country to seek restitution for the recent Yamasee murders of trader Matthew Smallwood and his employees. As with the Carolina agents who came before him, Glover found it difficult to convince Lower Creeks to kill Yamasees, due to the Creeks' close marital and adoptive ties to that people and lingering pro-Spanish sentiment in towns such as Coweta and Apalachicola. After spending more than three months among the Creeks, Glover had little to show for his efforts, when on 16 March he received word that two scalps had come to Cussita. Glover made haste to that town, receiving the scalps from the hand of a Cussita chief named Licka, who revealed that it was not the Cussitas who had brought in the scalps but rather the Yuchis. As Glover reported: "The two scalps was brought in by five Euchees who was sent out to break the way by Licka and give the following accounts of their expedition. They met with seven Spaniards and three yamasees at or near the Appalachee old town killing beef, and fired on them, killed one Spaniard, one indian, and wounded another Indian and took eight of their guns, seven of which were English trading guns."[20]

That the Yuchis were bold enough to kill Yamasees at a time when other Lower Creek towns hesitated to do so may reflect the Yuchis' relative strength at that time. For reasons that are not exactly clear (Glover believed that Creek practices of infanticide and abortion were the cause), by the middle of the 1720s the Yuchi population was on the rise, just as the Creek population seems to have been dwindling. In March 1725 Glover reported that "it is observed that the Indians decay everywhere except the Youchees." Glover's census taken at that time affirms this observation. The Yuchi village was then home to 180 men, 200 women, and 150 children, making by it by far the most populous of the Chattahoochee towns. In contrast, the combined population of the politically prominent towns of Cussita and Coweta was less than that of the Yuchis. The ancient "mother town" of Apalachicola came in a distant third with a mere 230 souls.[21]

In one sense the Yuchi act of taking Spanish and Yamasee scalps hints at their willingness to act independently of Creek wishes. Glover's journal reveals, however, that the Yuchis, by exploiting inter-town factionalism among the Lower Creeks, were playing a more subtle political game. As the two preeminent "head towns" among the Lower Creeks, both the Cowetas and the Cussitas could stake claim to the Yuchis' allegiance. It just so happened that the Cussitas, more eager to fulfill English demands, were at odds with the Cowetas, who tended to protect Yamasee and Spanish interests. Cleverly, it seems, the Yuchis procured and redeemed the scalps in a way that recognized Cussita's preeminence, even if only symbolically. Glover's journal indicates, for example, that Licka, the headman of Cussita, personally sent the Yuchi war party on its errand to Florida, hinting that Cussita leaders claimed the right to command Yuchi warriors, who in this case appear not to have acted merely on their own initiative. Moreover, the delivery of the scalps to Glover followed a recognizable chain of transmission, from the Yuchis, to Licka, then to Glover, thus making the scalpings a Cussita act, which may have softened the perception that the Yuchis had behaved in an insubordinate manner toward the Cowetas.

Nevertheless, the Yuchis' bold stroke against the Yamasees and Spaniards under the auspices of Cussita authority appears to have put them in a precarious position, requiring them to abandon their homes on the Chattahoochee River. The timing of their proposed departure suggests that this was the case, for upon hearing of the Yuchis' actions, Glover soon reported: "The Euchees have broke up their town in the lower creeks and are now unsettled. I am endeavoring to get them to Savana town or the Pallchacolas whether they will or not I can't yet tell."[22] Banishment, of course, was and remains a powerful mechanism of control in Native communities, which claim that right on the grounds that group cohesion merits the excision of a community's intractable members. The Creeks famously exercised this right when they banished the Apalachicola man Tomochichi and his followers, who founded the town of Yamacraw in what became the colony of Georgia. At the same time, evidence seems to indicate that the Yuchi exile was partially voluntary, as they did not fly in haste but chose to remain among the Creeks for a while. "The Euchees," Glover wrote, "have promised me to move next fall [1728], but [I] could not get them to do it now."[23]

Extant records indicate that the Yuchis soon made good on their promise to move closer to South Carolina, choosing the environs of Fort Palachacola as their new home.[24] Anglican minister Francis Varnod, while on a missionary visit to the Palachacola garrison in the summer of 1729, made a brief stop in the nearby "new settlement of the Uchee Indians" to baptize a "molatto child belonging to an Indian trader."[25] The Yuchi settlement was therefore relatively well established when just three years later the Carolina Council ordered Glover (again) "to go to the Palachacolas and to meet with the Utchees who are settled thereabout," empowering him "to inform himself of the state of the Utchees and how they stand affected and to endeavor to keep them in the interest of the government."[26]

That the Yuchis were on poor terms with the Lower Creeks can be seen in an ongoing war they conducted with the Cowetas, who may have been instrumental in pressuring them to leave. The *South Carolina Gazette* reported on 8 October 1732 that "the Coweetas had killed 2 Euchees, one they cut off the head, and the other they scalped; there are 3 others missing, who tis supposed are killed or carried away prisoners."[27] The *Gazette*'s brief description of this attack is telling. Not only did the Cowetas have to go far out of their way to confront Yuchis living on the Savannah River, but also the ritual disfigurement of the victims suggests that they were killed intentionally for purposes of revenge. The relationship between the Cowetas and Yuchis remained tense when James Oglethorpe arrived on the Savannah bluff to establish the colony of Georgia in February 1733. Describing the Native peoples on Georgia's frontiers, Oglethorpe wrote, "There are in Georgia on this side of the mountains three considerable nations of Indians, one called the lower

Creeks. . . . The other two nations are the Uchees and the Upper Creeks, the first consisting of 200, the latter of 1100 men. We agree so well with the Indians that the Creeks and Uchees have referred a difference to me to determine which otherwise would occasion a War."[28] Oglethorpe did not specify the nature of this "difference," but the fact that the two nations appear to have needed his services as an intermediary suggests the continuation of hostilities up until the time of Georgia's founding.

The move to Palachacola and subsequent alliance with the colony of Georgia ushered in a new, if short-lived, era in Yuchi history, during which the Yuchis engaged in diplomacy and warfare largely independent of Creek influence, in ways that had proved politically imprudent (or dangerous) in the preceding decade. Their situation was somewhat analogous to that of their neighbors to the east, Tomochichi's Yamacraws. Like the Yamacraws, the Yuchis became closely connected to the nearby Georgia colonists and earned a measure of political *gravitas* by allying themselves with Oglethorpe's regime. The records of the Salzburger immigrants, who settled on the Savannah River just below the Yuchi town at Palachacola, preserve numerous accounts of Yuchis trading with the local settlers and visiting them informally when they crossed into Salzburger territory.[29] The Yuchis, moreover, assisted Georgia leaders as hunters and guides, accompanying James Oglethorpe on his sojourns to Fort Frederica and to the southern frontier between Georgia and La Florida.[30]

Importantly, the Yuchis' close relationship to the Georgians drew them into that era's imperial military conflicts, in particular the long-standing dispute with Spain over the "debatable land" that became Georgia. During the 1730s and the subsequent War of Jenkins' Ear, the Yuchis conspicuously served as important allies to Oglethorpe and the British, more so relative to their small size than the Creeks living on the Chattahoochee. The Yuchis, for instance, are disproportionately represented in many of the war accounts that estimate the number of Indian allies fighting on behalf of the British. During the 1740 siege of St. Augustine, Oglethorpe estimated that twenty to thirty Yuchis lost their lives, singling them out for favorable treatment because they "have lately suffered so much for the sake of the English and are always ready to come out for war." The number of Yuchi dead in this instance stands out for the very reason that British officials made no such estimate (high by eighteenth-century Native standards) for Creek casualties. Georgia officials Thomas Ayres and William Stephens corroborate this evidence with explicit references to their attempts to recruit Yuchis and Savannah River Chickasaws for that very same siege.[31]

On the one hand Yuchi participation in Georgia military endeavors might be read as evidence of their subservience to the regime in Savannah. From a different perspective, however, providing military assistance to the British can also be seen as evidence that the Yuchis were then acting independently of Lower Creeks, who remained reluctant to commit to the British cause and were remarkably absent from the bloodiest encounters. In addition to fighting, Yuchi leaders appear to have negotiated with British commanders independent of direct Creek influence, thereby raising the possibility that the Yuchis did not at that time consider themselves "vassals" of the Lower Creeks. While Yuchi opinion on the matter does not, unfortunately, survive in the historical record, much can be inferred from their actions, suggesting a sustained period of engagement with the Georgia colonists that took place largely outside the orbit of Creek influence.

It remains unclear whether the Lower Creeks accepted the Yuchis as an independent entity. We do know, however, that many Creeks remained suspicious of them. In the summer of 1735, for instance, an Indian war party killed seven Yamacraws encamped near the Altamaha River. Tomochichi, who first reported the incident to Georgia officials, quickly fingered the Yuchis as the guilty party. The belief that the Yuchis were the murderers then appears to have become widespread, as both the Yamacraws and Lower Creeks perpetuated the rumor that the Yuchis had done the killing. Subsequent investigations exonerated the Yuchis of the murders, but only after the English had offered a credible alibi for the Yuchi man accused of leading the hostile party (he was at his home in a Yuchi town at the time).[32] Though the Yuchis were ultimately found innocent of the charges, the fact that Yamacraws and Lower Creeks were so quick to blame the Yuchis—and willing to entertain the rumor—suggests a lingering animosity.

Yet one does observe that Lower Creek leaders became more accepting of the Yuchis beginning in the mid-1730s. It is often said that familiarity breeds contempt, and in this instance the reverse appears equally true; the Yuchis' removal to Palachacola may actually have enhanced the ability of both parties to get along at a comfortable distance. Evidence for a possible "thaw" in the Yuchi-Creek relationship can be seen in the example of Ellick, a Cussita headman, who married three Yuchi women, with whom he lived at Palachacola during the 1730s. Notwithstanding Benjamin Hawkins's later portrayal of this plural marriage as a source of animosity toward Ellick, his marriage appears to have helped solidify ties between Creeks living on the Chattahoochee and the Yuchis.[33] Nor did Ellick's status permanently suffer, as he would eventually return to the Creek Nation in the 1760s as a prominent speaker and influential representative of Cussita, his town of origin. Creek leaders, in fact, seem to have recognized his potential value as a go-between with the Yuchis. In April 1735, after Oglethorpe and Tomochichi had returned from their famous voyage to England bearing gifts from the Georgia Trustees, Tomochichi saw fit to name Ellick, the "Chief man [who] lives at Ewchee town," a recipient.[34] As Georgia officials had pressured Tomochichi to distribute the presents in a politically expedient manner, we may presume that the Yamacraw chief's act of naming Ellick a recipient reflected a more widespread recognition of his—and by association, the Yuchis'—political importance.

Even Coweta's leaders appear to have reached a détente with the Yuchis. In 1736 Chigelly of Coweta was summoned to Fort Frederica to explain the web of relationships that existed between the Creeks, the Yuchis, and the Cherokees. Chigelly told the English that the Creeks and Yuchis were on good terms, explaining "the Uchees and we are friends," and adding that "if we meet with any

of the Cherokees, either we or they must die."[35] On one occasion in
1743 Creek leaders even took it upon themselves to solicit gunpow-
der from the Georgia government on the Yuchis' behalf, an occurrence that might have been unthinkable a decade earlier.[36]

Eventually, though, the expansion of the Georgia colony brought
the Yuchis and Creeks together again, causing them to erect a new
relationship upon foundations of the old, albeit under circumstances that may not have been of the Yuchis' choosing. As it was, the Yuchi settlement at Palachacola, for which proximity to Georgia had
initially proven advantageous, soon proved otherwise. Steady English encroachment prompted them disperse and give up the lands
upon which they had lived since 1732. By 1741 the Yuchis had already largely abandoned the area. As William Stephens reported
that year, the Palachacolas fort "was once the habitation of a tribe
of Euches, who deserted it a few years since, chusing to settle farther up; but a few of them frequent it still, with some vagrant Creeks
among them, occasionally; and one Thomas Wiggin, an Indian Trader, keeps stores there."[37] The presence of "vagrant Creeks" among
the Yuchis is telling, as it indicates that the ties between the two remained significant in spite of the Yuchis' exile. Thus when the Yuchis considered making a new home for themselves, the Chattahoochee valley was the logical choice. Writing many years after the fact,
Benjamin Hawkins suggested that none other than Ellick of Cussita played an instrumental role in finding a new home for the Yuchis. Ellick, Hawkins wrote, "collected all the Uches, gave them the
land where their town now is, and there they settled."[38] By the early 1750s a new Yuchi village emerged on the Chattahoochee, bringing their exile a generation earlier full circle.

By returning to the Chattahoochee, the Yuchis may unwittingly
(or perhaps willingly) have ceded much of the ability to act independently of Creek influence that they had exercised during their period
of exile. Hawkins's suggestion that Ellick "gave them land" sheds
some light on the nature of the Yuchis' political relationship to Cussita. As the "owners" of the lands upon which the Yuchis built their
town, the Yuchis remained there at the pleasure of the Cussitas, who

likely demanded a degree of symbolic recognition of that fact, if not outright political obedience. Though in day-to-day life the Yuchis and their Creek hosts appear to have forged a generally civil relationship, occasional difficulties could and did punctuate longer periods of relative calm. In particular, Yuchi actions that seemed to threaten the Lower Creeks' standing with the British caused Creek leaders to assert their right to correct Yuchi behavior.

The following incident is indicative of this lingering sense of Yuchi political inferiority among Lower Creeks. In the spring of 1758, with the threat of war raging in all quarters, a party of Yuchis stole fourteen horses from a white settlement on the Ogechee River, leading to the deaths of three settlers. Such an act threatened to draw Georgia's wrath against the Lower Creeks, who feared that they would be blamed for the incident. Whoyanne, an Apalachicola headman who happened to be in Savannah at that time, expressed concern to Georgia officials that "the white people can't distinguish Indians of different nations," therefore making it "possible the Creeks may be blamed for what other Indians do." Whoyanne then promised to return home and inform his people of the incident, agreeing to "acquaint the Uchees (who have head-men and wise-men among them)" with the details of the incident, so "that they might admonish their people."[39]

Whoyanne's promises notwithstanding, the Lower Creeks failed to bring in the Yuchi murderers as the summer waned. On 3 August Georgia officials sent agent Joseph Wright to the town of Chehaw, where Wright made explicit his government's demands for the heads of the three murderers. The Chehaws, however, refused to carry out the punishments, pleading that "they could not give an answer until they consulted the Cussetaws and Cowetas." Three more days of heated negotiations ensued between Coweta and Yuchi leaders, during which the Yuchis refused to punish the murderers on the grounds that they had lost several of their own people to the depredations of white settlers. Finally, on 9 August at Chehaw, Lower Creek leaders agreed to punish the three guilty Yuchis, which led to the death of one and the flight of the other two (whose fates are not known).

Ellick, not incidentally, offered to round up the two refugees, further indicating that the Cussitas considered themselves responsible for the Yuchis' behavior toward outsiders.[40]

Again, the pattern of events that took place after the murders is suggestive not only of the primacy of Coweta and Cussita among the Lower Creeks but also of their perceived right to exercise control over the Yuchis. First of all, Whoyanne's speech in Savannah, in which he refers to the Yuchis as "other Indians," betrays a Lower Creek tendency to regard the Yuchis as outsiders. Equally noteworthy is the fact that the Chehaws and other lower Creek leaders declined to take action themselves and left it to Coweta and Cussita to determine the fate of the suspected Yuchi murderers. Largely because of Coweta's and Cussita's influence, Lower Creeks arranged for the execution of one of the Yuchi suspects, against the expressed wishes of the Yuchi chief. When considered in the light of Creek notions of kinship, this pattern was logical for the Cowetas and Cussitas. As caretakers of the Lower Creek–Georgia alliance, they had a duty to revenge the deaths of their English allies, with whom they had signed treaties for three generations and for whom they were obliged to obtain "satisfaction" when murders were committed. As hosts of the Yuchis, which entailed obligations both to protect and to correct them as if kin, it was their responsibility in this instance to punish the Yuchis as their own.

Just as leaders of the Lower Creek towns of Coweta and Cussita could and did sacrifice Yuchi lives to avert diplomatic crises, the Lower Creeks also tended to relegate the Yuchis to an inferior role in Anglo-Creek diplomacy. Practically speaking, what this meant was that the Yuchis had little voice in momentous political affairs—land cessions, imperial alliances, "satisfaction" for murders, and the like—that affected them as much as the Creeks. This is not to say, however, that the Yuchis were excluded from *all* diplomacy, as Yuchi leaders at Palachacola occasionally negotiated their own agreements and exchanged ritual gestures with British officials. Whether this was a voluntary assertion of their independence or a sign of the Yuchis' status as "vassals," the important point is that Yuchis played no vital role in *Creek* diplomacy, and we should therefore question simplistic assumptions of their continuous political "participation" in Creek affairs.

Though written by Englishmen and susceptible to bias, treaties and related documentary material are valuable resources for examining the internal and external political affairs of Indian peoples. Not only do treaty minutes capture the grievances and aspirations that Indian leaders wanted to communicate to their European counterparts, but also they shed light on internal political arrangements. For example, Indian leaders who signed treaties did not do so randomly but tended to allow the most prominent members of the political community—most often from the most politically important towns—to make their marks first. Also, the exclusion of certain individuals or the underrepresentation of particular towns might hint of internal disagreements or factional disputes within the nation.

It is therefore interesting to observe that the Yuchis were not directly involved in Anglo-Creek treaty diplomacy in the early to mid-eighteenth century. For example, Yuchis appear not to have taken part in the first such treaties ratified between the Creeks and South Carolinians between 1705 and 1732.[41] Nor did they participate in the early rounds of diplomacy with the more recently established colony of Georgia, beginning with James Oglethorpe's first treaty with the Lower Creeks, completed in Savannah on 21 May 1733. Agreed to by "the head men of the Coweta and Cussita towns," treaty minutes record prominent speeches by Yamacraw chief Tomochichi, a "relative" of Tomochichi's from the town of Oconee, and the chief of Coweta himself. In all, the forty-four men present represented eight different Lower Creek towns. Nowhere are the Yuchis mentioned in the conference minutes or the text of the treaty itself. Most telling is a speech given by Coweta mico Yahou-Lakee, in which he laments the recent loss of two Creek towns, which had rendered their nation "weak." Hoping to see the Lower Creeks restored to their former grandeur, Yahou-Lakee praised the Yamacraws for founding a new town and called upon the Yamasees to do the same, so that "our nation shall be restored to its ten towns."[42] The Yuchis, though recently exiled like the Yamacraws, did not figure into Ya-hou-Lakee's equation, which hints that the Cowetas considered the Yuchis perpetual outsiders rather than an exiled part of their nation.

As with the treaty negotiations of 1733, the Yuchis also seem not to have been on hand for the ceremonial distribution of presents from the Georgia Trustees that took place in June 1735, made memorable as the event that inspired Chigelly of Coweta to recount the Cussita "Migration Legend."[43] In all, more than forty-two Creek leaders witnessed the proceedings, representing nine Creek towns. Several weeks later the Upper Creeks came to Savannah to receive their share of the presents. The Yuchis instead conducted their affairs separately before Oglethorpe in a ritual conducted eleven months later at Fort Frederica, for which the Yuchis received "muskets, red and blue cloth, powder, lead," and an assortment of other goods.[44] We may surmise that the presents were distributed in this manner because both parties—Oglethorpe and his Yuchi guests—regarded the Yuchis as a distinct entity rather than as "vassals" when it came to cross-cultural diplomacy.

As on previous diplomatic endeavors, Oglethorpe's 1739 treaty with the Lower Creeks, concluded at a time when the Yuchis and Creeks were on more amicable terms, provides no indication that the Yuchis played any role in its negotiation. At the time Oglethorpe's purpose was to solidify his relationship with the Creeks in order to present a united Creek-British front in anticipation of war against Spain and, as is revealed by a careful reading of the text, to solidify Georgia's territorial claims. This time Oglethorpe made the journey to Coweta personally to conduct affairs. At Coweta, Oglethorpe sat with leaders from eleven different Creek towns, and records indicate that no Yuchi leaders were on hand, in spite of the fact that Oglethorpe's entourage passed through the Yuchi town on 8 July.[45] Georgia officials, in fact, attempted to stir the marital spirit among the Yuchis separately, commissioning one William Grey on 29 September to proceed to the Yuchi communities near Augusta to recruit warriors, roughly five weeks after Lower Creek leaders ratified their own treaty with Oglethorpe in Coweta.[46]

The Creeks' tendency to exclude the Yuchis from diplomacy may have had the effect of lowering the Yuchis' reputation among Europeans, who likewise tended to overlook the Yuchis when conducting diplomacy with Indian tribes. Spanish officials, for example, seem not to have regarded the Yuchis as part of the Lower Creek polity. In 1738 officials in Cuba sent one Alonso Marquez del Toro into Lower Creek territory to distribute gifts and buy the Creeks' allegiance in anticipation of war with Britain. Toro, upon the advice of an Indian man familiar with the Lower Creeks, drew up a list of the towns targeted to receive the presents. His list, which included eleven Lower Creek towns, omitted the Yuchis entirely.[47] Likewise, British officials who compiled information concerning the political loyalties of Creek towns (to the British, the French, etc.) tended to regard the Yuchis as politically unimportant. One anonymous report, made in 1758 and intended for the eyes of South Carolina governor William Henry Lyttelton, claimed that the Yuchis were "taken no great notice of by neither the French nor English."[48] This perception may have been due, in part, to the relatively small size of their town. The Yuchis' town, which boasted fifty gunmen, was at that time but a third the number of the Cowetas and Cussitas.[49]

Given their diplomatic invisibility, the Yuchis had to engage in Anglo-Creek diplomacy indirectly, most likely through Ellick, the Cussita headman. Ellick, by virtue of his grant of land and marital ties to the Yuchis, may have spoken on the Yuchis' behalf as he rose to prominence as a go-between for the Creeks and British during the era of the French and Indian War. By 1763 he had become one of the leading spokesmen for the Lower Creeks and, as the British had conferred upon him the honor of "Great Medal Chief," was ubiquitous in the diplomatic talks and treaties conducted by Creek and British leaders during the 1760s. He was a leading Lower Creek signer of three treaties agreed to at Augusta (in 1763, 1767, and 1768), one at Picolata (1764), and at one at Pensacola (1765), to name but a few. One could imagine that Ellick, in speaking on behalf of the Lower Creeks, also represented the wishes of Yuchi leaders, as it was not unheard of for a Creek town to appoint the chief of a neighboring, closely related town to speak on its behalf. While this scenario is plausible, Ellick appears never to have engaged in diplomacy officially as a representative of the Yuchi town and instead signed treaties on behalf of Cussita.[50]

The Yuchis, though, began to play a more direct role in the politics of the Creek Nation during the French and Indian War, when the Georgia colony sought Creek alliances to counter an expected assault from the French and their Indian allies. Toward that end Henry Ellis, royal governor of Georgia, invited a large Upper and Lower Creek delegation to Savannah to solidify the alliance. The Creek delegation's arrival in late October 1757 prompted the weeklong negotiations that led to Ellis' Treaty, ratified in Savannah on 3 November. Three prominent Creek headmen, speaking on behalf of twenty-one Creek towns, dominated the negotiations that week, in particular the Wolf of Muccalassee and Stumpe and Togulki of Coweta. Though no Yuchi voice was set down in the Georgia Council's records, council minutes confirm the presence of at least one Yuchi "head man" during the talks preceding the ratification of the treaty.[51] Extant evidence does not allow one to identify or confirm the presence of that individual, but the final draft of the treaty indicates that the Yuchis were among the twenty-one towns that consented to it, making the 1757 document the very first that the Yuchis signed in conjunction with the Creeks.

From that point onward, the Yuchi presence at diplomatic talks became more conspicuous, most likely because they were now physically located amid the Lower Creeks, and the endurance of their decades-old political relationship (however defined) seemed to merit their inclusion. The Treaty of Paris (1763) had officially brought the Seven Years' or French and Indian War to an end, but British officials found that they had much work left to do in shoring up Indian alliances. Particularly important was the need to fix vaguely defined boundaries between the Creek Nation, the colony of Georgia, and the new colonies of East and West Florida, which the British had acquired from Spain by virtue of the treaty. Beginning with the 1763 Congress at Augusta, British and Creek officials met on at least six occasions to discuss these and other matters relating to trade and frontier hostilities. Yuchi leaders known as Bever and Phipa were on hand at the congress held at Picolata in 1765 to fix the boundary between the Creeks and East Florida and signed a treaty on behalf the Creek nation as representatives of Yuchi town.[52] Two years later an unnamed "Eutche King" attended a trade conference held by British Indian superintendent John Stuart at Augusta, and in the fall of 1768 Yuchi warriors Presto and Phipa (again) took part in another round of talks held with Georgia officials, and signed off on yet another boundary treaty penned at Augusta.[53]

While present, though, it is clear that Yuchi leaders partook in diplomacy only intermittently and usually in a supporting role. Rarely if ever did Yuchi leaders sign the official "talks" that frequently changed hands between Lower Creek and British leaders. Even when Yuchi leaders were present at the various congresses, treaty minutes indicate that they remained a silent, shadowy presence. At no time did a Yuchi representative make his voice heard during the official diplomatic exchange at either the Picolata or Augusta conferences. More telling, though the British sought to win influence among the Creeks by naming influential men "medal chiefs," no Yuchi leader appears to have garnered this honor prior to the outbreak of the American Revolution.[54]

As with foreign diplomacy, extant evidence of eighteenth-century Green Corn Ceremonies (*posketv*) also hints at the Creeks' tendency to exclude the Yuchis from their inner circles. Briefly, posketv (from which the English name busk derives) was and is today the Creek version of the annual Eastern Woodland Green Corn Ceremony, usually consisting of up to eight days of fasting, feasting, speech making, and the ritual relighting of a town's sacred fire. In part a ceremony celebrating the first fruits of the year's harvest, the Green Corn Ceremony also served and still serves as an important means for ritually renewing the relationships among closely related clans and towns—those who, to put it in the Creek idiom, shared "the same fire." From a functionalist perspective, then, an examination of the participants in any given Green Corn Ceremony ritual may give us some indication of the connectedness between Creek towns or the lack of it.

Though it was rare for early eighteenth-century European intruders to witness—much less to understand—Creek rituals, circumstantial evidence of the Green Corn Ceremony held in Coweta in 1750 offers a clue that the Yuchis, despite living just ten miles downstream, remained outside the orbit of Coweta ritual life. It happened that year that Abraham Bosomworth, seeking to court Creek support for his sister-in-law Mary's claims against the Georgia government for disputed lands within the colony (Mary was half-Creek and likely related to Coweta's chiefs), ventured to Coweta during the Green Corn Ceremony, perhaps intentionally, knowing that most Creeks were likely to be home at that time. Two days after the completion of the Green Corn Ceremony rituals Bosomworth called together Creek leaders then in Coweta to put their mark on prepared documents acknowledging Mary's right to the lands in question. Tellingly, representatives from five Chattahoochee towns—Cussita, Hitchiti, Apalachicola, Chehaw, and Osuche—were on hand and thus likely participants in the recent Coweta Green Corn Ceremonies. Acmucieche of the Upper Creek town of Tuckebatchee was even on hand, perhaps in recognition of the long-standing relationship between the two as "friend towns." Significantly, the Yuchis were not on hand in Coweta that day. Though such an omission may indicate Yuchi disapproval of Bosomworth's scheme, it is probable that the Yuchis had not attended the Coweta Green Corn Ceremony because they and the Cowetas did not consider themselves to be of "the same fire."[55]

What, then, are we to make of the official U.S. government assertion that the Yuchi tribe has "continuously been part of the political system of the Creek Confederacy since the 18th century"? Should we take British officials at their word and assume that the Yuchis were little more than "vassals" of the Creeks, who at times treated the Yuchis in ways that seem to support the assertion? The evidence presented here calls for a more nuanced understanding of Yuchi relations with the Creeks in the early to mid-eighteenth century. It should be remembered that the Yuchis entered the orbit of Creek life at a time of widespread dispersals of Indian populations due to disease, warfare, enslavement, imperial warfare, and the lure of trade. Thus their on-again-off-again immersion into the Creek fold likely indicates Yuchi aspirations to position themselves favorably in this environment rather than their desire somehow to become "Creek." While Native understandings of territorialism and politics make it feasible that the Creeks demanded, and the Yuchis accepted, terms similar to that of vassalage, we should remember that this characterization is more a product of British and Creek views of political history. Therefore, we should not assume that the Yuchis—like vassals in a variety of other contexts—readily accepted the asymmetrical terms of their political relationship. When opportunities arose, as we have seen, the Yuchis could and did act independently. The Creeks' tendency to render the Yuchis invisible in diplomatic affairs suggests that politically speaking, the Yuchis were "in" but not "of" the Creek Nation—which hints at an even bigger issue. Perhaps there is a connection between the Yuchis' political invisibility and their well-known ethnic distinctiveness; often excluded from the fabric of Creek political life, the Yuchis may have embraced the status of "outsider" as a kind of defense mechanism that enabled them to cope with a persistent Lower Creek hegemony as well as to preserve their ancestral social, cultural, linguistic, and historical distinctiveness.

Acknowledgments

I would like to thank Jason Baird Jackson for his editorial assistance and for sharing his expertise on Yuchi history and ethnology, all of which made this chapter possible. I also wish to extend thanks to the other participants in the 2004 American Society for Ethnohistory panel where this volume got its start for sharing their ideas and helping to refine my own.

Notes

U.S. Department of the Interior, Office of Federal Acknowledgment, "Summary under the Criteria and Evidence for Proposed Finding against Federal Acknowledgment of the Yuchi Tribal Organization," Document no. Yto Voo1 Doo5, 11 July 1995, 9–11.

1. Jason Baird Jackson, *Yuchi Ceremonial Life: Performance, Meaning, and Tradition in a Contemporary American Indian Community* (Lincoln: University of Nebraska Press, 2003), 4.

2. "William Stephens and the Georgia Assistants to Benjamin Martyn, July 19, 1750," in *Early American Indian Documents*, 20 vols., vol. 11: *Georgia Treaties 1733–1763*, ed. John T. Juricek (Frederick MD: University Publications of America, 1989), 200 (hereafter cited as GT).

3. The Oxford English Dictionary Online, www.oed.com, Definitions, vassal, #2c and #3.

4. Oxford English Dictionary Online, definition #1.

5. On the Appalachian origins of the Yuchis, see John Worth's contribution to this volume as well as John Swanton, *Early History of the Creek Indians and Their Neighbors* (Washington DC: Government Printing Office, 1922), 289–90; Jackson, *Yuchi Ceremonial Life*, 27; John E. Worth, "The Lower Creeks: Origins and Early History," in *Indians of the Greater Southeast: Historical Archaeology and Ethnohistory*, ed. Bonnie McEwan (Gainesville: University Press of Florida, 2000), 285–286.

6. A. S. Salley Jr., ed., *Journal of the Commissioners of the Indian Trade of South Carolina, September 20, 1710–April 12, 1715* (Columbia SC: State Company, 1926), 70–71.

7. Anonymous, "Indian Villages Map, ca. 1715," in William P. Cumming, *The Southeast in Early Maps*, 3rd ed. (Chapel Hill: University of North Carolina Press, 1998), plate 46A; Worth, "The Lower Creeks," 285.

8. On the Ocmulgee trading post, see Gregory Waselkov, "The Macon Trading House and Early Indian-European Contact in the Colonial Southeast," in *Ocmulgee Archaeology, 1936–1986*, ed. David Halley (Athens: University of Georgia Press, 1994), 190–96.

9. Salley, *Journal of the Commissioners*, 58.

10. On the early trade regime in South Carolina and origins of the Yamasee War, see Verner Crane, *The Southern Frontier, 1670–1732* (Durham NC: Duke University Press, 1928), 71–186; James Merrell, *The Indians' New World: Catawbas and Their Neighbors from European Contact through the Era of Removal* (Chapel Hill: University of North Carolina Press, 1989), 49–91; Stephen Oatis, *A Colonial Complex: South Carolina's Frontiers in the Era of the Yamasee War, 1680–1730* (Lincoln: University of Nebraska Press, 2004), 24–132.

11. On the pan-Indian alliance and its overtures to Spanish Florida, see "Governor Francisco Corocoles y Martinez to the King, July 5, 1715," Archivo General des Indias–Audiencia de Santo Domingo, legajo 834, fols. 4–5, microfilm; Oatis, *Colonial Complex*, 112–13.

12. Mark Boyd, "Diego Peña's Expedition to Apalachee and Apalachicolo in 1716," *Florida Historical Quarterly* 28 (1949): 1–27.

13. Mark Boyd, "Documents Describing the Second and Third Expeditions of Lieutenant Diego Peña to Apalachee and Apalachicolo in 1717 and 1718," *Florida Historical Quarterly* 31 (1952): 109–39, see 117, 122, 134.

14. For the details of my argument, see Steven C. Hahn, *The Invention of the Creek Nation, 1670–1763* (Lincoln: University of Nebraska Press, 2004), 29–47, 66.

15. William Cronon, *Changes in the Land: Indians, Colonists, and the Ecology of New England* (New York: Hill and Wang, 1983), 59.

16. Joshua A. Piker, *Okfuskee: A Creek Indian Town in Colonial America* (Cambridge MA: Harvard University Press, 2004), 115.

17. "Contract between the Chief of San Luis and the Chacato Refugees at Escavi, December 12, 1694," in *Visitations and Revolts in Florida, 1656–1695*, ed. John Hann (Tallahassee: Florida Bureau of Archaeological Research, 1993), 187–88.

18. On the hierarchical nature of systems of reciprocity, see Claude Lévi-Strauss, "Reciprocity and Hierarchy," *American Anthropologist* n.s. 46 (1944): 266–68. For a fuller discussion, see Claude Lévi-Strauss, *Structural Anthropology*, trans. Claire Jacobson and Brooke Grundfest Schoepf (New York: Basic Books, 1963), 132–63.

19. Hahn, *Invention of the Creek Nation*, 121–48.

20. "Charlesworth Glover, Journal 1727–28," in *Records in the British Public Record Office Relating to South Carolina*, vol. 13, ed. W. Noel Sainsbury, transcripts, South Carolina Department of Archives and History, Columbia, 117–145, quotation on 145.

21. Because of Glover's long history of interaction with the Creek Nation, and the access he had to them as the commanding officer at Fort Moore, I generally accept his census numbers. However, I do not accept infanticide and abortion as the causes of Lower Creek population loss. It seems unreasonable to me that a people trying to recover from wars with the English and the Cherokees would have engaged in such practices on a broad scale. Glover intended his census for the Anglican Church's missionary establishment, the S.P.G., and may have alluded to what he considered "heathen" practices as a way of rekindling stalled missionary efforts among the Indians. In my view, the most likely explanations for these demographic trends involve disease, warfare, and dispersal of Lower Creeks who settled in Chislacaliche's town or among the Upper Creeks. As the evidence for this is wanting, though, this hypothesis remains speculative. For the census numbers, see A. S. Salley,

"The Creek Indian Tribes in 1725: Charlesworth Glover's Account of the Indian Tribes of March 15, 1725," *South Carolina Geneological and Historical Quarterly* 32 (1931): 241–42.

22. "Charlesworth Glover, Journal 1727–28," 13:150.

23. "Charlesworth Glover, Journal 1727–28," 13:167.

24. It should be noted that archaeologist Thomas Foster has argued that the probable Yuchi town site on the Chattahoochee River was continuously occupied throughout the eighteenth century. While it is feasible that a few Yuchis remained there, the historical evidence for their occupation of Palachacola on the Savannah River between 1729 and 1741 seems incontrovertible. Further research will therefore be needed to reconcile the historical and archaeological data. For now, my instinct is that a ten- to twenty-year hiatus of Yuchi occupation would difficult to discern archaeologically, particularly given the inconclusive evidence for a distinctive Yuchi material culture. It may also be the case that the temporarily abandoned town site was occupied occasionally by Creek families, thus leading to the impression that the town was continuously occupied. See Foster, this volume.

25. "Francis Varnod to the S.P.G. Secretary, September 4, 1729." Records of the Society for the Propagation of the Gospel, Letter Series "B", Volume 4, document no. 235 (pages unnumbered).

26. South Carolina-Council Journal August 16, 1732, British Public Record Office, CO 5/434, microfilm, South Carolina Department of Archives and History, Columbia, no page or folio number.

27. *South Carolina Gazette*, 8 October 1732.

28. "James Oglethorpe to the Trustees of Georgia, March 12, 1733," in Juricek, *GT*, 11–12.

29. See Piker, this volume.

30. For Yuchi activity at Fort Frederica, see Kristin Hvidt, ed., *Von Reck's Voyage: Drawings and Journal of Philip Georg Friedrich von Reck*, ed. Kristian Hvidt (Savannah GA: Beehive Press, 1980), 39–40. Von Reck insinuates that some Yuchis agreed to accompany Oglethorpe and the Yamacraws to Florida that year.

31. This is not to deny Creek involvement in the War of Jenkins' Ear. My argument, however, is that several small tribes living in close proximity to Georgia, such as the Yuchis, Savannah River Chickasaws, Yamacraws, and Tomohetans, proved to be more reliable allies during that period, often volunteering for the more difficult missions while the Chattahoochee Creeks generally preferred scouting and keeping the paths clear of Spanish soldiers. For further explanation see Hahn, *Invention of the Creek Nation*, 173–85. For examples

highlighting the recruitment and actions of Yuchi fighters, see "Thomas Eyre's Account of Mission to Cherokees Sept. 29, 1739," in Juricek, *GT*, 100; "Journal of William Stephens, Oct. 22, 1739," in *Colonial Records of the State of Georgia*, vol. 4 (Supplement), ed. Allen Candler, Kenneth Coleman, and Milton Ready (Atlanta: Franklin Printing, 1908), 436; and William Stephens, *A Journal of the Proceedings in Georgia*, entry for 24 November 24, 1739 (London, 1742; repr. March of America Facsimile Series, no. 37, Worcester MA, 1966), 199. On Oglethorpe's estimates of Yuchi dead and comments, see "Oglethorpe to William Stephens, Sept. 25, 1741," in Juricek, *GT*, 104. Spanish officials likewise identified the Yuchis among the Indian attackers. "Manuel de Montiano to the King, July 6, 1740," in *Collections of the Georgia Historical Society*, vol. 7 (Savannah: Printed for the Society, 1909), 56–58.

32. "Thomas Causton to the Trustees, June 20, 1735," in Juricek, *GT*, 55.

33. On Ellick's marriages, see Benjamin Hawkins, *A Sketch of the Creek Country in the Years 1798 and 1799*, in *The Collected Works of Benjamin Hawkins, 1796–1810*, ed. H. Thomas Foster II (Tuscaloosa: University of Alabama Press, 2003), 62s (s denotes *Sketch*).

34. "Thomas Causton to Patrick Mackay, April 10, 1735," in Juricek, *GT*, 53.

35. "James Oglethorpe, Talks with the Lower and Upper Creeks, 'Second Audience,' July 3, 1736," in Juricek, *GT*, 73.

36. "Interpreters' Report on Oglethorpe's Talk with Chehaw War Captains, April 22, 1743," in Juricek *GT*, 109.

37. "Journal of William Stephens, Feb. 7, 1741," in Candler et al., *Colonial Records of the State of Georgia*, vol. 4 (Supplement): 85–86.

38. Hawkins, *Sketch of the Creek Country*, 62s.

39. "Provincial Council of Georgia, Talk with Chehaws and Cussitas, May 26, 1758," in Juricek *GT*, 280–81.

40. "Governor Joseph Wright, Report on Talks with the Lower Creeks, Sept. 8, 1758," in Juricek, *GT*, 284–85.

41. South Carolina authorities and the Creek Indians ratified three known treaties between 1705 and 1732. Specific evidence for the Indian towns and individual leaders involved in the treaty making process is available for the treaties of 1705 and 1732, but little is known about the 1717 preliminary agreement that put an end to the Yamasee War. For examples, see the "Treaty of 1705," in *Indian Treaties: Cessions of Land in Georgia, 1705–1837*, ed. J. E. Hayes (Atlanta: Georgia Department of Archives and History, 1941), 1; a copy of the 1732 treaty between South Carolina and the Creeks can be found in J. H. Easterby, ed., *The Journal of the Commons House of Assembly, 1736–1739*, The Colonial Records of South Carolina, series 1, 10 vols. (Columbia: South Carolina Archives Department, 1951–86), 1: 108–11.

42. "First Conference with the Lower Creeks, May 18–21, 1733" and "Oglethorpe's First Treaty with the Lower Creeks at Savannah, May 21, 1732," in Juricek, GT, 12–16.

43. "The Cussita Migration Legend," in *Colonial Records of the State of Georgia*, vol. 20, ed. Allen D. Candler, Kenneth Coleman, and Milton Ready (Athens: University of Georgia Press, 1974), 20:387.

44. "Baron Von Reck's Account of Oglethorpe's Meeting with the Yuchis, May 11, 1736," in Juricek, GT, 65.

45. "See Lieutenant Thomas Eyre's Account of Oglethorpe's Journey to Creek Country, July 8–September 15, 1739," and "Oglethorpe's Second Treaty with the Lower Creeks at Coweta, August 11, 1739," in Juricek, GT, 94–96.

46. "Thomas Eyres's Account of His Missions to the Cherokees, September 29–April 20, 1740," in Juricek, GT, 100.

47. "Juan Marquez del Toro, Diary, entry for February 22, 1738," Archivo General des Indias–Audiencia de Santo Domingo, 2593, Seville, Spain, available on microfilm in John Worth Collection, Randell Research Center, Pineville, Florida, reel 4, no. 1.

48. "Report on Indians, anonymous, ca. summer 1758," William H. Lyttelton Papers, Clements Library, Ann Arbor, Michigan.

49. "Oglivie to Thomas Gage, July 8, 1764," Thomas Gage Papers–American Series, Clements Library, Ann Arbor, Michigan.

50. Ellick is a ubiquitous presence in the paper trail of Anglo-Creek diplomacy from the year 1759 onward. For an early extant reference to Ellick as "Great Medal Chief," see "Superintendent Stuart's Trade Conference with Lower and Upper Creeks at Augusta, May 28–June 6, 1767," in Juricek GFT, 29.

51. See "Provincial Council of Georgia: Conference with the Upper and Lower Creeks, October 25, 29, and November 3, 1757," and "Ellis' Treaty with the Upper and Lower Creeks, November 3, 1757," in Juricek GT, 265, 270.

52. "Treaty of Picolata, November 15, 1765," in *Early American Indian Documents*, 20 vols., vol. 12: *Georgia and Florida Treaties, 1763–1776*, ed. John Juricek (Bethesda MD: University Publications of America, 2002), 12:466 (hereafter cited as GF TREATIES).

53. "Superintendent Stuart's Trade Conference with Lower and Upper Creeks at Augusta, May 28–June 6, 1767," and "Congress with the Lower Creeks at Augusta, and Boundary Treaty with the Creeks, Nov. 12, 1768," in Juricek, GF TREATIES, 29, 63, 70.

54. Such is my conclusion based on a perusal of extant materials that specify the names of "Great" and "Lesser" medal recipients. For examples, see "Superintendent Stuart's Trade Conference with the Lower and Upper Creeks,

May 28–June 6, 1767," and "Congress with the Lower Creeks at Augusta, Nov. 12, 1768," in Juricek, *GF Treaties*, 29, 65.

55. "Confirmation by Malatchi and Other Creek Headmen of Mary Bosomworth as Princess with Authority to Negotiate over Lands and the 'Confirmation Deed' from Malatchi and other Creek Headmen to the Bosomworths for the Yamacraw Tract, both August 2, 1750," in Juricek *GT*, 204, 209–10.

7. Reconsidering Coalescence
Yuchi and Shawnee Survival Strategies in the Colonial Southeast

~

In the first decade of the twentieth century an unnamed Yuchi informant told the ethnologist Frank Speck that the Yuchi, or *coyaha*, "came from the sun." In contrast, "the Shawnee came from above. The Creeks came from the ground, [and] the Choctaws came from the water." The four tribes eventually met and "mingled together in friendship . . . smoked together . . . and held a council." Initial conversations led them to consider a kind of multi-ethnic union. But after much contemplation, the Yuchi and their neighbors believed that it would be best for "each tribe going its own way and living alone."[1] In this way Yuchi explanations of their origin carefully distinguish between the Yuchi and their non-Yuchi neighbors. Even the Yuchi language is a genetic isolate. The Yuchi have maintained a commitment to their own unique identity, manifested in language, cosmology, ritual, and residence patterns, from the seventeenth century to the present.

At the same time, neither the Yuchi nor their Shawnee allies saw themselves in isolation from Indian country. Theirs is not an uncommon history, driven by unfettered independence. Rather, it is a story of the integrative function of violence in the colonial Southeast. In the late seventeenth and early eighteenth centuries the Indian slave trade made violence a survival strategy. And yet that same violence often worked against coalescence by making multi-ethnic unions contested and ephemeral. Virgin soil epidemics, and the slave raids that often coincided with them, may explain how small bands of Yuchis and Shawnees—from thirty to five hundred people—journeyed between, within, and among much larger English, Cherokee, and Creek worlds. Amid the destruction and reordering of peoples and their cultures in the early colonial world, Shawnees and Yuchis often appear at sites of conflict and discord. This comparative assessment of Yuchi and Shawnee peoples suggests some of the ways small societies avoided coalescence in the colonial Southeast.

In both the Shawnee and Yuchi cases, the archival record is fragmentary and silent for long periods in their history. When Shawnee and Yuchi people do appear in the sources, their beliefs and values are filtered through Creek, British, and American sources. For example, the Natchez Indian and Creek Indian agent George Stiggins castigated the Yuchi, stating that "in all conversations among themselves or not they speak their own barbarous tongue." Stiggins was particularly bothered by their commitment to maintaining Yuchi lifeways. He acknowledged that the Yuchi "are so attached to their own tongue and mode of living that very few of 'em make any use of, or can converse in the national tongue."[2] The Yuchi unwillingness to speak Muscogee (Creek) frustrated Stiggins and other advocates of Creek nationalism. But in the nineteenth century, when Stiggins offered this commentary, the Yuchi language had become a symbol of a deeper contest between an emerging Creek Nation and the tribal towns wedded to them. Linguistic diversity worked against coalescence. Tribal townspeople spoke one of four Muscogean languages: Creek, Hitchiti, Alabama, and Koasati. In addition, Yuchi and Shawnee were also spoken in a handful of Lower and Upper Creek towns.[3] In the nineteenth century, language became a major obstacle to Creek nationhood.

Neither coalescent nor ethnogenetic, the two non-Muscogean peoples, the Yuchis and Shawnees, confused those who knew them. How did they fit within the emerging Creek Confederacy? Their shared history as outliers within a larger, Muscogean-speaking world must explain, in part, why the Yuchis consider the Shawnees to be their "longtime friends." Life on the margins of larger Indian confederacies and powerful colonizers was not easy for either community. As early as 1714 the Carolinian John Lawson described the Shawnees as a "shifting, wandering people" who have "changed their settlements many hundred miles." Writing in 1755, the British Indian agent Edmond Atkin described the Shawnees as "stout, bold, cunning, and the greatest Travellers in America."[4] British and Creek sources on the Yuchis and Shawnees alternate between guarded respect and outright hostility. Yuchi and Shawnee history must be filtered through the prejudices of eyewitnesses who assumed that both groups were either dependent vassals of the Creeks or renegade interlopers with little right to the land they occupied in the Southeast. As children of migration, both the Shawnees and Yuchis seemed to be in constant search of a place to call home.

Their fierce commitment to independence, fostered in part by their historic alliance, is remarkable. Neither the Shawnee nor the Yuchi became Creek or Cherokee, Iroquois or Choctaw. In 1908 approximately 500 Yuchis remained, while there were approximately 1,650 Shawnees in that same decade.[5] Nevertheless, most historians have rushed to describe the Southeast as an Indians' "new world"; a place in which Indian people largely abandoned earlier identities and adopted new customs, and new polities, suited to life in a culturally plural world. The Catawbas and Creeks coalesced in the seventeenth and eighteenth centuries, but these multi-ethnic confederacies included strikingly autonomous towns.[6] In 1708 the soldier, slaver, and Carolina Indian agent Thomas Nairne described the "progression of on[e] village out of another." He wrote that "as for authority," southeastern Indians "look on their own Village to be independent . . . and free to manage their affairs as best pleases themselves." Resilient tribal towns existed alongside and sometimes within larger, more powerful, coalescent communities.[7] The paradigm of coalescence in a new world fails to explain the political realities of the peoples and cultures of the colonial Southeast.

Thomas Nairne understood that Indian identities emanated from tribal towns rather than from the larger confederacies to which they were sometimes joined. We must now seek to explain the symbiotic relationship between tribal towns and larger, coalescent polities. For the Shawnee and Yuchi, linguistic and cultural differences account for some of their independence. But in the main, both peoples reimagined themselves as the regional, tribal, and colonial contexts in which they lived changed over time. The sheer inventiveness of these small societies is staggering. And in the Shawnee and Yuchi cases, violence became a survival strategy. In the early colonial period, Shawnee and Yuchi towns appeared at vital crossroads of the traffic in human beings. First the Shawnee, and then the Yuchi, became portable slaving societies, and they placed their villages in dangerous borderland zones. Scholars estimate that at least fifty thousand Indians were enslaved in the colonial Southeast. But as the Indian slave trade subsided after the 1715 Yamasee War, Yuchi and Shawnee townspeople became mercenaries and auxiliaries of both the British and the Creek Confederacy. As refugees, the Shawnee and Yuchi converted their knowledge of the land and its peoples into an asset. Both were well armed, and both had the linguistic and diplomatic skill to make sense of fragmented Woodland Indian worlds. We must understand the deliberate economic and geographic choices they made through the lens of culture, for the preservation of their unique identities motivated Yuchi and Shawnee actions. Their tribal towns became the proving grounds for their long struggle against genocide and assimilation. By examining their colonial era tribal towns, we may get a better understanding of how the modern Shawnee and Yuchi survived the chaos and disorder of colonization.[8]

More often allies than enemies, the Shawnee and Yuchi survived on the periphery of colonial, Creek, and Cherokee worlds. Examining the intersections, as well as the divergences, of their respective histories reveals clues about how small societies survived, and sometimes thrived, even as emergent Indian confederacies encouraged coalescence. Their histories are suggestive and fragmentary, for there were long periods in which the Shawnee and Yuchi successfully avoided warfare and conflicts over trade. These long periods of relative peace do not appear in the archival record. In contrast, Yuchi and Shawnee understandings of the past—drawn largely from oral histories—emphasize the exact opposite of warfare and trade. A close examination of their oral histories shows that intermarriage and "helping out" with each other's rituals have always been the beating heart of their centuries-long alliance. In this way, Shawnee and Yuchi histories, from the present to the past, exist in a kind of parallel universe. But if we follow the stories across space and time, the stories Shawnee and Yuchi people tell about themselves and their special relationship encourage us away from battlefields and trading posts. Theirs are stories of continuity and survival. And their stories may enable us to cross over into complex Woodland Indian worlds in which allied tribal towns, often related through intermarriage, used violence and the rituals associated with it to define who they were and to carve out a valued place for themselves in the Southeast.

~

More than one hundred years ago Yuchi interlocutors told Frank Speck about their "strong feeling of friendship" for the Shawnee. Similarly, in 1935, an Absentee Shawnee named Jim Clark made sure that the ethnohistorian Erminie Wheeler-Voegelin learned about the Shawnee version of their historic alliance. Clark told the story of two Shawnee brothers who, in the 1830s, decided to ditch a brother of theirs who was prone to daydreaming with a gun in his hand. He was a poor hunter, and his brothers were convinced that his carelessness would cause their death. In fact, their brother was so careless that his kinsmen concluded "it doesn't matter what tribe we find, we'll stay there." And so the two Shawnee brothers left, "without telling their brother." Eventually, they were taken in by a band of Yuchi Indians, and the Shawnee brothers soon married into that community. According to Clark, there "got to be a fair sized Shawnee-Yuchi village," and this caused the allied tribes to move toward what is now Sapulpa, Oklahoma. The Yuchi-Shawnee community became known as "Big Pond," because "that full-blooded Shawnee man's name who founded their village was Big Pond." Clark's story of intermarriage and migration became his way of explaining why the Absentee Shawnees help out during the Yuchi Green Corn Ceremony.[9]

Writing in the 1850s, the amateur historian Thomas Woodward observed that "if the Uchees and Shawnees were not originally the same people, they had lived so long and so near each other as to become pretty well acquainted with each other's language." Woodward lived among the Creeks in Alabama, and he migrated west to Texas in the 1840s. It was here that Woodward encountered Spybuck, a Shawnee then living on the Southern Plains. In January 1842 Spybuck met with Woodward along the Washita River. According to Woodward, he was traveling with "a few Cherokees, some Choctaws, one or two Chickasaws, and a Delaware." Spybuck's delegation reflected the wide range of Shawnee migrations and the alliances built across the colonial world. Like Spybuck, Woodward brought the peoples and their tragic histories from the Southeast with him to Texas. Woodward "had some Uchee negroes that spoke the Uchee, Creek, and Hitcheta." And so it was that Spybuck, speaking Uchee with Woodward's multilingual "Uchee negroes," described how the Shawnees had been "forced back from the Savannah and the settlements of the Musqua, in Alabama and Georgia."[10] These sources offer the first evidence we have of the antiquity of the Yuchi-Shawnee alliance. Spybuck knew his history, and it was a history grounded in the Southeast.[11]

Fortunately for us, confusion regarding the relationship between the Yuchi and Shawnee languages helps us trace their historic alliance. Today some linguists mistake Yuchi with the Siouan language family.[12] But in the colonial era, observers erroneously believed that Yuchi was a dialect of Shawnee. For example, the travel writer and naturalist William Bartram, writing in the 1770s, described the Yuchi language as "altogether or radically different from the Creek or Muscogulge tongue, and . . . called the Savanna or Savanuca tongue." Bartram was right to differentiate Yuchi clearly from Muscogee. But local traders led him to believe that Yuchi was "a dialect of, the Shawanese."[13] Ties between the Yuchi and Shawnee were so close that

FIGURE 4. "Indians going a-hunting." Given the artist's association with the Yuchi and the men's distinctive hairstyle, these are probably Yuchi men pictured in hunting dress. Painted on the colonial frontier of Georgia in 1736 by Philip Georg Friedrich von Reck or someone in his retinue. NKS 565 4° (Von Reck's drawings), 25 verso. The Royal Library, Copenhagen, Denmark.

For discussion of this image and the collection from which it comes, see Hvidt, *Von Reck's Voyage*, 126–27. The image is online at http://www.kb.dk/permalink/2006/manus/22/eng/25+verso/?var=.

Bartram, along with local traders, had a difficult time differentiating between the two.

As early as 1700 the Jesuit missionary Jacques Gravier noted that both Yuchis and Shawnees could speak each other's languages. On a trip down the Mississippi, probably near modern Memphis, Gravier encountered "a pirogue of Taögria," or Yuchi. Gravier noted the Yuchis' affinity for English trade goods, and he was surprised to learn that they could "say a few words of Illinois." However, the exchange between the Yuchi and the Jesuit improved considerably when they both began speaking "the Chaouanoua tongue."[14] While intermarriage and alliance probably explains the Yuchis' fluency in

Shawnee, it is also true that by the eighteenth century, Shawnee had become a trade language. Writing in 1708, the Anglican missionary Francis Le Jau noted that "the Savannah Tongue . . . is understood all over these Northern Parts of America, even in Canada."[15]

Colonial observers often identified Indian people by their primary language. But more often, Native peoples such as the Shawnee and Yuchi used distinctive hairstyles and material ornamentation to differentiate between themselves and others. One of the 1736 drawings of Philip Georg Friedrich von Reck illustrates the Yuchis' distinctive "top-knot hairstyle" (fig. 4). In 1753 Shawnee warriors wore a single feather attached to a roach haircut. When asked to explain, the Shawnee simply replied that "all our Indians dress the same way." Hairstyles helped warriors differentiate between friend and foe. According to Von Reck, "they cut the upper part of the head hair from those they have conquered in order to see from what nation and tribe they are."[16] Shawnee men further distinguished themselves by partially severing the auricle of each ear, and then using trade silver and other metal objects to stretch the lobes of their ears over time.[17]

Snap judgments regarding language often determined whether a person lived or died. In May 1751 settlers between the Congaree and Savannah thought they were safe when two Indians "came here about dark and sat down very civil." A survivor of the encounter knew they were Shawnees because her husband could "talk their tongue." But unfortunately for her husband and her family, these Shawnees were from Ohio, not Carolina, and as a result, they regarded the settlers as strangers, murdering her husband and her children as they slept in their beds. In the colonial period, Indian identities were highly contingent, and their village affiliation often became the best gauge of their intentions. In another colonial encounter, Cherokees in pursuit of Creek warriors thought they had cornered the Creeks in a cabin after nightfall because they "heard people talk in the Creek tongue." But as the Cherokees fired on the cabin, two white men emerged, one of whom had been wounded by the volley. In this multilingual world, language was an imperfect means of determining a person's identity.

Across Indian country, language, hairstyle and dress embodied striking differences between contiguous tribal towns. Between 1773 and 1776 the writer and naturalist William Bartram toured Creek country, and he noticed incredible variation in the Creek Confederacy's influence over the sixty to seventy towns in its sphere of influence. The Yuchis, in particular, "claim a very extensive territory over which they claim an exclusive property." Rather than challenge Yuchi claims, Bartram noticed that members of the confederacy were "cautious of affronting the Uches so generally yield for their common interest and safety."[18]

The Shawnee thought of themselves as members of one of five patrilineal divisions, or society clans. Two of the five Shawnee divisions, the Kispokotha and Thawekila, dominated the Shawnee migration to the Southeast. These autonomous and migratory kin groups were often separated by vast distances and unique ethnic landscapes. Moreover, the divisions—Kispokotha, Mekoche, Thawekila, Pekowitha, and Chalagawtha (Chillicothe)—fulfilled different functions.[19] For example, chiefs came from either the Thawekila or Chalagawtha divisions, while the Kispokothas regulated war. According to tribal elder George Blanchard, "at one time we lived in different clans so if you needed somethin' you traveled to visit them. If you needed medicine you visited the Mekoches, if you needed war you visited the Kispokothas."[20] The Shawnee towns that dotted the colonial Southeast, then, were also kin groups based on the divisions. The Savannah River Shawnees tended to come from the Thawekila division, while the Sawanogi Shawnees within the Upper Creek Confederacy tended to come from the Kispokotha division.[21]

As refugees in colonial woodlands, the Shawnees carried these core components of their identities with them to the Southeast. Warfare with the Iroquois prompted the Shawnee exodus to the Southeast. Between 1669 and 1671 Iroquois warriors attacked Shawnee villages in the Ohio Valley.[22] In 1673 the Illinois told Marquette that the Shawnees "live on the banks [of the Ohio], and are so numerous that I have been informed there are thirty-eight villages of that nation." However, Marquette learned that they were "a very harmless people" who were constantly attacked and taken captive by the Iroquois "because they have no firearms."[23] By 1675 these "mourning wars" had devastated Indian communities throughout the lower Great Lakes. The Iroquois either killed or ritually incorporated those they attacked. Captives thus assumed a new Iroquois identity, as the physical embodiment of fallen kinsmen.[24] Victims of Iroquois war parties thus faced a stark choice: absorption into Iroquois society or incessant, genocidal war. Faced with such a choice, the Shawnees began a long migration from the Ohio Valley. Louis LeClerk de Milford, a Frenchman living within the Creek Nation at the end of the eighteenth century, believed that the Iroquois attacks prompted the Shawnees to "implore the protection of the Muskogees." According to Milford, "the Creeks took them in and assigned them land in the center of the nation."[25] But at this time the Muscogee Confederacy was not in a position to subordinate the Shawnees to their interests.

Those who survived joined one of several different migrations into the Southeast.[26] Nicholas Perrot, a *coureur de bois*, or "brush runner" who was considered to be an illegal trader by New France, had lived with the Shawnees in Illinois. He told of the Iroquois driving the Chaouanons south to Carolina.[27] In the summer of 1670 in the vicinity of the Roanoke River, the explorer John Lederer located a band of Shawnees whom he described as the "Rorenock or Shawan."[28] Four years later the slaver and doctor Thomas Woodward met two Shawnees at the Westo village along the Savannah River, near modern Augusta, Georgia. Woodward was surprised to learn that the Shawnees had been living "twenty days journey West Southwardly from them." The Shawnees brought with them "Spanish beeds and other trade as presents, makeing signs that they had comerce wth white people." French colonizers also located the Shawnees in Spanish Florida, where they "trade with Europeans who pray as we do, and use Rosaries, as well as Bells for calling to Prayers. According to the description given us, we judge them to be Spaniards."[29]

Between the 1650s and the 1720s the middle Savannah River became a haven for survivors of Iroquois warfare. Paradoxically, those who withstood death, captivity, and the loss of identity at the hands of the Iroquois went on to become slavers for the English. In fact, the Savannah River became a center for the shipment of Indian slaves from the interior Southeast to port towns such as Charles Town. In the late 1650s the Erie—northern Iroquoian speakers who originally inhabited the region south of Lake Erie, between what are now Buffalo, New York, and Toledo, Ohio—began appearing along the Savannah River. Between 1654 and 1656 their linguistic kin, the Five Nations Iroquois, devastated the Erie in a series of mourning wars. Those who survived abandoned their homeland, moved southeast, and became known as the Westo.[30] First Virginians, and then Carolinians, traded guns to the Westo for Indian slaves, sold mainly to planters in Jamaica, Bermuda, and the Leeward Islands. The Westos ultimately settled on the middle Savannah River because it provided easy access to the Mission Indians of Spanish Florida as well as Cherokee and Creek targets through the river's intersection with the Tennessee River drainage.[31] Even those Englishmen who helped bring about the Indian slave trade were startled by what they saw at the Westo village. Woodward noted that the Westo would "hang the locks of haire of Indians that they have slaine" from the rafters of their longhouses. Under constant threat of attack, they built a double palisade along the inland side of the town and a single one facing the river's edge.[32]

In 1674 Shawnee refugees visited the Westos' village on the Savannah River, warning them of an impending attack by the Lower Creek town of Cussita, which had joined with Chickasaw and Cherokee allies. At least temporarily, Westo and Shawnee newcomers allied themselves against their Creek, Cherokee, and Chickasaw enemies. But their allegiance to each other proved temporary. By 1680 the Shawnees turned against the Westos. In 1680 by allying themselves with the English and the Yamasees, Shawnee warriors devastated the Westos. The Shawnees rejected Westo attempts to end the war. The Lords Proprietors noted that the Shawnees captured Westo peace messengers, who "were taken & sent away to be sold." The proprietors tried to explain Shawnee treachery: "If there be peace with ye Westohs and Waniahs," they wondered, "where shall ye Savanahs get Indians to sell ye Dealers in Indians."[33] The Shawnee answer to this question, like that of the Westos before them, was to capture Indian slaves wherever they could find them. Discerning English-allied tribes from French or Spanish allies became increasingly difficult as the seventeenth century drew to a close. Woodward seemed to play a role in the 1680 Westo War. In 1674, after recruiting Shawnees to Carolina, Woodward told them to return in four to five months, "wth deare skins, furrs, and young slaves."[34]

Between 1680 and 1708 the Shawnees built a life for themselves along the Savannah River by obliging Woodward's request for Indian slaves. They established three villages on or near Beech Island, on the east side of the Savannah River, across from modern Augusta, Georgia. South Carolina's former governor, John Archdale, seemed pleased with the new Shawnee arrivals. He noted that by 1680 the Shawnees in Carolina accounted for such numbers that they were able to reduce the Westos "from many thousands . . . to a small Number" until the Westos, "the more Cruel of the two, were at last forced quite out of that Province."[35] Again like the Westos before them, the Shawnees became slavers who lived precariously, surrounded by larger though less well-armed groups of townspeople and English traders huddled along the Ashley River and the coastline.

The pressures of the slave trade and the vast depopulation of the Indians forced Shawnee slavers to take risks that eventually undermined their relationship with South Carolina. In November 1707 an English trader reported that Shawnees "had fallen on ye Northern Indians & had carried severall our Indian slaves away with them." Carolinians suspected that the Shawnees were selling English-allied Indians in North Carolina, Virginia, and Maryland. And in the years that followed, the English tried to bend the Shawnees to their will through a mixture of diplomacy and force. As a result Shawnees began secretly leaving the colony. These Shawnee "deserters" congregated along the Patapsco River, in the Chesapeake Bay watershed.[36] Carolina sent a delegation north to Maryland to induce them to return. Also in 1707, South Carolina's James Moore led what amounted to an "armed posse" of Creek Indians against Shawnees who threatened to attack the Catawba and abscond with their prisoners.[37] As Algonquians originally from the Ohio Valley, Savannah River Shawnees called upon long-standing ties with northern tribes, including the Iroquois, Susquehanna, and Lenape. Their return to the border between Maryland and Pennsylvania signaled the acceptance of life within the Iroquois "covenant chain."

In these years Shawnees stepped up attacks on English-allied Indian towns, and they sometimes killed or captured Indian slaves. Carolinians swiftly retaliated. In February 1708 the Carolina assembly paid the "Northward Indians," probably the Catawba, "fifty guns a Thousand flints 200tw of powder 400 tw of Bulletts . . . to attack the said Indians our Enemies." Catawbas who brought in either a scalp or a Shawnee prisoner got to keep their guns.[38] Shawnee out-migration from the region certainly increased as a result. But a 1708 census indicates that some Shawnees stayed behind, residing in one of their three towns, which could field a combined force of 150 warriors.[39]

In the first decade of the eighteenth century, the English became particularly adept at coordinating warriors from various towns in large-scale attacks on their enemies. For example, in 1704 James Moore and only fifty Englishmen led a force of more than a thousand Creek warriors against the Apalachee in northwest Florida. Those who were not killed or sold in the British West Indies were forcibly relocated to the Savannah River region. By 1710 the Yuchi had relocated to the middle Savannah River as well.[40] As a result "Savannah Town" became a much more diverse place, inhabited by peoples originally from across the Eastern Woodlands who were drawn to it through a combination of fear, force, and the lure of European goods.

The Carolina proprietors did what they could to stem the Shawnee out-migration from Carolina. Informants among the traders and new arrivals at Savannah Town kept the English appraised of their movements. In 1707 rumors circulated about Shawnee intentions after "Cundy, an Indian Woman and Wife to one of the traders, reported that the Savanas intended to goe away."[41] The Anglican missionary Francis Le Jau confirmed these rumors in 1708 when he reported that "one of the Savannah Town's Inhabitants went away from us . . . and are joined with our enemies."[42] In 1710 Le Jau observed that the Shawnees continued to "keep about the places where the Westos lived, but perhaps are not so numerous."[43]

It is hard to discern the reasons why small numbers of Shawnees stayed behind. But those who did joined forces with neighboring Yuchis and Apalachees. During the Tuscarora War of 1711–12, Yuchi, Shawnee, and Apalachee warriors defended English plantations from possible attack. In 1711 the Carolina assembly created a force of Indians for protection, to include "100 from the Savannahs and Appalacheas and Tohogoligo."[44] Tohogoligo is the Algonquian word for Yuchi (today the Shawnee word for Yuchi is Tahogaliiki). References to the "Tohogoligo" confirm that Carolinians used the Shawnee word for Yuchi to identify them. Second, the Shawnee, Yuchi, and Apalachee used violence—the armed defense of British settlements—to underscore their value to colonizers. By creating a defensive buffer between Tuscarora warriors in North Carolina and settlements such as Charles Town, Shawnees, Yuchis, and Apalachees maintained their importance.[45]

During the first two decades of the eighteenth century, warfare diminished Indian populations in the Southeast as never before. English traders turned away from newcomers to the region, such as the Westo and Shawnee. Powerful confederacies, such as the Creek, Cherokee, Choctaw, and Chickasaw became slavers, and they targeted small societies such as the Yuchi, Shawnee, and French-allied tribes of the Gulf Coast. Traders allied with larger, coalescent communities encouraged this transition, from the middle Savannah River towns to the confederacies of the interior Southeast. As discussed by Brett Riggs elsewhere in this volume, the most spectacular reflection of this reality came in 1714, when a Yuchi town named Chestowe, situated near the Cherokees on the Middle Tennessee River, was attacked by a Cherokee force. Ostensibly, a rogue British trader named Alexander Long inspired the slaughter over a

soured trade relationship with the Chestowe Yuchi.[46] When Cherokee warriors surprised their village, the Chestowe Yuchi understood
that those who survived the attack would be enslaved and sold into
slavery, most likely in the British West Indies. This was a fate worse
than death, and it was all too familiar to tribes such as the Yuchi.
According to a trader named James Douglas, "the Euchees killed
their own People in the War House to prevent their falling into the
Hands of the Cherikees."[47] Fear of enslavement drove the Yuchi to
kill their own people as defeat became imminent.

The attack on Chestowe threatened to engulf the entire region in
a general war, as allied tribes on both sides considered retaliation.
Both Alexander Long and the Cherokees nearly waged a surprise
attack on the Yuchi and Shawnee villages along the Savannah River in order to prevent them from retaliating on the Chestowe Yuchis' behalf. The Cherokees claimed that "they were told by the white
people since Chestowe was cut off they ought to goe cut off the other Euchees att the Savana Town or else there would be no Traval-
ing."[48] Alexander Long and his Cherokee henchmen realized that
ethnically related towns frequently came together for mutual defense.
While the Middle Tennessee River and the Savannah River seem geographically distant to us now, colonial Americans understood that
"the headwaters of the Savannah interlaced with the sources of the
Tennessee."[49] Yuchis and Shawnees on the Savannah River thus had
easy access to Chestowe. They could—and would—seek justice for
their fallen kin. It was only through long hours of careful diplomacy—what Indian people called "covering the dead"—that the British were able to avert further bloodshed.

By 1715 the English hunger for Indian slaves had diminished Indian populations throughout the Southeast. English-allied tribes
became vulnerable to kidnapping and enslavement as hunters did
what they could to obtain English trade goods. Rogue traders, encouraged by the planter elite, fueled the cruelty. Aggrieved Indian
communities joined forces against the Carolinians, and they began
the Yamasee War on Good Friday, 15 April 1715, with a massacre
of settlers around Port Royal. On 14 April the Carolinian Thomas

Nairne, a man who had once bragged about convincing the Chickasaws that "slave catching was much more profitable than formal haranguing," attempted to stem the bloodshed. Nairne, along with two other men, rushed to the Yamasee town of Pocataligo, only to be captured and killed. The Yamasees vented their rage on Nairne by tying him to a post and sticking hundreds of lighted wood splinters into his body. He died slowly, by fire, over a period of days. Tribes who had been allies of the English, including "Crick Indians, to whom the Yamoussees, Savana, and Apalachi Indians are joined," suddenly became their enemies. Carolinians feared this alliance because they could field "2000 stout men" against the colonists.[50]

The Carolinians certainly knew their attackers. In July 1715 Francis Le Jau described how approximately six hundred warriors from the "Yamousees, Apalachee's Savanas & other Southern Indians . . . burn'd about 30 houses, Destroy'd all the Horses Cattle and Plantations they could." Historian William Ramsey argues that the Yuchis and Lower Ochese Creeks were included in the southern arm of the Yamasee War. Yuchi townspeople along the Savannah River were major participants in the war. Uchee Island, located "16 miles above Fort Augusta," was a short distance north of Savannah Town, on modern Beech Island. While only 67 Shawnee warriors, and another 166 women and children remained at Savannah Town in the census of 1715, 130 Yuchi men lived with their wives and children at two Yuchi settlements above modern Augusta, Georgia, in that same year.[51]

These changing circumstances compelled Savannah River Shawnees to continue their out-migration from the region. By the 1720s the Shawnee population dropped considerably, from the Savannah River to the border between western Maryland and Pennsylvania.[52] In 1725 the Savannah Town trader Charlesworth Glover conducted a census of Indian towns in the Southeast. In it he noted that the there were thirty Shawnees remaining at Savannah Town, only eight of whom were men. In contrast, there were 530 Yuchis at the time. For Glover, the 1725 census confirmed that the Indians seemed to "decay everywhere." The lone exception to this demography of decline, Glover recorded, were the "Youches." Surprisingly, in 1725, they represented the "highest Number of Souls in the 3 provinces."[53]

The thirty Shawnees who remained at the town that bore their name may have coalesced into any number of the Indian towns that remained along the Savannah River. There were simply too few of them to survive independently. In contrast, the Yuchis seem to have rebounded from the massacre at Chestowe. Some degree of political centralization seems to have occurred as well. As late as 1737 the Chickasaw war chief Mingo Ouma created a map of the Southeast that defined the Yuchis' place in this world. While Mingo Ouma identified Muscogee towns such as Coweta and Okfuskee, he did not locate these towns within an overarching "Creek" national synthesis. His preference for towns, rather than confederacies or nations, reflects the fact that in the early 1700s the Creek Confederacy was still in its infancy. According to historian Joshua Piker, "centralized power above the level of an individual town was practically nonexistent." Tellingly, Mingo Ouma understood the Yuchis to be allied with both the British and the lower Creek town of Cussita. In contrast, Mingo Ouma did not include Shawnee towns on his map of the colonial Southeast. His silence regarding the Shawnees illustrates the extent of upheaval and migration endured by Native peoples in the eighteenth century. Regional contexts changed frequently in the colonial world.[54]

While most of their Shawnee allies moved north, Yuchi survivors of the Yamasee War moved farther south, toward the English and German settlements along the border between South Carolina and Georgia. Between 1728 and 1755 several Yuchi towns remained on the middle and lower Savannah River. Silver Bluff, on the east side of the Savannah River near modern Aiken, South Carolina, and Mount Pleasant, near modern Savannah, Georgia, were two Yuchi towns of particular importance. The Yuchi shift from trading centers such as Savannah Town toward the borderlands with Spanish Florida reflects a deeper transition, from slavers to mercenaries. Yuchi survival depended on their ability to defend English settlements from Indian attacks emanating from Spanish Florida. Then, as before, Yuchi warriors fought in multi-ethnic forces, organized and led by prominent officials from South Carolina and Georgia. War in defense of British settlements enabled the Yuchi to live in close proximity to colonizers.

But the constancy of war transformed the ritual life of southeastern tribes such as the Yuchi. While organized violence ensured Yuchi survival, it also meant that rituals of war came to dominate Yuchi culture in the first half of the eighteenth century. English and German allies of the Yuchi attended such rituals, for they functioned to sanctify the taking of life in warfare. As a result we have some records of these ceremonies. For example, in 1736, the Yamacraw chief Tomochichi and the Yuchi chief Umpeachy performed a war dance prior to their attack on St. Augustine. Tomochichi and Umpeachy's people "made a ring, in the Middle of which four sat down, having little Drums made of Kettles, cover'd with Deer-skins." These four men, "beat and sung," while "others danced, being naked to their Waists." The ritual culminated when the "chief warriors . . . stood out" and "describ'd (by Actions as well as by Words) which way he had vanquish'd the Enemies of his Country." According to ethnologist Jason Jackson, these ritual elements are consistent with Algonquian war rituals, including those of the Shawnee, Kickapoo, and Delaware. Yuchi ritual performance reflected the values and beliefs of Native peoples from the lower Great Lakes rather than those from Muscogean-speaking worlds of the Southeast.[55]

Even in rituals associated with war, Yuchi conceptions of gender set them apart from their Creek neighbors. Creek rituals of war typically included rituals of fasting and purification, and women were excluded from these ceremonies. In 1772, while on a diplomatic mission among the Upper Creeks, David Taitt witnessed a series of ritual events designed to bring success for men "going off to war the next day." Central to the evening's ceremonies was the powerful emetic known as black drink, made from the plant *Ilex vomitoria*. After taking black drink, Taitt joined the men in a sweat lodge, followed by the "usual Ceremoney of Smoking Tobacco." In everything from warfare to planting, the complementary but sex-segregated world of the Creeks contrasted with that of the Yuchis. The Indian agent Benjamin Hawkins was struck by the fact that at Yuchi Town, "the men take part in the labors of the women." As a keen observer of the Muscogee people, Hawkins noticed that the Yuchi were outliers in terms of both gender and language.[56]

After 1715 some Yuchi people hoped to avoid border warfare. Those who were interested in peace founded another village on Laurel Bay, northwest of Beaufort, South Carolina. Yuchis joined a multi-ethnic community there, and they became known as "Settlement" or "Parched-corn" Indians because, according to the self-proclaimed "English Chickasaw" James Adair, they "chiefly use it for bread, are civilized, and live mostly by planting." Adair may have overstated the Yuchis' ability to live by planting alone. Prominent Englishmen, including the planter William Bull, supported the Laurel Bay community.[57]

By the middle years of the eighteenth century, the Savannah River and Laurel Bay settlements lost ground to Yuchi Town, on the Chattahoochee River, at the modern site of Fort Benning. Life among the Lower Creeks seems to have offered a degree of autonomy that diminished with each year for the Carolina Yuchi. In 1729 Yuchi Town emerged as the predominant Yuchi community within the Lower Creek Confederacy and was associated with the Creek town of Cussita in particular. Over time, Yuchi Town became the mother town for the Yuchi people. Writing in the 1770s Bartram described "Uche Town" as "the largest, most compact and best situated Indian town I ever saw." Bartram noted that the town was "full of youth and young children," and he estimated that somewhere between one thousand and fifteen hundred people lived there.[58] If so, the Yuchi population had recovered significantly since the 1725 census. Moving from 530 people to more than a thousand in fifty years suggests that Yuchi Town was composed of Yuchi people not accounted for in Glover's census. By the 1770s Yuchi people from across the Southeast had largely consolidated on the Chattahoochee River.

At the same time, Shawnee towns proliferated in both the Southeast and Ohio as the colonies of South Carolina, Maryland, and

Pennsylvania became increasingly difficult places for Indian people to live. In the 1730s and 1740s Shawnees either founded or settled within three different Upper Creek towns. The largest, Sawanogi, was located southeast of the Alabama town of Mucclassee on the Tallapoosa River. The British trader John Spencer operated a trading post dubbed "Little Savannah House," and he served a multi-ethnic community including Shawnees, Alabamas, Creeks, and Yuchis. Farther to the east lay the Creek town of Ecunhutke. The resident trader, John Eycott, noted that he served Creeks "and the Savanoes." Finally, a third contingent of Shawnees settled far to the north, on a tributary of the Coosa River, near the Creek town of Coosa. As such, this last town was affiliated with the Abeika people, one of three ethnic groupings who composed the Upper Creeks. However, most Shawnees seemed to have strong ties to the Alabama towns, particularly Mucclassee, in the middle of the eighteenth century.[59]

Time and again, Shawnees described a decentralized world in which kinship and alliance determined Native American destinies. As one Shawnee from Wakatomica in eastern Ohio explained, "I am a Shavanah, and Head of a Town," but "we are distributed by different Names." Shawnee towns, composed of a series of interrelated kin, made intensely local decisions. But local decisions often imperiled other Shawnee towns, especially during the French and Indian War. Shawnees in the Upper Creek Confederacy struggled to draw boundaries between themselves and their Shawnee kinsmen in the Ohio Valley. As with the Yuchi, Shawnee identities diverged according to their village affiliation. By the middle of the eighteenth century Ohio Shawnees who were allied with the Cherokees stepped up attacks against the Catawbas and, in some cases, the Laurel Bay Yuchis. In contrast, Shawnees at towns such as Sawanogi lived within the Upper Creek Confederacy as violence between the Creeks and Cherokees escalated. At the same time, Shawnees associated with the French trader Peter Chartier moved into the Upper Creek Confederacy. Their arrival, coming in the decade prior to the French and Indian War, jeopardized all Shawnees residing in the Southeast. Not surprisingly, ten Shawnee headmen from an Upper Creek Shawnee town near Abihka tried to convince Governor Glen of "their good affection for the English upon any occasion."[60]

In these years larger confederacies such as the Creek and Cherokee, as well as French and British colonizers, hoped that the Shawnees would help them create an intertribal alliance that stitched together the southern and northern tribes. Sawanogi, the Shawnee town opposite Mucclassee, seems to have been founded in 1737, when French observers noted that Shawnees had arrived in the Alabama towns to mediate peace talks between the Cherokees and the Lower Creek town of Coweta.[61] The Shawnees acted as "guarantors of peace" between these communities. They were few in number, for the Marquis de Vaudreuil, the governor of French Louisiana, noted that "seventy or eighty" Shawnees had "come from Canada . . . to settle among the Alabamas."[62] By the 1730s their long diaspora from the Ohio Valley meant that Shawnees had the geographic and linguistic range to bring disparate peoples together. For a brief period, between 1737 and 1748, Vaudreuil hoped that the Shawnees might bring about a general peace between the French-allied peoples of the *pays d'en haut* and the French- and British-allied confederacies of the Southeast. However, the intensely local nature of Indian country worked against French plans for a grand alliance against the British in the years leading up to the global war between the French and British. In 1744 Vaudreuil himself admitted that "each village has its own chief who, with his warriors, follows the course that seems good to him, so that they are so many small republics."[63]

By the 1750s English-allied towns such as the Laurel Bay Yuchis became easy targets for Cherokee, Iroquois, and Shawnee war parties from the northeast. In 1751 alone, a single Seneca war party killed twenty-five Yuchis and dragged ten captives back with them to western New York. Northern Indian attacks increased in the years leading up the French and Indian War, and many colonial officials believed that the attackers had been manipulated by the French. In 1753 South Carolina governor James Glen overreached when a local militiaman named David Godin captured six Shawnee warriors on their way to assault the Laurel Bay community. He explained that the settlement Indians "are upon many Accounts very service-able to us." Glen's explanation suggests that the Laurel Bay Yuchis provided the British with intelligence regarding Indian country. The Yuchis understood the dynamics of Indian country in ways that the British did not. But more important, the British called on settlement Indians to hunt down runaway slaves. According to Edmond Atkin, those "still living in our settlements" played a vital role in perpetu-ating the slave economy by ensuring that black slaves could not es-cape and unite with Indians of the interior Southeast.[64]

~

Even after 1717, when the Yamasee War effectively ended the Indi-an slave trade, neither the Yuchi nor the Shawnee freed themselves from its legacy. For the Shawnee, the killing and capture of Indian people remained central to manhood and the achievement of sta-tus in Shawnee society. Well into the 1760s Shawnees sometimes referred to their victims as slaves. Initially Shawnees viewed their captives as little more than war trophies. But if they survived the or-deal, captives' humanity was restored and they became full-fledged members of Shawnee society. For much of the eighteenth century Shawnee taking of captives resembled Iroquois models of warfare.[65]

In the 1750s Wakatomica Shawnees from Ohio and Overhill Cher-okees from Chota joined forces and attacked Catawba and Settle-ment Indians in North and South Carolina. In 1753 six Shawnee men were apprehended along the Lower Salkehatchie River, near the Yu-chi community of Laurel Bay. They told their captor, Captain Go-din, that "they were Cherokees and looking for Utchees." After be-ing imprisoned in Charles Town, the Shawnees acknowledged their true identities. In fact, they were Chalagawtha Shawnees from the town of Wakatomica, along the Muskingum River, in what is now Ohio. Chalagawtha Shawnees claimed the right to speak, and to lead, on behalf of the Shawnee people. As such, their capture had repercussions throughout Indian country. Their headman, Itawach-comequa, denied hunting Yuchis, claiming instead that he "came to find my friend Shirtier [Peter Chartier]." In a separate interrogation a Shawnee boy admitted to carrying a slave halter with him, in case he "took any prisoners and tied him, I might put it round his neck." Though their attackers were unsuccessful, the Shawnee men admitted that they had been a part of six unique expeditions against the Laurel Bay community. A planter named Morgan Sabb identified the Shawnees from an earlier encounter, also along the Salkehatchie River, in 1751. Governor Glen became further convinced of their guilt when a Yuchi named King Tom came to Charles Town jail, pointed to Itawachcomequa, and claimed that the Shawnee chief had taken him prisoner twice. King Tom described how on both occasions Itawachcomequa had "carried [him] to the Cherokee country."[66]

Cherokee intermediaries did their best to free Itawachcomequa and his Shawnee kinsmen. They warned Governor Glen that holding the Shawnees in prison would surely imperil Carolina and the rest of British North America. Little Carpenter of the Cherokees did not vindicate Shawnee actions. But he did warn Glen that "for the sake of the white people that come among us," he would be wise to set them free. If, instead, Glen chose to hold the Shawnees for their attacks on the Yuchis, "the 5 Nations will join these people, and some of the Cherokees" will do the same. Sure enough, when three Shawnees managed to escape from the Charles Town jail, they laid waste to frontier settlements as they made their way back to Wakatomica. Old Hop, the headman at Chota, blamed Governor Glen, who "did not do well by the Savannahs." As if to illustrate his point, the Chalagawtha headman Itawachcomequa, died shortly after breaking out of jail in Charles Town. Old Hop chided Glen, explaining that he should "have killed them," or done something more so that "they could never return back to their own people." Since the captives had made their escape, the Overhill Cherokees understood that a chain of interrelated and allied towns would mobilize for war against the British. Glen hoped that Woodland Indian peoples would yield to his will. Instead, Glen watched with horror as Indian towns from Alabama to New York learned of his ill-treatment of the Shawnee prisoners.[67]

For their part, the Wakatomica Shawnees could not understand

Governor Glen's defense of the Settlement Indians. In the proving ground of slavery and American land hunger, Shawnees had adopted racialized notions of identity; they complained that "their business was with red and not white people." Unlike their Yuchi victims, Wakatomica Shawnees migrated west, beyond the Appalachian Mountains. But their capture and imprisonment illustrates that even those Shawnees who desired a measure of autonomy remained wedded to British North America. For Skiagunsta of the Cherokees, "red" and "white" worlds were inseparable, for he admitted that "every necessary thing in life we must have from the white people." By the middle of the 1750s Governor Glen and the Carolinians continued to value the Yuchi, Catawba, and coastal groups allied with Carolina because "they form part of our Barrier, and if they are cut off, a Door will be left open to the French Indians." Each distinct vision of Indian-white relations came into collision as headmen made ultimate decisions about their people's destiny.[68]

By the 1780s Sawanogi remained a distinctively Shawnee community. British observers noted that there were Yuchi Indians living among them. At both Yuchi Town and Sawanogi, Shawnees and Yuchis managed to retain a coherent sense of their distinctiveness even while the authority of the Upper Creeks increased after the American Revolution. The superintendent of Indian Affairs in the Southeast, Benjamin Hawkins, recognized that the Shawnees at Sawanogi retained "the manners of their countrymen to the N.W."[69] But life in Creek country was not easy. Observers noticed that a shared sense of oppression, of marginalized status, bound them together. Writing in 1901 the Swiss linguist Albert Gatschet noted that "the Creek Indians always nurtured a clandestine aversion towards the Yuchi and call them slaves (*salafki*)."[70]

The Indian slave trade created ephemeral alliances that necessitated frequent removals. Political and military alliances did not lead to cultural coalescence in the Southeast. Like language, ritual also came to define differences between Indian towns. Today, Shawnees and Yuchis "help out" at each other's ceremonial grounds. However, most Shawnees like to point out that their form of the Stomp Dance is more of a social than a religious ritual. Shawnees convey this belief by noting that they do not take "red root" medicine, which is an element of some stomp dance ceremonials among the Yuchis.[71] These contemporary observations serve to remind us of the cultural subtleties that Native people, across space and time, have used to maintain their unique ethnic identities. Military alliances and trade relationships based on Indian slavery are unreliable gauges of belief and identity. But if we follow Yuchi and Shawnee oral histories into past worlds, we may learn more about the nature of their historic alliance. In the 1840s a Shawnee man named Spybuck knew enough of his history to link himself to the Savannah River Shawnees. His story of survival and adaptation acknowledged the vital role that intertribal alliances have played in Shawnee history. Nevertheless, Spybuck acknowledged the Yuchi creation story, which rejects coalescence, preferring instead a world with "each tribe going its own way."

Acknowledgments

I would like to thank Yuchi Tribal Chairman Andrew Skeeter for inviting me to deliver this paper at the 2010 Yuchi History Conference. Thanks also to Jason Baird Jackson, Joshua Piker, and Robbie Ethridge for their comments and suggestions as I developed this essay.

Notes

1. Frank G. Speck, *Ethnology of the Yuchi Indians,* ed. Jason Baird Jackson (Lincoln: University of Nebraska Press, 2004), 143.

2. For Yuchi nouns and notions of animacy, see Mary S. Linn, "Yuchi and Non-Yuchi: A Living Classification," *Florida Anthropologist* 50 (1996): 189–96; George Stiggins, "A Historical Narration of the Geneaology, Traditions, and Downfall of the Ispocoga or Creek Tribe of Indians," in *A Creek Source Book,* ed. William C. Sturtevant (New York: Garland, 1987), 22–23.

3. Willard B. Walker, "Creek Confederacy Before Removal," in *Handbook of North American Indians,* vol. 14, *Southeast,* ed. Raymond D. Fogelson (Washington DC: Smithsonian Institution, 2004), 373.

4. John Lawson, *A New Voyage to Carolina,* ed. Hugh Talmage Lefler (Chapel Hill: University of North Carolina Press, 1967), 173–74; Wilbur R. Jacobs, ed., *Indians of the Southern Colonial Frontier: The Edmond Atkin Report and Plan of 1755* (Columbia: University of South Carolina Press, 1954), 65.

5. Population figures for the Shawnee at the turn of the century are complicated by the fact that the Loyal Shawnee, today's Shawnee Tribe of Oklahoma, were then considered members of the Cherokee Nation. As a result, it
is difficult to assign a precise figure to the three federally recognized Shawnee
tribes of today. The best estimate of the total Shawnee population between
1900 and 1905 is 1,800 people, For incomplete census data, see U.S. Department of Interior, *Annual Report of the Commissioner of Indian Affairs*, [1905],
202; U.S. Department of Interior, *Annual Report of the Commissioner of Indian Affairs*, [1903], 280.

6. James H. Merrell, *The Indians' New World: Catawbas and their Neighbors from European Contact through Removal* (New York: Norton, 1991);
Colin G. Calloway, *New Worlds for All: Indians, Europeans, and the Remak-
ing of Early America* (Baltimore MD: Johns Hopkins University Press, 1997).

7. Alexander Moore, ed., *Nairne's Muskhogean Journals: The 1708 Expedition to the Mississippi River* (Jackson: University Press of Mississippi, 1988),
62–63. Maureen Meyers, "From Refugees to Slave Traders: The Transformation of the Westo Indians," in *Mapping the Mississippian Shatter Zone: The
Colonial Indian Slave Trade and Regional Instability in the American South*,
ed. Robbie Ethridge and Sheri M. Shuck-Hall (Lincoln: University of Nebraska
Press, 2009), 97; on Catawba coalescence, see Merrell, *The Indians' New World*.

8. Stephen Warren and Randolph Noe, "The Greatest Travelers in America:
Shawnee Survival in the Shatter Zone," in *Mapping the Mississippian Shatter Zone*, ed. Robbie Ethridge and Sheri M. Shuck-Hall (Lincoln: University
of Nebraska Press, 2009), 169.

9. Speck, *Ethnology of the Yuchi Indians*, 11. For Jim Clark's story, see
"Big Pond or Sapulpa [Yuchi] Shawnee Group," folder 277, box 31, Erminie
Wheeler Voegelin Manuscript Collection, Ayer Modern Manuscripts, Newberry Library, Chicago. The Big Pond ceremonial ground has now become a
part of the Sand Creek ground. See Jason Baird Jackson, *Yuchi Ceremonial
Life: Performance, Meaning, and Tradition in a Contemporary American Indian Community* (Lincoln: University of Nebraska Press, 2003), 47–48. Linguist Mary S. Linn argues that the Yuchi word for "Big Pond" is "Big Water."
In contrast to Clark's opinion, she believes that "Big Pond" looks like a place
name in Yuchi, rather than, as Clark suggests, a Shawnee word or name. Mary
S. Linn, pers. comm., 10 October 2010.

10. Thomas S. Woodward, *Woodward's Reminiscences of the Creek, or
Muscogee Indians, Contained in Letters to Friends in Georgia and Alabama*
(Montgomery AL: Berrett and Wimbish, 1859), 41. The Spybuck name is fa-
mous among the Bird Creek Shawnees in and around Sperry, Oklahoma.

11. Ethnologist Frank Speck certainly believed that the Yuchi-Shawnee alliance was quite old. One of his interlocutors was Charley Wilson, "a Shawnee of the band affiliated loosely with the Yuchi and Creeks since very early times and now with them in the northwestern part of the Creek Nation." See Frank G. Speck, "Ceremonial Songs of the Creek and Yuchi Indians," *University of Pennsylvania, University Museum, Anthropological Publications* 1 (1911): 157–245, 241.

12. For examples of the confusion regarding the Yuchi language as a Siouan language, see Edward Sapir, "A Bird's Eye View of American Indian Languages North of Mexico," *Science* 54 (1921): 408; Mary R. Haas, "The Proto-Gulf Word for Water (with Notes on Siouan-Yuchi)," *International Journal of American Linguistics* 17 (1951): 71–79. See also Linn's chapter in this volume.

13. Woodward, *Woodward's Reminiscences of the Creek, or Muscogee Indians*, 40; William Bartram, *Travels, and Other Writings: Travels through North and South Carolina, Georgia, East and West Florida* (New York: Library of America, 1996), 317.

14. The Illinois word for Yuchi, *taogaria*, was probably adopted from the Shawnee word for Yuchi, *tahokale*. See Jason Baird Jackson, "Yuchi," in *Handbook of North American Indians*, vol. 14, *Southeast*, ed. Raymond D. Fogelson (Washington DC, 2004), 428. For Gravier's account, see Reuben Gold Thwaites, ed., *The Jesuit Relations and Allied Documents*, 71 vols. (Cleveland: Burrows Brothers Company, 1896), 65:115.

15. Francis Le Jau, *The Carolina Chronicle of Dr. Francis Le Jau, 1706–1717*, ed. Frank J. Klingberg (Berkeley: University of California Press, 1956), 49.

16. William L. McDowell Jr., ed., *Documents Relating to Indian Affairs, May 21, 1750–August 7, 1754*, The Colonial Records of South Carolina, series 2, vol. 2 (Columbia: South Carolina Archives Department, 1958), 424; Kristian Hvidt, ed., *Von Reck's Voyage: Drawings and Journal of Philip Georg Friedrich von Reck* (Savannah GA: Beehive Press, 1980), 40.

17. Charles Callender, "Shawnee," in *Handbook of North American Indians*, vol. 15: *Northeast*, ed. Bruce G. Trigger (Washington DC: Smithsonian Institution, 1978), 632. For the earliest known painting of a Shawnee warrior, by Marin in 1796, see Louis Houck, *A History of Missouri: From the Earliest Explorations and Settlements until the Admission of the State into the Union* (Chicago: R. R. Donnelley, 1908), 213.

18. Gregory A. Waselkov and Kathryn E. Holland Braund, eds., *William Bartram on the Southeastern Indians* (Lincoln: University of Nebraska Press, 1995), 146.

19. Contemporary Shawnee spellings of the divisions are *kesepokofi, pekowefi, mekoga, galikifi*, and *hifiwakela*.

20. George Blanchard, interview with Stephen Warren, 27 October 2005.

21. Swanton believed that the Shawnees in Carolina were members of the Hathawekela division. See John R. Swanton, *Early History of the Creek Indians and Their Neighbors* (Washington DC: Government Printing Office, 1922), 317. Noel Schutz makes the case that the Sawokli and Thawekila are the same division. See Noel Schutz, "The Study of Shawnee Myth in an Ethnographic and Ethnohistorical Perspective," PhD diss., Indiana University, 1975, 377–81. The strongest documentary evidence for the Thawekila Shawnee–Savannah River connection comes from James LeTort, who gave an account of the Indians at Alleghany: "200 Okewela [Thawekila] families lately from S. Carolina to Ptowmack, & from thence thither; making 100 men." Quoted from "Number of Indians, 1731," in *Pennsylvania Archives: Selected and Arranged from Original Documents in the Office of the Secretary of the Commonwealth*, vol. 1, comp. Samuel Hazard (Philadelphia PA: Joseph Severns and Company, 1852), 1:301–2.

22. For the best comprehensive analysis of Shawnee migrations to date, see Jerry Eugene Clark, "Shawnee Indian Migration: A System Analysis," PhD diss., University of Kentucky, 1974, 21–22. For the three attacks on the Shawnee, see José António Brandão, *"Your Fyre Shall Burn No More:" Iroquois Policy toward New France and Its Native Allies to 1701* (Lincoln: University of Nebraska Press, 1997), table D.1; see also Cadwallader Colden, *The History of the Five Nations Depending on the Province of New-York in America, 1742 & 1747* (Ithaca NY: Cornell University Press, 1958); Pierre Francois Xavier de Charlevoix, *History and General Description of New France*, 6 vols. (New York: J. G. Shea, 1866–72), 3:74–75.

23. Pere Joseph Marquette, "An Account of the Discovery of Some New Countries and Nations in North America," in *Historical Collections of Louisiana, Embracing Translations of Many Rare and Valuable Documents Relating to the Natural, Civil and Political History of that State*, ed. B. F. French (New York: Wiley and Putnam, 1846–53), 2:202.

24. For more on "mourning wars," see Allen Greer, *Mohawk Saint: Catherine Tekakwitha and the Jesuits* (Oxford: Oxford University Press, 2005), 12–14; Daniel K. Richter, *The Ordeal of the Longhouse: The Peoples of the Iroquois League in the Era of European Colonization* (Chapel Hill: University of North Carolina Press, 1992), chap. 3.

25. Louis LeClerc de Milford, *Memoir or a Cursory Glance at My Different Travels & My Sojourn in the Creek Nation* (Chicago: R. R. Donnelley, 1956), 184. Historian Angie Debo maintained that "a tradition of Creek-Shawnee friendship going back to the dim days of their legendary history." See Angie

Debo, *The Road to Disappearance: A History of the Creek Indians* (Norman: University of Oklahoma Press, 1941), 56.

26. Erminie Wheeler-Voegelin believed that shortly before the historical period, "Shawnee began drifting southward from their northern location. The path they followed probably lay along the eastern Piedmont." See Erminie Wheeler-Voegelin, "Mortuary Customs of the Shawnee and other Eastern Tribes," *Indiana Historical Society, Prehistory Research Series* 2 (1944): 227–444, 373.

27. See Nicholas Perrot, "Memoir on the Manners, Customs, and Religion of the Savages of North America," in *The Indian Tribes of the Upper Mississippi Valley and Region of the Great Lakes*, 2 vols., ed. Emma Helen Blair (1911; repr., Lincoln: University of Nebraska Press, 1969), 1:226.

28. John Lederer, quoted in Charles A. Hanna, *The Wilderness Trail: Or the Ventures and Adventures of the Pennsylvania Traders on the Alleghany Path*, 2 vols. (New York: AMS Press, 1972), 1:122.

29. Verner Crane dated the Shawnee arrival in Carolina to the Westo War of 1680–81. However, we know from Henry Woodward's relation that the Shawnee had at least visited the Savannah River in 1674 (this Woodward is not to be confused with the Woodward who met Spybuck in the 1840s). Verner W. Crane, *The Southern Frontier, 1670–1732* (Durham NC: Duke University Press, 1928), 334. See Henry Woodward, "A Faithfull Relation of My Westoe Voiage," in *Narratives of Early Carolina: 1650–1708*, ed. Alexander S. Salley (New York: Scribner's Sons, 1911), 133. Thwaites, *The Jesuit Relations*, 47:145, 147. See also Nicholas Perrot, "Memoir on the Manners, Customs, and Religion of the Savages of North America," 146.

30. Marian E. White, "Erie," in *Handbook of North American Indians*, vol. 15: *Northeast*, ed. Bruce G. Trigger (Washington DC: Smithsonian Institution, 1978), 412–16; for a more recent treatment of the Westo, and an explanation of their identification with the Erie, see Eric E. Bowne, *The Westo Indians: Slave Traders of the Early Colonial South* (Tuscaloosa: University of Alabama Press, 2005).

31. Verner W. Crane, "An Historical Note on the Westo Indians," *American Anthropologist* 20 (1919): 331–37, 335.

32. Woodward, "A Faithfull Relation of My Westoe Voiage," 134.

33. Cited in Chapman J. Milling, *Red Carolinians* (Chapel Hill: University of North Carolina Press, 1940), 85.

34. Woodward, "A Faithfull Relation of My Westoe Voiage," 134.

35. John Archdale, "A New Description of that Fertile and Pleasant Province of Carolina, by John Archdale, 1707," in *Narratives of Early Carolina, 1650–1700*, ed. Alexander S. Salley Jr. (New York: Scribner's Sons, 1911),

277–312. See also John T. Juricek, "Indian Policy in Proprietary South Carolina, 1670–1693," MA thesis, University of Chicago, 1962, 121–24.

36. Alexander S. Salley Jr., ed., *Journal of the Commons House of Assembly*, November 12, 1707 (Columbia, SC: State Company, 1941), 38, 46.

37. Alexander S. Salley Jr., ed., *Journal of the Commons House of Assembly*, June 12, 1707 (Columbia SC: State Company, 1941), 27–28; for "armed posse," see William L. Ramsey, *The Yamasee War: A Study of Culture, Economy, and Conflict in the Colonial South* (Lincoln: University of Nebraska Press, 2008), 110.

38. Alexander S. Salley Jr., ed., *Journal of the Commons House of Assembly*, February 10, 1708 (Columbia SC: State Company, 1941), 62. For a fuller description of the conflict between the Shawnee and Carolina, see Alan Gallay, *Indian Slave Trade: The Rise of the English Empire in the American South, 1650–1717* (New Haven CT: Yale University Press, 2002), 210–11.

39. Taken from "A Report of the Governor and Council, 1708," in *The Colonial South Carolina Scene: Contemporary Views, 1697–1774*, ed. Roy H. Merrens (Columbia: University of South Carolina Press, 1977), 35. Swanton, *The Early History of the Creeks*, 317, agrees but says these three towns were on the Savannah River, citing W. Noel Sainsbury, ed., *Records in the British Public Record Office Relating to South Carolina*, 5 vols. (Columbia: Historical Commission of South Carolina, 1928–47), 5:208.

40. John E. Worth, "Razing Florida: The Indian Slave Trade and the Devastation of Spanish Florida, 1659–1715," in *Mapping the Mississippian Shatter Zone: The Colonial Indian Slave Trade and Regional Instability in the American South*, eds. Robbie Ethridge and Sheri M. Shuck-Hall (Lincoln: University of Nebraska Press, 2009), 301; on the Yuchi arrival on the Savannah River, see Daniel T. Elliott's chapter in this volume.

41. Worth, "Razing Florida," 17.

42. Le Jau, *Carolina Chronicle*, 39. See also David H. Corkran, *The Creek Frontier, 1540–1793* (Norman: University of Oklahoma Press, 1967), 58. Prior to his death Randolph Noe struggled unsuccessfully to trace many of the primary source roots of Corkran's findings. For this reason *The Creek Frontier* should not be used to substantiate factual claims about the colonial Southeast.

43. Le Jau, *Carolina Chronicle*, 49, 68.

44. Crane, "An Historical Note on the Westo Indians," 334.

45. George Blanchard, interview with Stephen Warren, 27 October 2005; Gallay, *Indian Slave Trade*, 211, 267.

46. For an extended treatment of the Cherokee attack on Chestowe, see Gallay, *Indian Slave Trade*, 319–22, and Brett Riggs's chapter in this volume.

47. William L. McDowell Jr., ed., *Journals of the Commissioners of the Indian Trade, September 20, 1710–August 29, 1718*, The Colonial Records of South Carolina, series 2, vol. 1 (Columbia: South Carolina Archives Department, 1955), 56.

48. McDowell, *Journals of the Commissioners*, 1:54.

49. Verner W. Crane, "The Tennessee River as the Road to Carolina: The Beginnings of Exploration and Trade," *Mississippi Valley Historical Review* 3 (1916): 3–18, 10.

50. Moore, *Nairne's Muskhogean Journals*, 39, 21; Le Jau, *Carolina Chronicle*, 175.

51. For Shawnee villages on the Savannah River, see Guillaume Delisle, maps XV, XVII, in *Indian Villages of the Illinois Country, 1670–1830: Atlas and Supplement*, comp. Sarah Jones Tucker (Springfield: Illinois State Museum, 1975). For attacks on Carolina settlements, see Le Jau, *Carolina Chronicle*, 164, 180. On Yuchi inclusion in the "Southern Indian" contingent of the Yamasee War, see William L. Ramsey, *The Yamasee War: A Study of Culture, Economy, and Conflict in the Colonial South* (Lincoln: University of Nebraska Press, 2008), 101; on the Yuchi towns on the Savannah River, see Kenneth Coleman, ed., *The Colonial Records of the State of Georgia*, vol. 31: *Trustees' Letter Book, 1745–1752* (Athens: University of Georgia Press, 1986), 31:115; for Shawnee and Yuchi population figures, see Ramsey, *Yamasee War*, 110.

52. Warren and Noe, "The Greatest Travelers in America," 174–76.

53. For the Glover census, see A. S. Salley, "The Creek Indian Tribes in 1725," in *South Carolina Historical and Genealogical Magazine* 32 (1931): 240–41.

54. Joshua Piker, *Okfuskee: A Creek Indian Town in Colonial America* (Cambridge MA: Harvard University Press, 2004), 17; a reproduction of the 1737 Chickasaw map can be found in Gregory A. Waselkov, "Indian Maps of the Colonial Southeast," in *Powhatan's Mantle: Indians in the Colonial Southeast*, ed. Peter H. Wood, Gregory A. Waselkov, and Thomas Hatley (Lincoln: University of Nebraska Press, 1989), 298. This map is presented and discussed in Piker's chapter in this volume.

55. Francis Moore, *A Voyage to Georgia: Begun in the Year 1736* (London: Jacob Robinson, 1744), 71–72; for a deeper analysis of this War Dance, see Jason Baird Jackson, "A Yuchi War Dance in 1736," in *European Review of Native American Studies* 16 (2002): 27–32; for more on the Yuchi defense of English settlements in Georgia and South Carolina, see Steven C. Hahn, *The Invention of the Creek Nation, 1670–1763* (Lincoln: University of Nebraska Press, 2004), 181–82.

56. "Journal of David Taitt's Travels from Pensacola, West Florida, to and through the Country of the Upper and the Lower Creeks, 1772," in *Travels*

in the American Colonies, ed. Newton D. Mereness (New York: Macmillan, 1916), 516; Benjamin Hawkins, "A Sketch of the Creek Country in the Years 1798 and 1799," in *Collections of the Georgia Historical Society*, vol. 3, pt. 1 (Savannah: Printed for the Society, 1848), 58–59.

57. Daniel J. Tortora, ed., "'A Faithful Ambassador': The Diary of Rev. William Hutson, Past of Independent Meeting in Charleston, 1757–1761," *South Carolina Historical Magazine* 108 (2007): 32–100, 43, n. 205; James Adair, *The History of American Indians*, ed. Kathryn Holland Braund (Tuscaloosa: University of Alabama Press, 2005), 346.

58. Bartram, *Travels, and Other Writings*, 316–17.

59. McDowell, *Documents Relating to Indian Affairs*, 128–29.

60. McDowell, *Documents Relating to Indian Affairs*, 427, 215.

61. Jacobs, *Indians of the Southern Colonial Frontier*, 64–66. See also Ian Steele, "Shawnee Origins of Their Seven Years' War," *Ethnohistory* 53 (2006): 657–87, 658–61.

62. Patricia Kay Galloway, *Mississippi Provincial Archives*, vol. 4: *French Dominion, 1729–1748* (Baton Rouge: Louisiana State University Press, 1984), 146–47, 222

63. Galloway, *Mississippi Provincial Archives*, 4:216.

64. McDowell, *Documents Relating to Indian Affairs*, 47. For a full explanation of the role of Settlement Indians in slavery, see Gallay, *Indian Slave Trade*, 348–49; Jacobs, *Indians of the Southern Colonial Frontier*, 44–45.

65. Dwight L. Smith, "Shawnee Captivity Ethnography," *Ethnohistory* 2 (1955): 29–41.

66. Excerpts from the interrogations come from McDowell, *Documents Relating to Indian Affairs*, 421, 424, 432. These same Shawnees change their story and try to explain that they were in South Carolina to attack their traditional enemies, the Catawba. However, they were captured on the Lower Salkehatchie River, very near Laurel Bay, far south of Catawba Territory. For these reasons, King Tom's story about being captured by Shawnees makes sense. Historian Ian Steele takes the Shawnees at their word and argues that they wanted to capture Catawbas. See Steele, "Shawnee Origins of Their Seven Years' War," 661.

67. McDowell, *Documents Relating to Indian Affairs*, 246–47, 465.

68. McDowell, *Documents Relating to Indian Affairs*, 432, 453, 437.

69. Benjamin Hawkins, "A Sketch of Creek Country," 15.

70. Albert S. Gatschet, "Towns and Villages of the Creek Confederacy in the XVIII and XIX Centuries," in *A Creek Source Book*, ed. William C. Sturtevant (New York: Garland, 1987), 389.

71. George Blanchard, interviews with Stephen Warren, 27 October 2005 and 11 June 2005. For more information on red root medicine, see Jackson, *Yuchi Ceremonial Life*, 228–29. The use of red root medicine in connection with square ground ceremonies is also central to the practices of the Creek, Seminole, and Cherokee in present-day Oklahoma.

8. To the Backcountry and Back Again
The Yuchi's Search for Stability in the Eighteenth-Century Southeast

~

There is an odd dichotomy in scholarly discussions of the Yuchi. On the one hand, when we talk about Yuchi relations with non-Yuchi, we emphasize instability and conflict. The Yuchi, we note, moved frequently; they had a host of enemies; their alliances were ephemeral and frequently broken.[1] The historical record can certainly be made to support this view of Yuchi history. Thus, in 1728, a British agent reported: "The Euchees have broke up their Town in the Lower Creeks and are now unsettled." Possibly bowing to British pressure, they "Settled" in the British backcountry by 1732. Once there, they were attacked at least twice by their Creek ex-neighbors and developed such bad relations with the British colonists that they were labeled as "the worst of all" the Indians. By 1741 a Georgia official considered them "a scattered Nation, often moving, and changing their Place of Settlement"; later that year another Georgian wrote that "they have abandoned their old dwelling places" in the lower Savannah River valley. These experiences evidently left the Yuchi "very much impaired in Number and Strength and reduced to a very low state," making them the sort of people who "flee from other Indians." Not surprisingly, they fell under Creek influence again. They "were called" back to Creek country in 1751, although only after "the women and children" in one of their villages on the

Savannah River were killed by northern Indians and a Yuchi community on the South Carolina coast lost five of its people to raiders who claimed to be Cherokees. By 1752 the Yuchi were described as "a kind of Vassals to [the Creeks], and reside[d] among them."[2] In this telling, Yuchi relationships with outsiders appear to range from the dysfunctional to the deadly, and the Yuchi's place in the world seems profoundly unsettled.

On the other hand, the chaos and hostility disappear when we discuss Yuchi society and culture. In this context the Yuchi appear unusually stable and successful. They preserved their language and culture; they jealously guarded their autonomy; they remained recognizably Yuchi even as other small nations were blending into the eighteenth century's emerging confederacies.[3] And again there is evidence to support this reading. Thus, Yuchi of the late eighteenth century were said to "retain all their original customs and laws and . . . [to have] adopted none of the Creeks." Their language at the time, a colonist noted, was "altogether or radically different from the Creek or Muscogulge tongue," and an early twentieth-century Creek story about "the Creator" giving languages to all the Indians suggests a Native perspective on this difference: "He found that there were still some Indians whom he had not provided for. These were the Yuchi. Having no language for them, he kicked them in the buttocks saying 'Ba!' which explains why the Yuchi have such an unintelligible speech." The Yuchi's own language inscribed this story's sense of difference into their daily lives—"Animacy in Yuchi is divided into two classes: those who are members of the Yuchi tribe and those who are not"—without in any way accepting the Creek narrative's implication of inferiority. In fact, the Yuchi knew themselves to be Tsoyaha, "Children of the Sun," a uniquely favored people whose ceremonies ensured the continuity of this world and its many peoples. "If the Yuchi perish," said the Sun in a Yuchi origin narrative, "I will not face this world. I will turn my face away, and there will be darkness upon the earth, and it will even be the last of the earth." The Yuchi were therefore content to remain "in confederacy with the Creeks, but [did] not mix with them"; they were not alarmed when they were "taken no great Notice of by neither French nor English." And who could blame them? After all, their main community, according to a British observer in the 1770s, was the "best situated Indian town I ever saw," a "populous and thriving" place "full of youth and young children." Even the Yuchi houses — "large and neatly built . . . [with] the appearance of red brick walls" and "neatly covered or roofed" — bespoke an enviable, enduring, and distinctly Yuchi way of life.[4]

In terms of Yuchi society and culture, then, we have emphasized stability and continuity; in terms of Yuchi relations with the surrounding world, we have emphasized crisis and change. Bringing these two visions of Yuchi life together into one narrative requires — to oversimplify dramatically — finding change within the continuity or continuity within the change. I suggest that we pursue the latter course and search for continuity within the Yuchi's changing relations with non-Yuchi. I say this because the ethnographic literature has convinced me that Yuchi social and cultural continuity was real, that these people were able to remain recognizably Yuchi linguistically, culturally, and socially.[5] The factors that propelled the Yuchi in this direction certainly centered in their relations with one another, but their ability to preserve a distinctly Yuchi way of life was also directly linked to the continuities they were able to create in their dealings with the outside world. It was these relationships that provided the Yuchi with the social and material resources necessary to carve out a degree of autonomy during the eighteenth century. Yuchi stability and continuity, in short, was neither confined to nor divorced from their relations with other Yuchi.

The years in which the Yuchi immigrated to, lived in, and emigrated from the British backcountry represent a particularly worthwhile venue for exploring this people's ability to create enduring ties to outsiders. Two characteristics of this period — the late 1720s through the early 1750s — make it especially significant. To begin with, because of temporary proximity to literate European colonists, this is the time in the early history of the Yuchi when they are most visible in the historical record. These years have therefore been critical to historians' understandings of the Yuchi. There may have been more important eras in Yuchi history, but historians perforce behave like the drunk in the old joke who looks under the lamppost for his car keys because that's where the light is: they tend to confine their research to the area illuminated by the documents.[6] Second, the backcountry years are the period when Yuchi relations with non-Yuchi seem to have been most disordered. In less than twenty-five years, it appears that the Yuchis first severed their ties to the Creeks, then embraced new bonds with the British, and finally broke those bonds and reestablished their ties to the Creeks. The seeming confusion of the backcountry years, then, and the visibility of those very years in the historical record have encouraged us to emphasize chaos and disruption when we discuss Yuchi relations with non-Yuchis. Those same characteristics, however, offer us the opportunity to reexamine and rewrite this aspect of Yuchi history. After all, the light provided by Yuchi proximity to the British colonists affords us a welcome chance to watch colonial-era Yuchis in action. More important, if the Yuchi found ways to forge stable relations with non-Yuchis despite the crises of the backcountry years, then that represents a strong indication of their ability to establish long-lasting bonds with outsiders in other, less chaotic (and less visible) periods of their history. The Yuchis' time in the backcountry, in other words, offers us a window onto their persistent and frequently successful efforts to forge and maintain stable relations with outsiders. It is time we recognized the continuities in this aspect of the Yuchis' lives and this period of their history.

These continuities begin with the fact that some Yuchi remained in Creek country even as others moved to the British backcountry in the late 1720s and early 1730s. Soon after the 1728 breakup of their Lower Creek community, the Yuchi "settled" another town in Lower Creek country. The new town, in the words of Benjamin Hawkins writing seventy years later, was located "where the [Yuchi] town now is"; a Chickasaw map from 1737 showed a Yuchi town in approximately this location (see fig. 5).[7] People from this town appear occasionally in the British colonial records. Thus, in 1735 a

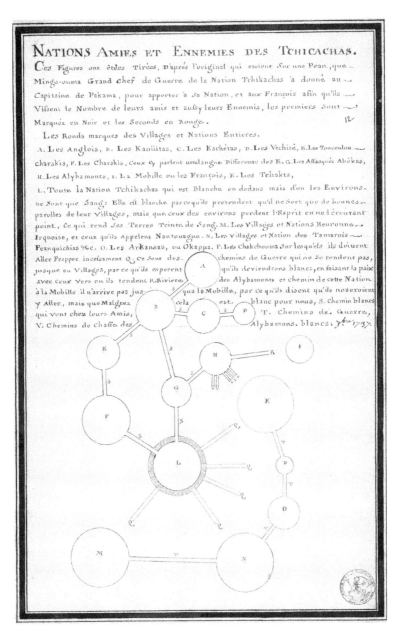

FIGURE 5. A French copy of a Chickasaw/Alabama map of 1737. For a discussion of how to read this map, see note 7. From the Archives Canada–France. The map is online at http://bd.archivescanadafrance. org/acf-pleade-3-images/img-server/FRCAOM/FRCAOM_F3290_12/ DAFCAOM03_F3290001201_H.jpg.

Creek headman whom Georgia officials planned "to invite down" to Savannah lived "at Ewchee town" among the Lower Creeks. That same year, a "Mico of the Uchesses" consulted with a British agent in Lower Creek country about bloodying the path between the Lower Creek and the Spanish in Florida; he then took "25 men . . . to war," returning to "his own Town with Colours flying." In 1742 the same leader who was invited down in 1735 was described as "one of the Headmen of the Euchee . . . in the lower Creeks." By November 1749, two years before the Yuchi were "called" back to Creek country, a Yuchi "King" and "Head Warriour" arrived in Savannah as part of a delegation from "the Lower Creek Nation," and the following year three British traders took out licenses for Yuchi communities among both the Lower and Upper Creeks.[8] It is clear, then, that some Yuchis chose to preserve their connections with the Creeks, and it is likely that these ties were based on something more substantial than mere proximity. After all, headmen from Yuchi and Creek towns traveled together, and Yuchis "engaged, together with the Creeks, in War against the Cherokees." Contacts of this sort, and the continued presence of Yuchis in Creek country, help to explain a 1736 comment by a Creek headman: "the Uchees and they were friends."[9]

One other thing about these Creek country–dwelling Yuchis is clear: their connections were especially strong with one Creek town and one Creek headman. Again and again the documents show that the Yuchis had a very close bond with Aleck and, to a lesser extent, with his hometown of Cussita. In the examples cited above, Aleck was the headman invited down from Creek country in 1735. The invitation referred to him as living "at Ewchee town," but when he arrived in Savannah he was described as "Mico, or King . . . from the Cussitaws."[10] Aleck was also the headman mentioned in 1742, when he was identified as "one of the Headmen of the Euchee and Cussetaw Towns in the lower Creeks." Moreover, the 1737 Chickasaw map shows that the Cussitas were the Yuchis' only connection to their Creek neighbors. The existence of a Yuchi-Cussita alliance is suggested by records from the late 1720s, when these towns were two of the three Creek communities that would not make peace with the Spanish-allied Yamasee; the Yuchi, in fact, went to Cussita to present a British agent with scalps from a Spaniard and a Yamasee. This Cussita-Yuchi bond evidently grew stronger in 1729 when, as Hawkins wrote,

> an old Chief of Cussetuh, . . . Captain Ellick, married three Uchee wives, and brought them to Cussetuh, this act being greatly disliked by his townspeople. Their opposition determined him to move from Cussetuh; he went down opposite where the town now is, and settled with his three brothers, two of them had Uchee wives. He after this collected all the Uchees and gave them land where the town now is, and there they settled.[11]

Hawkins's description of Cussita-Yuchi hostility is called into question by the number of eighteenth-century connections between the two peoples and by the testimony of modern Yuchis who continue to speak of ties to Cussita forged by a headman's marriage to Yuchi women.[12] Hawkins was on firmer ground, though, when he discussed Aleck and his brothers. It is likely not a coincidence, for example, that "Uchee Will" was "the head" of Tadpole, a small Yuchi village, in the late eighteenth century and that one of Aleck's brothers was named Will.[13] As for Aleck, his 1729 marriage followed by one year the break-up of the first Yuchi town among the Lower Creeks. Aleck evidently gathered some of his in-laws and founded a new Yuchi town in Lower Creek country. Because he remained a Cussita—from the mid-1750s to the late 1770s he was referred to as a headman from this town—he could bind the Yuchi to this important Lower Creek community.

The Yuchis' ties to Aleck were evidently enduring enough that—even as the town he founded in Lower Creek country persisted—Aleck eventually followed some of his in-laws to the British backcountry. In 1746 Aleck was present at a backcountry meeting during which South Carolina's governor chastised the Creeks because "some of your young People have been so rash and imprudent, as to kill six of the Euchee's our Friends, who are settled amongst

us, and have carried off others as Slaves." Aleck's presence may, indeed, have encouraged the governor to address the Yuchis' grievances, but the fact that Aleck was one of the Creeks who, according to
the governor, "have never been in Carolina before since my Arrival" in December 1743 suggests that he had not yet moved to the area
himself. By 1749, however, Aleck had "Settled" (along with another headman and "13 Indians and their Families") in the backcountry, and he and his followers were reported to "generally reside in
[Georgia's] Settlements" in 1754; three years later, he "applied for
a Grant of a Piece of Land." By 1760 he had moved back to Creek
country but "talked of returning to [the British] Settlements," a proposal on which he evidently made good, since he complained of Euro-American trespassers in 1761 and 1763. His "Cow penn" was
just on the Creek side of the boundary line in 1765, but in 1766 he
agreed to give up his "Plantation." He may then have moved to Doctor Town, another Creek backcountry community; if so, he likely
maintained a residence in the backcountry until at least 1775. The
available evidence, while thin, suggests that he undertook several of
these moves at the urging of his Yuchi wives. Thus, in 1760, Aleck's
talk of moving back to the British "Settlements" was prompted by
"His Wives . . . often complaining" about their standard of living
among the Creeks. Three years later, at least one of these women
moved to the South Carolina backcountry with "a Party of Euchee Indians." Aleck claimed that she was "taken" and "carried" off,
and asked the British for help in recovering her; but his wives' previously expressed preference for backcountry living and the presence of this woman's Yuchi kinsmen strongly suggest that this was
a marital argument, not wife stealing. If so, the Yuchi woman evidently made her point, since Aleck probably retained a home in the
backcountry for another decade.[14]

For the Yuchi, then, moving to the area around the British settlements did not mean abandoning ties to their Creek neighbors.
Nor did the Yuchi have to create relationships with their new British neighbors from scratch. They retained, for example, their connections to South Carolina's government, connections forged during

the earlier Yuchi occupation of several sites in the Savannah River valley. As early as 1712, South Carolina had sought to prevent the Yuchi—who had become allies in the colony's war against the Tuscarora—from "deserting" their communities near the colony and "goeing to the French." Three years later, with the onset of the Yamasee War, the Yuchi did abandon these towns, moving west to Creek country and no doubt straining their relationship with South Carolina. However, by the time of the 1723 arrival in Charleston of Toucopagee, "a beloved Man of the Euchees," Yuchis were again in diplomatic contact with the colony, and by the late 1720s they were taking part in South Carolina-sponsored attacks on the Yamasees. Thus, when the Yuchis broke up their Lower Creek town in 1728, it was no surprise that a Carolina official attempted to recruit the refugees to move back to the colony's western frontier: "The Euchees have promised me to move next fall, but [I] could not get them to do it now."[15]

The Yuchi were as good as their word. By 1731 they were in the process of establishing a new backcountry life. In the winter of that year, John Macgilvery and Company submitted two petitions to South Carolina's government. One sought permission to trade with the Yuchi, a signal that they were reconstituting their community; the other asked that "the Uchee Indians" be given "a Quantity of Corn," a bulky, difficult to transport commodity that could only have been intended for people living near South Carolina. The following year Carolina sent an agent to the Yuchis' new town at Mount Pleasant, five miles up the Savannah River from the colony's Fort Palachacola. He was "directed to inform himself of the State of the Utchees, and how they stand affected and endeavour to keep them in the Interest of the Government." The colony, moreover, put its money where its mouth was, authorizing the agent to distribute £100 worth of presents to the Yuchi.[16] South Carolina officials came to consider the Yuchi as "under our Protection," but since the colony made plans to mobilize Yuchi warriors to fend off the Spanish in 1737, 1738, 1742, and 1743, the Yuchi likely saw the relationship as a reciprocal one. The occasional "Complaints made by the Inhabitants of this Province against the Euchee Indians" — "grown to a very great Pitch of Insolence"; "Insolence and Disorders"; "the Liberties they take" — suggest the confidence with which Yuchis approached their Euro-American neighbors. The Yuchis knew, of course, that they "live[d] amongst [South Carolina's] Settlements," but they had reason to believe that the colonists depended on men like "Jenkins the head Man of the Euchees" who were "ready to come with his people if the Spaniards should ever come again." While the Yuchis resided in the backcountry, therefore, they did not hesitate to visit Carolina officials — sometimes in numbers the colonists found excessive — and even after they returned to Creek country, Yuchis might show up in South Carolina's capital to remind its leaders that although they had "settled for several years now . . . in the Lower Creek Nation," they "were friends to the English."[17]

Yuchis who moved to the backcountry likewise retained their connections to certain British traders. Thomas Wiggan, for example, traded among the Creeks in the 1720s. He based his Lower Creek operations in Cussita, and perhaps the Yuchi encountered him through their own ties to this town; or perhaps they knew him first as a kinsman of Eleazer Wiggan, with whom the Yuchi had traded prior to the Yamasee War. In either case, it seems clear that the Yuchi knew Thomas Wiggan before the breakup of their first Lower Creek town. Wiggan, it should be noted, also had "long standing" connections to Mount Pleasant, where he "[kept] Stores."[18] The Yuchi who settled there after leaving Creek country thus had a familiar British face nearby, one who — because of his continuing ties to Cussita — could also connect them to friends and family among the Lower Creeks. Wiggan was likely the "Indian Trader who lived" in the "town of Uchee Indians" at Mount Pleasant in the mid-1730s, and he traded with the Yuchis into the 1740s. By that point he had been named the commander of Georgia's fort at Mount Pleasant, where he continued to deal with Yuchis; archaeological evidence suggests that "it was quite likely" that Yuchis "not only lived around the fort, but also within it." The food and pottery that Yuchi women provided the garrison testifies to the enduring nature of their people's ties to Thomas Wiggan, ties that may have outlived this particular trader.[19] For example, it is tempting to speculate that the John Wiggen mentioned in a 1764 letter from a Yuchi town in Creek country was Thomas's son (and perhaps Eleazer's grandson). More concretely, it is clear that Thomas's employee John Ladson carried on his employer's Yuchi connections. Ladson was on Wiggan's payroll by 1727; by 1743 he had settled near Wiggan in Mount Pleasant; by 1752, after the Yuchi return to Creek country, Ladson was described simply as "Trader in the Utchees." And in an interesting coincidence, the 1764 letter from a Yuchi town that mentions John Wiggen also passes along a talk from "Allick & the principle Men of the Cussitaws" criticizing the activities of "Ladson's half breed Son."[20] The letter, in other words, brings together ties—to the Wiggans, to Ladson, to Aleck, to Cusseta—that both pre-dated the Yuchis' time in the backcountry and remained a part of Yuchi life well after they returned to Creek country.

Enduring ties of this sort were a valuable commodity in the colonial Southeast, but the Yuchi also used their years in the backcountry to form new relationships with their British neighbors. Doing so must have seemed a necessary survival strategy for a people attempting to establish themselves in an area dominated by Euro-Americans. The Yuchi were quite successful, for example, in cultivating ties with the newly founded colony of Georgia and particularly with General James Oglethorpe, the colony's leader. After being in the colony for only two months he agreed to serve as a mediator between the Yuchis and the Creeks, and he repeatedly defended Yuchi lands against encroachments by Georgia settlers, asserting finally that "[s]ome may fancy that because their Land is not planted, therefore there is no Hurt in taking it from them, but the Indian Nations have as much Right to their Woods as an English Gentleman has to a Forest or a Chace, and they are more necessary to them since the Venison is the Flesh that enables them to pay the English for their Goods." The Yuchi formalized this relationship in 1736, sending "a sizable deputation" to Savannah, where "[t]he Indian king gave a long speech, an alliance was concluded and gifts were exchanged." They honored their commitment by serving in large numbers during Georgia's wars with Spanish Florida, receiving in return not simply Oglethorpe's defense of their lands but also supplies and the ability to use Georgia as a place of refuge when threatened by other Native peoples.[21]

With Oglethorpe's departure in 1743, however, the Yuchis' relationship with Georgia cooled perceptibly. Georgia's officials ceased protecting Yuchi lands, and some of Georgia's colonists had long since made it clear that "the bad Uchee Indians" were unwelcome neighbors; the Yuchi, for their part, had their own complaints about the Euro-Americans' unneighborly behavior. These problems notwithstanding, the Yuchi continued to maintain their Georgia connections even after moving back to Creek country. Their diplomatic ties to Georgia's leaders remained strong enough that a newly arrived governor predicted a Yuchi visit, "it being Customary upon the arrival of a new Governor, for the neighbouring Indians to come to him, to renew the Peace." The governor may have seen such visits as a burden, but from a Yuchi perspective, they worked, allowing the Yuchi to include Georgia's leaders in their network of friends. Thus, for example, when a series of tit-for-tat murders involving Yuchis and backcountry colonists threatened to end the Yuchi-Georgia relationship in the late 1750s, the Yuchi drew upon their ties to Aleck to salvage their connections to Georgia: "In the end it was left by some of the Euchee Headmen to Aleck, to consult . . . privately about getting the [Yuchi] Fellow [accused of the murders] to be killed." By the following spring, Yuchis were again aiding Georgia against its enemies, with a "Party" of Yuchis returning to Savannah to report both their success in killing three Cherokees and the death of their headman, Istichago, "who before he expired ordered them to acquaint the Governour that he died contended in having so manifested his Friendship to the English." The governor commended the Yuchis for bravery, offered consolation over the loss of their headman, and remarked that "the Regard his Excellency had for their Chief should extend to the Son he had left behind him, who, although a Child, should receive constant Proofs of his Bounty." The meeting ended with Georgia's leader promising that he would "always look upon the Uchees as his Brothers," a fitting description of the relationship that the Yuchis had cultivated with Georgia's officials for almost three decades.[22]

Other relationships the Yuchi formed while in the backcountry were less formal. Most of these ties left only the most ephemeral of traces in the historical record, traces that both suggest the existence of long-lasting connections and leave modern observers struggling with unanswerable questions. What did it mean, for example, when Oglethorpe sent a note "to a certain woman (Hewitt) living among these [Yuchi] people in which she is requested to come to [Ebenezer] with the chief of these Indians to discuss in detail several matters"? Had James Hewitt, a British trader with ties to the Yuchi, married a Yuchi woman? Or had Hewitt married a Euro-American who "speaks their language"? If so, had she learned Yuchi from her neighbors at Mount Pleasant?[23] Or, to take another example, why do we find references in the 1750s and 1760s—well after most Yuchis had returned to Creek country—to the "local Uchee Indians" and to Yuchis "haunt[ing] our Settlements, as they constantly do, especially about Mount Pleasant"? Is it significant that at least a few of these Yuchis spoke some English? Why did Georgia's governor feel it was necessary to remind the colonists during a 1774 Creek-British crisis that "all trade and intercourse whatever" with the Yuchi was prohibited in any "part of this [pro]vince"? And the questions go on. Why did Morgan Sabb go out of his way to confront a party of northern Indians intent on attacking a backcountry Yuchi village in 1751? Why did Mr. Drayton allow a group of Yuchis to settle on his "Plantation" as late as 1765?[24]

It is hard not to conclude that in at least some of these cases, we can see the flip side of the complaints other colonists directed at the Yuchi. Yuchis and Euro-Americans, these snippets suggest, could and did get along. And some of the relationships the Yuchi forged while living in the backcountry were likely enduring ones. Consider, for example, their ties to South Carolina's lieutenant governor William Bull. In 1715, during the Yamasee War, Yuchis had been part of a war party that destroyed dozens of plantations, but they left the Bull family church untouched. During the early 1740s Yuchis were living in Grenville County, as were the Bulls, and Lieutenant Governor Bull helped defuse tensions between the Yuchis and their Euro-American neighbors. He continued to pass on news about the Yuchis into the 1750s, and the Yuchis continued to live within eight to ten miles of his plantation. In 1751 he asked to be reimbursed £100 "for Corn supplied the Euchee," and the next year a visitor reported that two Yuchis were at his plantation. The Yuchis' ties to the Bull family endured at least until 1765 — fifty years after they spared the Bull's church — when South Carolina's government thought the lieutenant governor's son should deliver a message to Yuchis who were still living in South Carolina. And the Yuchis likely formed similar — and similarly enduring — personal relationships with less well-placed colonists too. So, for example, in 1738 John Miller was described as someone "who keeps Stores at Augusta to serve the Indian Traders." Did he also, during his time in Augusta, get to know the Yuchis who lived a few miles south of town? It is impossible to know, but by the late 1750s and continuing into the 1760s and 1770s he was repeatedly identified with some variant of the phrase "a trader from the Eutchies."[25] Possibly his later affiliation was an echo of a relationship like that between the Bulls and the Yuchis, a relationship the Yuchis created and maintained while living in the backcountry.

Fortunately for historians, though, while the Yuchi were in the backcountry, they established other informal relationships that are easier to trace. Take, for example, the Yuchi connection to the Galphin-Barnard family of Indian traders. George Galphin began trading with the Lower Creeks in the late 1730s. At some point during the 1740s he started a plantation at Silver Bluff, south of Augusta and only two miles north of a Yuchi backcountry community. By 1751 Yuchi ties to Galphin were such that South Carolina's governor simply wrote they "live . . . at Silver Bluff."[26] These ties survived the Yuchis' return to Creek country. By 1757 Galphin was described as "of the Uchy Town in the Lower Creeks," and two years

TIMPOOCHEE BARNARD
AN UCHEE WARRIOR

PUBLISHED BY F. W. GREENOUGH, PHILAD.ª

FIGURE 6. Timpoochee Barnard as pictured around 1825 by
Charles Bird King in a lithograph by J. T. Bowen, as published in 1842
by Thomas McKinney and James Hall in their *History of the Indian
Tribes of North America*. The image is online at http://content.lib.
washington.edu/u?/mckenneyhall,587.

later he wrote that "the Euches was my sole Dependents"—that is, trading partners. This was not true—Galphin had "Dependents" all over Creek country and was most closely connected to the town of Coweta—but it was plausible enough that South Carolina's governor promised "to prevent . . . any . . . Interloper from interfering in your Trade." Galphin remained involved with the Yuchis until at least 1768, when he outfitted a trader bound for a Yuchi village. Another trader in that village at the same time was outfitted by Edward Barnard.[27] This was not a coincidence: the Barnards had strong ties to both the Yuchi and Galphin, ties that evidently dated to the Yuchis' years in the backcountry. John Barnard had command of Georgia's fort at Mount Pleasant by 1744, and he assumed some of Thomas Wiggan's accounts; he was most certainly in close contact with the Yuchi. Timothy Barnard was Galphin's nephew and partner, a trader to the Yuchi, the husband of a Yuchi woman, and the father of eleven Yuchi children. By century's end he and his family lived one and a half miles south of Beaver Dam, a Yuchi village; his son, Timpoochee Barnard (fig. 6), later assumed the title "Captain of [the] Uchees."[28] The Barnards' role in Yuchi life, like that of Galphin, was a legacy of the Yuchis' time in the backcountry.

Their personal charms aside, the Yuchis evidently invested time in Galphin and the Barnard family for reasons that went beyond friendship. Galphin was one of the most influential and prosperous traders of the eighteenth century, a man with a web of connections throughout the Native Southeast and the Euro-American world. The Barnards were not, perhaps, in this league, but they were nonetheless wealthy and well-positioned enough for Timothy Barnard to become the assistant to Benjamin Hawkins, the U.S. agent to the Creeks. Many of the Yuchis' connections, in fact, were to the influential and the powerful. This was true of their ties to Georgia and South Carolina's leaders, and it was also true of their contacts in Creek country. Aleck, for example, spoke for the Creeks at four conferences in the 1760s and was appointed a "Great Medal Chief" by the British; Cussita, Aleck's hometown, was centrally featured in the Creek origin story and remained "first in rank" among Creek towns at century's end.[29] The Yuchi, then, picked their friends with care. And once such relationships were established, the Yuchi showed an impressive ability to maintain them. Whatever else we take from their long-term ties with certain individuals and polities, it is clear that these connections challenge the stereotype of the Yuchi as an insular and hostile people adrift in an unwelcoming world.

Nevertheless, I am most emphatically not arguing that the Yuchi always got along with their Native and European neighbors. It is clear both that they did not and that this was to some extent a two-way street, with the Yuchi meeting insult with insult, hostility with hostility, aggression with aggression. Even leaving aside the uninformed "Yuchis are thieves" type of comments, the number of people who disliked the Yuchis in the eighteenth century is striking, as is Yuchi unwillingness to give an inch in conflicts with their neighbors. I have seen nothing like it in the records from the period, and it is tempting to speculate about the relationship between these conflicts and the Yuchis' cultural distinctiveness and sociopolitical continuity. Whatever the source or impact of this antagonism, however, the preceding discussion has shown that it is inaccurate to say the Yuchis fought with "the Creeks" or "the colonists." Instead, the Yuchis fought with some people and retained close ties to others. Thus it was no surprise to find that in less than two weeks' time, one Georgia colonist could write of Yuchis fleeing in fear after the arrival of a Creek party while another noted that the Yuchis were allied with the Creeks in a war against the Cherokees. It was also entirely in keeping with the Yuchi approach to outsiders that six months later, a Georgia minister could state that "the Uchee Indians . . . are very bad neighbors" only two days after Oglethorpe both noted that "I could not allow any settlements to be made" on Yuchi land and cautioned the same minister that "we must not injure the Indians, nor must they injure us."[30]

The Yuchi, it is clear, understood something that we tend to forget: the eighteenth-century Southeast was a place where nations and confederacies, colonies and empires, were not particularly cohesive entities. For a relatively powerless people intent on maintaining their cultural traditions and preserving their political independence, this lack of cohesion was a godsend. The Southeast was a place where the Yuchis could legitimately hope to have good relations with one set of Creeks or colonists and hostile relations with a different set.[31] In terms of the subject matter of this chapter, if we discuss Yuchi movements within the context of large-scale, homogeneous political units—from confederacy to colony and back again—their history looks chaotic. If we deemphasize the confederacy and the colony, however, and focus instead on the local and the personal, the chaos fades away and real continuities emerge. These continuities bring eighteenth-century Yuchi experiences into line with their more recent history of persistence and stability.

Notes

1. Chapman J. Milling, *Red Carolinians* (1940; repr., Columbia: University of South Carolina Press, 1969), 179–87; David Corkran, *The Creek Frontier, 1540–1783* (Norman: University of Oklahoma Press, 1967). Alan Gallay, *The Indian Slave Trade: The Rise of the English Empire in the American South, 1670–1717* (New Haven CT: Yale University Press, 2002), 16, 319–21, 335, 340.

2. For 1728, see W. Noel Sainsbury, ed., *Records in the British Public Record Office Relating to South Carolina, 1663–1782* (henceforth BPRO-SC), 36 vols., 13:150, microfilm, 11 reels in the collection of the Georgia Historical Society, Savannah. For 1732, see South Carolina's Council Journals (henceforth SC-CJ), 16 August 1732, South Carolina Department of Archives and History, Columbia. For the attacks, see BPRO-SC, 22:151; *South Carolina Gazette*, 30 June 1746. For "worst," see Allen D. Candler, Kenneth Coleman, and Milton Ready, eds., *The Colonial Records of the State of Georgia* (henceforth CRS-GA), 39 vols., 25:10 (vols. 1–19 and 21–26, Atlanta: Franklin Printing, 1904–16; vol. 20, Athens: University of Georgia Press, 1974; vols. 27–39, bound typescripts, available on microfilm at the University of Georgia). For 1741, see CRSGA, vol. 4 (Supplement): 122, and George F. Jones, Marie Hahn, Renate Wilson, and Don Savelle, eds., *Detailed Reports on the Salzburger Emigrants Who Settled in America . . . Edited by Samuel Urlsperger* (henceforth SALZ), 17 vols. (Athens: University of Georgia Press, 1968–95), 8:442–43. For "impaired," see CRSGA, 6:148. For "flee," see "John Tobler's Description of South Carolina (1754)," ed. Walter L. Robbins, *South Carolina Historical*

Magazine 71 (1970): 257–65, quotation on 264. For 1751, see William L. Mc-
Dowell Jr., ed., *Documents Relating to Indian Affairs, May 21, 1750–August
7, 1754,* and *Documents Relating to Indian Affairs, 1754–1765* (henceforth
DRIA), The Colonial Records of South Carolina, series 2 (Columbia: South
Carolina Archives Department, 1958, 1970), 1:170; for "women," see James
Adair, *The History of the American Indians,* ed. Kathryn E. Holland Braund
(1775; repr., Tuscaloosa: University of Alabama Press, 2005), 348. For 1752,
see CRSGA, 26:401. For the South Carolina coastal Yuchi, see the entry in SC-
CJ, 2 July 1751, containing "Accounts of Sundry murders, Violences and out-
rages Committed by a Band of Indians, upon our friendly and Neighbouring
Indians the Utchees settled among us near Port Royal." The accounts consist of
three letters—James Williams to Colonel John Mullryne, n.d.; Edward Morris
to Mullryne, n.d.; Thomas Wigg to Governor James Glen, 13 June 1751—later published in DRIA (1:78–79, 82). However, the published letters disguise the
fact that the victims of the attack were Yuchi. In the DRIA, the letters' one reference to the Yuchi was mistranscribed as "the Vetus" (1:78); moreover, the
DRIA reproduces only the letters themselves, not the council's discussion containing the above-mentioned reference to "Violences" visited upon the Yuchi.

    3. Angie Debo, *The Road to Disappearance* (Norman: University of Okla-
homa Press, 1941), 4, 195, 308; J. Leitch Wright Jr., *Creeks and Seminoles:
The Destruction and Regeneration of The Muscogulge People* (Lincoln: University of Nebraska Press, 1986), 110–11; Nancy Shoemaker, *A Strange Like-
ness: Becoming Red and White in Eighteenth-Century North America* (New
York: Oxford University Press, 2004), 93–94.

    4. Mark Van Doren, ed., *Travels of William Bartram* (1791; repr., New York:
Macy-Masius, 1928), quotations on 313 ("altogether," "in confederacy"), 312
("best situated"). Frank G. Speck, *Ethnology of the Yuchi Indians,* University
of Pennsylvania, Anthropological Publications of the University Museum, vol.
1 (Philadelphia: University Museum, 1909), quotations on 12 ("Creator"), 107
("perish"). Mary S. Linn, "Yuchi and Non-Yuchi: A Living Classification," *Florida Anthropologist* 50 (1997): 189–96, quotation on 190 ("Animacy"). Jerome
Courtonne, "List of Headmen of the Creeks," 17 October 1758 ("taken"), William H. Lyttelton Papers, Clements Library, University of Michigan, Ann Arbor. C. L. Grant, ed., *Letters, Journals, and Writings of Benjamin Hawkins,*
vol. 1: *1796–1801* (Savannah GA; Beehive Press, 1980), 313. For a contemporary Yuchi statement about their relationship to the sun, see the narrative provided by Newman Littlebear in Jason Baird Jackson, *Yuchi Ceremonial Life:
Performance, Meaning, and Tradition in a Contemporary American Indian
Community* (Lincoln: University of Nebraska Press, 2003), 69–73.

5. The ethnographic sources on Yuchi life that I have found most useful include Jackson, *Yuchi Ceremonial Life*; Jackson, "Yuchi," in *Handbook of North American Indians*, vol. 14: *Southeast*, ed. Raymond D. Fogelson (Washington DC: Smithsonian Institution, 2004), 415–28; Pamela S. Wallace, "Indian Claims Commission: Political Complexity and Contrasting Concepts of Identity," *Ethnohistory* 49 (2002): 744–67.

6. I am grateful to Richard D. Brown of the University of Connecticut for reminding me, in a non-Yuchi context, of the joke and, more important, for connecting it to the process of writing about peoples with relatively inaccessible pasts.

7. Grant, *Benjamin Hawkins*, 1:313 ("settled," "now"). For the map, see Gregory A. Waselkov, "Indian Maps of the Colonial Southeast," in *Powhatan's Mantle: Indians in the Colonial Southeast*, ed. Peter H. Wood, Gregory A. Waselkov, and M. Thomas Hatley (Lincoln: University of Nebraska Press, 1989), 292–343, especially 298, 329–32. Waselkov notes that this map contains "considerable geographical detail" but argues that its main function "was to portray social and political relationships" (300). Although the sociopolitical component of the map is striking, it is important that we not overlook what it has to tell us about spatial relations. The map was intended to be oriented east-west (that is, horizontally), but in order to read the key added by a French official it is always displayed on a north-south axis (that is, vertically). If the map is rotated clockwise ninety degrees—so that the circle "A" is on the right—then it becomes a remarkably accurate geographic depiction of the eighteenth-century Southeast. Read from east to west, it shows the British (A), the Lower Creek (B, C, D), the Upper Creek (G, H), and the Chickasaw (L). The Cherokee (E, F) are to the north of the Creek, while Mobile (I) and the Choctaw (K) are to the south and southwest respectively. Most important for the purposes of this essay, the three Lower Creek towns shown on map are presented in the correct geographic relationship to each other: first Coweta (B) in the north, then Cussita (C), and then Yuchi (D). I am grateful to Jeffrey Means for the suggestion that the map was intended to be read horizontally.

8. For 1735, see CRSGA, 20:316–18; for "Mico of the Uchesses," see CRSGA, 20:297, 400. For 1742, see J. H. Easterby, ed., *The Journals of the Commons House of Assembly*, The Colonial Records of South Carolina, series 1 (henceforth SC-JCHA), 10 vols. (Columbia: South Carolina Archives Department, 1951–86), 24 February 1742, 415, 418. For the 1749 party, see CRSGA, 6:295–97. For the Yuchis' presence, see "Presents Delivered by William Stephens ... to the Chieftains and Warriors," Joseph V. Bevan Papers, folder 5A, items 12 and 17, Georgia Historical Society, Savannah. For the traders, see

DRIA, 1:128–29. One of the traders, Stephan Forest, had apparently traded in one of these towns the year before; see CRSGA, 27:226.

9. For traveling, see, in addition to the previous note's references for 1735 and 1749, E. Merton Coulter, ed., *The Journal of Peter Gordan, 1732–1735* (Athens: University of Georgia Press, 1963), 48. For "War," see CRSGA, 4 (Supplement): 122. For "friends," see Robert C. McPherson, ed., *The Journal of the Earl of Egmont: Abstract of the Trustees Proceedings for Establishing the Colony of Georgia, 1732–1738* (Athens: University of Georgia Press, 1962), 175.

10. Unless otherwise noted, the quotations in this paragraph are drawn from the documents cited in notes 7 and 8. For "Mico," see CRSGA, 20:381–82.

11. Grant, *Benjamin Hawkins*, 1:313. For war with the Yamasee, see SC-CJ, 1 September 1726; for the scalps, see BPRO-SC, 13:145.

12. Jackson, *Yuchi Ceremonial Life*, 29–32. There is, however, one documented incident when Cussitas attacked Yuchis—a 1746 assault on a backcountry Yuchi community in which six Yuchis were killed and "many others" captured. The Lower Creeks later claimed that the Yuchis "deserved to be punishe'd" for leaving Creek country. If this claim is accurate, it suggests that Hawkins's much later report that Yuchi-Cussita hostilities stemmed from Aleck's marriage is inaccurate. Rather, it seems the Yuchis angered the Cussitas when they failed, from a Cussita perspective, to live up to their commitments. The ongoing nature of the Yuchi-Cussita relationship demonstrates that the two peoples found a way to defuse this crisis. For the attack, see BPRO-SC 22:151 ("many"); *South Carolina Gazette*, 30 June 1746. For the Cussitas, see SC-CJ, 11 March 1746. For the Lower Creeks, see Journal of South Carolina's Upper House of Assembly, 6 June 1747, 12, South Carolina Department of Archives and History, Columbia.

13. For Will, see CRSGA, 7:566–69. For "Uchee Will," see Grant, *Benjamin Hawkins*, 1:314. Will's real name may have been Huweley; SC-CJ, 22 November 1746.

14. The material on Aleck's movements after 1749 is drawn from Joshua Piker, "Colonists and Creeks: Rethinking the Pre-Revolutionary Southern Backcountry," *Journal of Southern History* 70 (2004): 503–40, especially 528. For Aleck in 1746, see *South Carolina Gazette*, 30 June 1746. For Aleck's wives, see Edmond Atkin to Henry Ellis, 25 January 1760, Henry Ellis Papers, folder 942, item 3, p. 15, Georgia Historical Society; CRSGA, 9:17–18.

15. For "deserting," see SC-JCHA, 15 May 1712; for "French," see William L. McDowell Jr., ed., *Journals of the Commissioners of the Indian Trade, September 20, 1710–August 29, 1718*, The Colonial Records of South Carolina, series 2, vol. 1 (Columbia: South Carolina Archives Department, 1955), 24.

For Yuchis in the Tuscarora War, see Gallay, *The Indian Slave Trade*, 267. For Yuchi-Yamasee relations, see BPRO-SC, 10:175; BPRO-SC, 13:145, 165; SC-CJ, 1 September 1726 and 15 November 1726. For 1728, see BPRO-SC, 13:150, 167.

16. SC-CJ, 18 January 1731 (Macgilvery), 3 March 1731 ("Corn"), and 16 August 1732 ("directed").

17. For "Protection," see BPRO-SC, 22:151; for "Settlements," see DRIA 1:85. For the plans, see SC-JCHA, 14 December 1737; SC-CJ, 8 April 1738, 27 August 1742 (Jenkins), 14 April 1743; SC-JCHA, 1 March 1743. For problems, see SC-JCHA, 27 May 1742 ("Complaints"), 26 March 1743 ("great Pitch"), 3 July 1744 ("Disorders"), 25 May 1742 ("Liberties"). For Yuchi visits, see SC-CJ, 26–28 May 1742 (excessive numbers) and 4 April 1761 ("friends"); DRIA, 1:431–33.

18. For Thomas Wiggan (called Wiggins in chapter 4 of this volume) in the 1720s, see SC-CJ, 1 September 1726, 24 August 1727, and 27 August 1727; BPRO-SC, 13:166. For Wiggan's house in Cussita, see SC-JCHA, 15 December 1736, 138–39; Anonymous, "A Ranger's Report of Travels with General Oglethorpe, 1739–1742," in *Travels in the American Colonies*, ed. Newton Mereness (New York: Macmillan, 1916), 218–36, especially 221. The former document mentions Wiggan interpreting for Aleck during a 1735 encounter in Cussita, although it is clear that Wiggan and Aleck disagree on the issue under consideration. For Eleazer Wiggan, see Gallay, *The Indian Slave Trade*, 320–21. If Thomas Wiggan's connections to the Yuchi began with Eleazer this would have been, at best, a mixed blessing given Eleazer's involvement in a 1713 plot to destroy a Cherokee-based Yuchi town. CRSGA, 4:86 ("long standing," "Stores"). For details on this plot, see chapter 3 of this volume.

19. For "Trader" and "town," see McPherson, *Journal of the Earl of Egmont*, 193. A Savannah merchant noted that "a near Nation called the Utchees" had multiple — "a few" — "Indian Traders," but this most likely refers to those traders who dealt not just with the Mount Pleasant Yuchi but also with those living around Augusta; John Brownfield to Thomas Tuckwell and Rowland Pytt, 6 April 1736, in John Brownfield's Copy Book, 1735–1740, microfilm in the Collections of the Georgia Historical Society; original in the Archives of the Moravian Church, Bethlehem, Pennsylvania. Daniel T. Elliott and Rita Folse Elliott, *Mount Pleasant: An Eighteenth-Century Yuchi Indian Town, British Trader Outpost, and Military Garrison in Georgia*, Lamar Institute Publication Series Report 10 (Watkinsville GA: Lamar Institute, 1990), 56; for food and pottery, see 30, 34. The ties with the garrison at Mount Pleasant may explain why the colonists in this area do not seem to have made the same complaints about Yuchi behavior that dot the records dealing with the other Yuchi backcountry communities, particularly those near Ebenezer and Fort Moore.

20. John Miller to John Stuart, 14 February 1764, in John Stuart to Thomas Gage, 11 April 1764, Thomas Gage Papers, Clements Library, University of Michigan, Ann Arbor. For Ladson in 1727, see BPRO-SC, 13:82; for 1743, see Thomas Stephens and Sir Richard Everhard, "A Brief Account of the Causes that Have Retarded the Progress of the Colony of Georgia in America [1743]," in *Collections of the Georgia Historical Society*, vol. 2 (Savannah: Printed for the Society, 1842), 88–161, especially 123; for 1752, see DRIA, 1:307. Ladson's son, Boson, was most likely not a Yuchi; see Claudio Saunt, *A New Order of Things: Property, Power, and the Transformation of the Creek Indians, 1733–1816* (New York: Cambridge University Press, 1999), 159, n. 105.

21. For mediation, see CRSGA, 20:14. For Oglethorpe and land, see "Letters from General Oglethorpe to the Trustees of the Colony and Others, from October 1735 to August 1744," in *Collections of the Georgia Historical Society*, vol. 3 (Savannah: Printed for the Society, 1873), 1–156, especially 35–37; Francis Moore, "A Voyage to Georgia, Begun in the Year 1735," in *Collections of the Georgia Historical Society*, vol. 1 (Savannah: Printed for the Society, 1840), 79–152, especially 102, 145–6; CRSGA, 6:147–48 ("Some may fancy"). For the alliance, see Kristian Hvidt, ed., *Von Reck's Voyage: Drawings and Journal of Philip Georg Friedrich von Reck* (Savannah GA: Beehive Press, 1980), 39; see also Jason Baird Jackson, "A Yuchi War Dance in 1736," *European Review of Native American Studies* 16 (2002): 27–33. For a concise statement by Oglethorpe regarding the Yuchis' military aid, see CRSGA, 6:147. For Yuchis taking refuge in Georgia, see CRSGA, vol. 4 (Supplement): 122; CRSGA, 26:38; SALZ, 15:69–70.

22. For Georgia officials dismissing Yuchi land claims, see CRSGA, 6:147–48; CRSGA, 26:26, 115. SALZ, 8:528 ("bad"); for a Yuchi-colonist conflict that nicely sums up each side's position, see SALZ, 8:436–38. For "Customary," see CRSGA, 27:64. For the murders, see Lachlan McGillivray to William Lyttelton, 3 September 1758, Lyttelton Papers, Journal of Joseph Wright's negotiations with the Lower Creeks, 20 July 1758 to 9 August 1758, in Henry Ellis to William Lyttelton, 8 September 1758, Lyttelton Papers; Edmond Atkin to Henry Ellis, 25 January 1760, Ellis Papers, 6–8, quotation on 8 ("In the end"). For the Yuchi party, see CRSGA, 8:295–97; for the headman's name, see CRSGA, 8:292.

23. Oglethorpe's note is quoted in SALZ 8:436. For James Hewitt's ties to the Yuchi, see CRSGA, 22 (part 2): 314; "Expence for the Cherokee, Chickasaws & other Indians that went with his Excellence General Oglethorpe on the Expedition to St. Augustine," 1740, Bevan Papers, folder 5A, item 31A.

24. For "local," see SALZ, 17:229; for "haunt," see Atkin to Ellis, 25 January 1760, Ellis Papers. For Yuchis who spoke English, see DRIA, 1:232; SC-CJ,

4 April 1761. For 1774, see *Georgia Gazette*, 27 April 1774. For Sabb, see DRIA, 1:431–3, 443. For Drayton, see SC-CJ, 22 February 1765.

25. For the Bull church, see William L. Ramsey, *The Yamasee War: A Study of Culture, Economy, and Conflict in the Colonial South* (Lincoln: University of Nebraska Press, 2008), 122. For the early 1740s, see SC-JCHA, 25 May 1742 and 3 July 1744. For a contemporary map showing Sheldon, the Bull's plantation in the area, see William De Brahm, "A Map of South Carolina and a Part of Georgia," in William P. Cumming, *The Southeast in Early Maps*, 3rd. ed., revised and enlarged by Louis De Vorsey Jr. (Chapel Hill: University of North Carolina Press, 1998), plate 59c. For Yuchi news, see SC-CJ, 23 August 1750; DRIA 1:421. For Yuchis living at "Laverill's Bay," near Sheldon, see DRIA 1:78; see note 2 to this chapter for this document's connection to the Yuchis. For corn, see SC-JCHA, 29 January 1751, 212. For 1752, see DRIA 1:232; for 1765, see SC-CJ, 22 February 1765. For Miller, see CRSGA, 4:203 ("Stores"). Atkin to Ellis, 25 January 1760, 7, Ellis Papers; John Miller to John Stuart, 14 February 1764, in John Stuart to Thomas Gage, 11 April 1764, Gage Papers; "David Taitt's Journal to and through [the] Lower Creek Nation," in *Documents of the American Revolution*, vol. 5: *Transcripts, 1772*, ed. K. G. Davies (Dublin, Ireland: Irish University Press, 1974), 273–82, quotation on 275 ("trader"); British Public Records Office, Colonial Office: America and West Indies, Plantations General, 1760–1784 (hereafter BPRO, CO) 5/77, fol. 164.

26. For Galphin's early career, see Kathryn E. Holland Braund, *Deerskins and Duffels: Creek Indian Trade with Anglo-America, 1685–1815* (Lincoln: University of Nebraska Press, 1993), 46. Braund notes (48) that Galphin "purchased [Silver Bluff] in the 1740s." For the location of the Yuchi town, see Adair, *History*, 348; for 1751, see DRIA, 1:170.

27. White Outerbridge to William Lyttelton, 24 March 1757, Lyttelton Papers; George Galphin to William Lyttelton, 5 April 1759, Lyttelton Papers; William Lyttelton to George Galphin, 4 June 1759, Lyttelton Papers. For Galphin and Edward Barnard employing traders at Buzzard Roost, see Deposition of William Frazier, 16 March 1768, in John Stuart to Thomas Gage, 2 July 1768, Gage Papers; for Buzzard Roost as a Yuchi village, see Robbie Ethridge, *Creek Country: The Creek Indians and Their World* (Chapel Hill: University of North Carolina Press, 2003), 64.

28. For John Barnard, see Daniel T. Elliot, *Ye Pleasant Mount: 1989 and 1990 Excavations*, Lamar Institute Publication Series Report 11 (Watkinsville GA: Lamar Institute, 1991), 17–18. For Wiggan signing a Creek account over to Barnard, see SC-JCHA, 6 April 1743, 363, 367. For Timothy's connections to Galphin, see BPRO, CO 5/80, fols. 80–81 (nephew), and Braund, *Deerskins*

& Duffels, 44–45 (partner). For Timothy as a Yuchi trader, see BPRO, CO 5/77, fol. 164; see also 5/81, fol. 296. For Timothy's family, see Grant, *Benjamin Hawkins*, 316; for the location of his house, see 313. For Timpochee, see Frederick Webb Hodge, ed., *Handbook of American Indians North of Mexico, Part 2* (Washington DC: Government Printing Office, 1910), 752 ("Captain"); Thomas L. McKenney and James Hall, *History of the Indian Tribes of North America*, vol. 2 (Philadelphia: F. W. Greenough, 1842), 25–28.

29. For Barnard as an assistant, see Grant, *Benjamin Hawkins*, 316. For Aleck at conferences in 1763, two in 1765, and 1768, see CRSGA 28(1):459; BPRO-SC, 30:73–74; Dunbar Rowland, ed., *Mississippi Archives, 1763–1766, English Dominion: Letters and Enclosures to the Secretary of State from Major Robert Farmer and Governor George Johnstone* (Nashville TN: Press of Brandon Printing Company, 1911), 197–8; CRSGA 9:667 and 10:575; BPRO, CO 5/70, fol. 89. For "Great Medal Chief," see BPRO, CO 5/70, fol. 86, and "At a Congress held at the Fort of Picolata," 1765, in James Stuart to Thomas Gage, 21 January 1766, Gage Papers. For the origin story and "rank," see Grant, *Benjamin Hawkins*, 326–27.

30. SALZ, 8:123 (fear); CRSGA, 8:122 (allied); SALZ, 8:442 ("bad") and 437 ("settlements," "injure").

31. For a Creek-centered discussion of this dynamic, see Joshua Piker, "'White and Clean' and Contested: Creek Towns and Trading Paths in the Aftermath of the Seven Years' War," *Ethnohistory* 50 (2003): 315–47; Piker, *Okfuskee: A Creek Indian Town in Colonial America* (Cambridge MA: Harvard University Press, 2004).

9. A Band of Outsiders
Yuchi Identity among the
Nineteenth-Century Florida Seminoles

~

The history of the Yuchi Indians in Florida is poorly known and not well understood. On the early end are seventeenth-century mentions of the Uchezes, on the later end we have Uchee Billy and Uchee Jack of Second Seminole War fame, with a long gap in between.[1] The picture is no brighter archaeologically. Ethnicity, a challenge to archaeologists in even the best of circumstances, has not been forthcoming from the slim archaeological record of the Florida Yuchi. The many unknowns are at once frustrating and invigorating. Mysteries still abound in southeastern ethnohistory. Rewards will come to new generations of scholars who are adept at merging archaeological discoveries with the documentary record. One such minor attempt is made here in the summary of evidence pertaining to the nineteenth-century Florida Yuchi. Most of this information derives from military and governmental attention given to the Florida Indians during the Second Seminole War (1835–42). This war resulted from the Indian resistance to their forced removal to Indian Territory and over its seven-year course brought the force of some 100,000 army regulars and militia to bear on the capture and collection of the 5,000 or so Native people whose occupation of Florida impeded expanded white settlement of the land. Historical documents from this period reflect the concern with this overall purpose but can nonetheless

FIGURE 7. Stone memorial commemorating the death of John Winfield
Scott McNeil, St. Augustine National Cemetery. Photograph by
Deborah L. Bauer.

serve as sources of ethnographic information. Such information is
particularly rich for the groups or bands comprising the larger entity collectively known as the Seminoles and much less so for the minority Yuchi population. We must try to make the best use of available information to reconstruct the Yuchi experience and place it
on the continuum of Yuchi culture and history. In doing so we dis-
cover that there are perhaps a few things that can be said about Yuchi identity during this time of great cultural upheaval and change.

We can begin by contemplating the lone public monument to the
Yuchi presence in Florida (fig. 7).[2] This is a simple gray slab in the
St. Augustine National Cemetery inscribed with the words "John
Winfield Scott McNeil, Killed by Uchee Billy, Mosquito Inlet, Sep-
tember 11, 1837." Here we have Uchee Billy's most famous inter-
section with recorded history, made memorable by the fact that the
nineteen-year-old McNeil was the nephew of President Franklin
Pierce.[3] McNeil and his 2nd regiment of Dragoons had crawled on

their hands and knees through the swamp to stage a dawn surprise attack on the Yuchi village, having been led to the small island refuge by a Seminole captured in a similar raid on King Philip's camp at dawn the day before.[4] Although truly surprised, the Yuchi managed to fire a few wild shots in the confusion, one of them from Uchee Billy piercing the breast of the gallant, unlucky lieutenant, the only military casualty of the day.

Details of the capture of Billy and his brother Uchee Jack from firsthand sources give us the most prolonged glimpses of Yuchi ways of life during this period, if we accept Billy and Jack as being representative.[5] The episode begins on 10 September 1837, when five companies of troops, guided by a Black Seminole informant, charge the camp of King Philip and his family in the vicinity of the Tomoka River, capturing him and ten of the eleven men, women, and children there, including one man named Tomoka John.[6] It is Tomoka John, not the Black Seminole, who leads the soldiers to the Uchee Billy camp some ten miles distant, suggesting that the Black Seminole did not know of this location. This could mean that the Yuchis were less connected to the Black Seminoles than was Philip; indeed, the Black Seminoles were known to have been in the area for the purpose of digging coontie roots for Philip and others, which they evidently were not doing for Billy's band, as we will see.[7]

Guided by Tomoka John but commanded by Lts. Peyton and the ill-fated McNeil, two fifty-man columns circled Billy's camp and lay concealed in the palmettos awaiting orders for a dawn attack on the morning of 11 September. The surprise attack, given away only by last-minute barking of Yuchi dogs, had the desired result, and amidst Yuchi war whoops and the firing of carbines, chaos quickly ensued. Here we can visualize the scene as described by one of the participants: "The wildness and interest of the scene was considerably augmented by the glaring eyes, streaming black hair and red-painted faces of the savages, as they danced and skipped about in fruitless efforts to escape. They evidently had not the time to make their toilet becomingly, for the reception of the early visitors; for we found them either perfectly naked, or only half clad with hunting shirts, their faces however covered with war-paint."[8] We learn further in this account that Billy had fired his weapon from behind a makeshift breastwork of bags of coontie, that there were "Indian spoils" in the camp that the soldiers were compelled to destroy, and that Tomoka John's participation in this excursion might have been inspired by the incentive to plunder Billy's camp. A number of Indian ponies were also taken. These ponies carried makeshift litters constructed of saplings and the many hides found in the camp, for the purpose of transporting the several wounded Indians and the body of McNeil.

From this description we can surmise several things. First, Billy and the Yuchis might have been little known to those Black Seminoles associated with Philip and apparently had no Black Seminoles of their own. Further, we learn that Tomoka John knew where the camp was and what it held, because he had recently lived there with Billy. This indicates some fluidity to band composition but an ultimate lack of allegiance to the Yuchi line. Both these observations reinforce the social separation between the Yuchi band and the neighboring Seminoles. This separation had some political expression as well, as we see in a story reported in the *Army and Navy Chronicle* on 6 May 1837 (months before the attack and Billy's capture) stating that the "runaway Creeks and Euchees are coming into this place," Fort Mellon, on the St. Johns River at Lake Monroe.[9] The "runaways," according to the paper, "express their desire to remain and emigrate with the friendly Creeks now at this place, in preference to moving off with the Seminoles."[10] A second report places Billy at Fort Mellon at this time.[11]

Materially, however, the Yuchis seem to have been indistinguishable from their Seminole counterparts. War paint, war whoops, hunting shirts, dried hides, use of coontie, even the location of the camp itself on a small pine island surrounded by wet swamp, are all in common with Seminole traits and are seen throughout Florida by mid-1837, a full year and a half into the Second Seminole War. As can be seen by reviewing the Yuchi archaeological record, material culture alone will not lead us to Yuchi identity in any simple way. I say this with the understanding that detailed excavations of a Florida Yuchi site have yet to be undertaken. When and if this happens, surprises may result from a more detailed examination of Yuchi materiality.

The capture of Billy and Jack did not entirely eradicate the Yuchi in Florida. Testimony from a captured Seminole warrior from the Withlacoochee River area west of Fort King (present-day Ocala) on 13 January 1837 indicates that a village of Euchees, together with a village of Tallassees and one of Choceochutties, comprised a camp living on Clear-water Creek, probably in the vicinity of present-day Crystal River on Florida's west coast, some eighty-five miles west of Billy's base at Spring Garden.[12] Minor mentions of Yuchis in 1841 place them at Fort Brooke during larger deportations of Seminoles, Creeks, Tallahassees, and Mickasukies.[13] In February of that year a single Yuchi guided a company of dragoons in the search for the Creek warrior Octiarche who was raiding settlements along the Suwannee River.[14] Given that person's familiarity with the terrain of the west-central region of Florida, it is possible that he derived from the Clear-water Creek village described. On 14 June 1842 a Halburta Harjo and three "Euchees" arrived with Seminoles at Fort Gibson during their deportation to Indian Territory.[15] On 22 February 1843 Yuchis were among the 250 Indians deported from Fort Brooke; these men were said to have been "faithful negotiators" and were therefore rewarded with their own special boat ride.[16]

By 1842 both the generals and the politicians begrudgingly realized that total removal of Florida Indians through military means would not be feasible. The escalating and increasingly effective military effort only hardened the will of those elusive few to remain in Florida. Given time, the establishment of trust, and the inevitable recognition on the part of the Indians that their future in Florida was doomed, they would soon enough give themselves up and join their brethren in Indian Territory, or so the thinking was in 1842. The immediate reality was that among the remaining warriors enumerated (70 Seminoles, 30 Mickasukies, 12 Creeks, four Choctaws) four of them were Yuchi.[17] We do not know if these men had families remaining with them and, if so, how many of the approximately 180 women, children, and elders still thought to be in the Florida swamps were Yuchi. We do see Yuchis included among Seminoles mentioned in the Charlotte Harbor area of the southwest Gulf coast in 1847.[18]

There also is single reference to a lone Yuchi residing with the Muskogee-speaking Chipco and his band north of Lake Okeechobee in 1849. Chipco's band was separated by language and distance from most of the remaining Seminoles in Florida, who were clustered in the Big Cypress or in the Everglades south of the lake. According to Indian agent William Casey, members of the Chipco group were called "outsiders" by the rest and were outlawed by the larger group at the Green Corn Dance and forced into further exile.[19] Although this person seems to be in the running for the "last" Yuchi in Florida, it is possible that this group or their descendants escaped the final episode of deportation in 1858 and thus contributed to the ancestry of the modern members of the Seminole Tribe and Miccosukee Tribe in Florida. Even so, we lose clear historical sight of the Yuchis after 1849, when their documented number had dwindled to one, and Seminole oral history seems not to have preserved their memory. Billy himself died in captivity in St. Augustine in mid-November 1837, several days before Wildcat's famed escape through the bars of their cell in Fort Marion.

Scholarly statements to the effect that the Yuchi in Florida contributed to emergence of the multiethnic Seminole are intriguing but remain unconfirmed.[20] For the years between 1821 and 1849 we can be reasonably sure that the various "Yuchi" of documentary mention were in fact some coherent association of people who were continuously perceived by the outside world as having a common "Yuchi" identity. It is true that most of these references (scattered and very few as they are) are from government or military sources and may therefore be perpetuating commonly held misperceptions rather than presenting ethnographic reality, but still it is reasonable to accept that for this nearly thirty-year period there were people in Florida that everyone, including themselves, recognized as Yuchi.

From the historical record emerge some general statements about the Yuchi during this period. One band or village lived in west-central Florida, north of Fort Brooke (Tampa) and south of the Suwannee River. A second and better-known band had their geographical center in the Spring Garden area of the St. Johns River.[21] This is on the east side of Lake Woodruff at or near Ponce de Leon Springs, northwest of present Deland, in the east-central region of Florida just inland from the Atlantic coastal strand. This was Uchee Billy's group. They were coerced into moving from their lands around the lake in 1823 by Joseph Woodruff, who coveted the fertile uplands that Billy had planted in corn.

Both Yuchi groups were recognized by others as having distinct identity. They were allied with the other bands who came to be called the Seminoles in the resistance effort but lived in their own villages and were politically separate from the Seminoles. Likewise they were politically separate from the Creeks. The documents also leave us with serious questions about genealogical connections between the Uchee Billy Yuchis of the post-1820s and some well-known Seminole lineages established in Florida prior to the 1821 transfer of Florida from Spain to the United States. After 1849 we have nothing, and before 1821 we have multiple threads that may or may not be connected.

One potential thread of consistency is the mention of Uchee Billy. We can know who the Yuchis were in part by answering the question: Who was Uchee Billy? Documents from the 1820s note him as a "chief."[22] They further indicate that he moved his town (and band) to the relatively inaccessible location on the St. Johns following the 1818 attacks by Andrew Jackson on the Mikasuki towns east of present-day Tallahassee in what was then Spanish Florida.[23] The Mikasuki connection is important because it places Uchee Billy in direct relationship with this stream of people who would eventually become known in the composite as the Seminoles. Charles Fairbanks goes so far as to state, based on an obscure military account, that the Mikasuki chief John Hicks (fig. 8) was Uchee Billy's father.[24] John Hicks (also known as Tokose Emathla) was a leader of

FIGURE 8. Tuko-See-Mathla, aka John Hicks, from an 1826 painting by Charles Bird King. Library of Congress Prints and Photographs Division, Washington DC, LC-USZC4-2904 (color film copy transparency); digital ID cph 3g02904, http://hdl.loc.gov/loc.pnp/cph.3g02904.

an eastern panhandle Mikasuki band displaced by Jackson's invasion, eventually resettling in the Alachua area before moving southwest into the Withlacoochee River swamps and Lake Tsala Apopka wetlands in the years prior to the Second Seminole War. To quote Fairbanks, "The close association of Uchee towns and Mikasuki indicates an amalgamation of originally different elements going on among the Seminole in this period."[25] But if Uchee Billy was in fact a Mikasuki by virtue of descent from John Hicks, then his distance from the proto-Seminoles was really not so great, and his identity as a "Yuchi" continuous with the once larger and much more dominant Yuchi groups of colonial Georgia is thrown into some doubt.

It is tempting to align Uchee Billy with Bartram's "Yuchi Town" of the upper Chattahoochee in a chain of descent, for example, but to do so and keep the John Hicks connection as still true means either that John Hicks married a Yuchi woman and then Billy as the offspring ended up with a name memorializing this relationship or that Yuchi and Mikasuki are basically inseparable as ethnographic constructs.[26] This does not seem to be a satisfactory solution given that "Mikasuki" and "Yuchi" bands or towns continue to receive distinct documentary mention in the period from 1820 to the 1840s. And if Billy was fathered by such a well-known Mikasuki as John Hicks, would having a Yuchi mother automatically designate him as a Yuchi? Was Uchee Billy really a Yuchi? What did others mean in calling him this? In what way was Uchee Billy Yuchi? In any case, by 1818 the name seems to have stuck, and Billy was considered a chief. An officer in the Jackson invasion reported that a town headed by Billy consisted of seventy-five persons and was located near the Mikasuki settlement east of present-day Tallahassee.[27] Fairbanks pushes the Mikasuki connection even further by suggesting that Billy's move to Spring Garden intentionally placed him in proximity to King Philip's band, also well-established Mikasukis who were militantly anti-American in their attitudes and actions but who stayed somewhat out of the mainstream of activity. The historian Mark Boyd accepts the designation of Uchee Billy as John Hicks's son (without citation), puts him in collusion with

Philip in the raiding and destruction of the St. Johns sugar plantations, and implicates him in the murder of a member of a plantation family.[28] This was followed up by the story, soon shown to be
false, of the retaliatory killing of Billy by soldiers in March 1836.[29]

Disentangling these issues is nearly impossible given the limitations of source materials and is made even more Gordian by the
sheer complexity of the times in which this story unfolded. To echo
Fairbanks, this was a time of cultural amalgamation, to which we
can also add the processes of fragmentation and ethnogenesis resulting from pioneering movements into new territory as complicat-
ing circumstances. The preceding summary very nearly exhausts
the known facts about the Yuchi in nineteenth-century Florida. The
question now becomes: Is there a productive way forward for Florida Yuchi scholarship?

Three broad areas of inquiry lend themselves to further exploration and have the potential to shape further knowledge about the
unique position of Yuchi ethnohistory in Florida. First, we can ask:
How did events and experiences in the early Territorial Period of
American Florida contribute to Yuchi social realignments? It is clear
that the Yuchis kept themselves apart from the main body of Seminoles (even if they too were decentralized) politically, economically, and culturally. The Seminoles too recognized the ethnic distinction of the Yuchi. There were powerful external forces acting on the
separate Seminole bands to promote the emergence of a "pan-Sem-
inole" identity, particularly in response to the joint governmental-
military efforts to remove or eradicate them, yet the Yuchi remained
apart and retained their singular identity.

Although Yuchi ethnogenesis has deep roots in the Southeast
before their experience in Florida, the ethnic reshaping undergone
by the various bands in the process of becoming Seminole in nineteenth-century Florida seems not to have occurred among the Yuchi. The Yuchi responded to external pressures differently and to
some extent resisted amalgamation. Looking at the list of chiefs (and
their towns) invited to the Treaty of Moultrie Creek proceedings in
September 1823, we see the absence of Yuchi even though the town

lists provided previously to the American delegation clearly identified them.[30] This indicates that the government left the Yuchi out of the recognition process that was the first step in removal, and it is therefore easy to see that the Yuchi would interpret this non-acknowledgment as a proxy approval of autonomy.

The second line of inquiry leads us to an anthropological puzzle. As contemporary Yuchis will quickly report, square ground ceremonies clearly were of vital importance to twentieth-century Yuchi. If square ground ceremonies were continuous from the early historic period through the twentieth century, is there any evidence (even if only inferred) of them among the Yuchi in Florida? This brings the related question: Did clans exist among the Florida Yuchi? Here we are confronted with demographic issues and questions of group size. Uchee Billy's social ties most likely were with Philip's band, but does this mean that the Yuchis and Philip's Seminoles shared clans? Would it have been possible for the Florida Yuchis, at least by the 1820s, to exist clanless? Anthropological thought experiments unfold and can be tested in the comparative anthropological literature.

The third line of investigation comes from archaeological research. Archaeological surveys in the Spring Garden–DeLeon Springs area have yielded Chattahoochee Brushed pottery sherds and a rolled metal Kaskaskia point for tipping arrows.[31] Brushed pottery is a minority ware in eighteenth-century Yuchi sites in Georgia, so its presence here is not unexpected.[32] The historical record of occupations in this area is not precise enough to attribute these artifacts exclusively to the Yuchi presence, and archaeological testing has been limited in scope; thus a sustained effort to define either a Yuchi or a Seminole archaeological record here has not occurred. The sherds of the familiar brushed pottery are scattered in several repositories and await what could be productive comparative reanalysis of both style and paste composition.[33] Such analyses would lead to productive understandings about technology and economy (by sourcing the clays) and, perhaps, social interactions and trade relations between Native peoples in Florida in the early to mid-nineteenth century. We might also explore further the possible connection of isolated finds of brushed pottery vessels along the St. Johns River to Yuchi occupations in the area.[34] These finds, and others along the Kissimmee River in south-central Florida, have not been convincingly attributed to historically identified Seminole groups in the region and, because of their geographical placement, suggest some relationship with the ethnographically known (and present-day) Creek-speaking Seminoles who now live on the Brighton Reservation on the northwest edge of Lake Okeechobee. These ceramics exist in various accessible repositories, and potential exists for them to be productively subjected to comparative technological study with the purpose of eliciting the behavioral, social, and cultural correlates of vessel attributes such as form, size, and variability in clays.

We can hope that the consideration of Yuchi ethnohistory in Florida will move beyond culture history and enter more anthropologically fruitful realms. To do so, we will have to take advantage of small clues and look for opportunities to expand our knowledge by using rich existing bodies of information to interrogate the Yuchi experience specifically. Coontie gathering is a case in point. We know from the Uchee Billy capture accounts that bales of gathered coontie were present at the Yuchi camp. We also know from abundant ethnohistorical accounts that coontie gathering and processing required scheduled movements to areas where the plants were locally abundant, that a division of labor made the actual harvesting economically efficient, and that the processing of the root to make edible flour required multiple steps to remove toxic plant poisons.[35] Given that the Yuchi seem to have lived in small and somewhat discrete, isolated groups, how would a commitment to coontie harvesting have been accomplished? What consequences might there have been for the labor relations between the Yuchi and neighboring bands of Seminoles and Black Seminoles? We do know that this kind of activity would have implications for the lived experience of the Yuchis and, if nothing else, this knowledge helps us animate them on the cultural and natural landscapes of nineteenth-century Florida.

From this brief account the limitations on Florida Yuchi ethnohistory should be abundantly clear. There is nothing remotely close to an ethnographic account of the Florida Yuchis from the early to the mid-nineteenth century. Ethnonyms are inconsistent, conflicting, paradoxical, and perplexing. The archaeological record remains unexplored and has not (yet) yielded to direct historic approaches. But what is known of the Yuchi story demonstrates that not all the Native ethnic and cultural dynamics operating in Seminole Wars–era Florida can be subsumed under the "Seminole" label. There is value in understanding, through specific case studies, that ethnogenesis is not an inevitable outcome but rather is the product of specific historical cultural contingencies, involving selective creative responses to the circumstances of the moment through the transmission (and invention) of cultural traditions, not through single causes and effects. The Yuchis seem to have been on the outside of the process of Seminole ethnogenesis, which was well under way during the Seminole Wars era.[36] The timing and tempo of the Yuchi ethnic process is distinct and not exactly in tune with the Seminoles. This observation forces us to confront the cultural and ethnic complexities that characterized the native postcolonial Southeast and takes our Yuchi frame of reference back to its pre-Florida roots. More precise understandings of the role and placement of the Florida experience in the broad continuum of Yuchi culture change awaits further research. Inasmuch as this research would elucidate broader processes of ethnogenesis and culture change, it would be doubly useful.

Notes

1. The name Yuchi is spelled different ways in the primary documents. The terms Euchee, Uchee, Yuchee, and other variants appear in the sources, all appearing to refer to the group or groups called here the Yuchi. Unless citing a specific source, I use the Yuchi spelling as consistently as possible to conform to modern usage. The name Uchee Billy seems most consistently to be spelled thus and I do not convert it.

2. There is (or was) a historical marker on private property in Walton County, in the Florida Panhandle, commemorating one Sam Story, also alleged to be Timpoochee Kinard, "Chief of the Euchees." There is a lively Internet debate about the Yuchi identity of this individual and strong historical

evidence to the contrary. Sources can be found at a link named "Sam Story," maintained by Baker Block Museum Educational Services, Baker, Florida, www.bakerblockmuseum.org and www.bakerblockmuseum.org/timpooch ee.htm (accessed 12 December 2010). Also see en.wikipedia.org/wiki/Sam _Story (accessed 1 December 2010). Some of the controversy results from failure to distinguish Timpoochee Kinnard, of Creek ancestry, and Timpoochee Bernard, a Georgia Yuchi.

3. John K. Mahon, *History of the Second Seminole War* (Gainesville: University of Florida Press, 1967), 212. This classic volume still stands as the basic modern reference work for the Second Seminole War.

4. John T. Sprague, *Origin, Progress, and Conclusion of the Florida War* (Gainesville: University of Florida Press, 1964), 216, 218. This is a detailed and comprehensive history of the Second Seminole War compiled by a participant in that conflict and citing many firsthand accounts and primary documents. Originally published in 1848, this study was reprinted in 1964 by the University Press of Florida, with an introduction by John K. Mahon, and more recently republished by the Seminole Wars Historic Foundation (Tampa FL: University of Tampa Press, 2000).

5. The *Army and Navy Chronicle*, published in Washington City and edited by B. Homans, compiled military documents and contemporary newspaper sources to create a digest of period military affairs. Listings for 6 and 8 May 1837, 18 September 1837, and 5 October 1837 describe Yuchi activities in the middle St. Johns River region, with the latter two citations detailing the attack on and capture of Uchee Billy. A second primary source is J. R. Motte's *Journey into Wilderness: An Army Surgeon's Account of Life in Camp and Field during the Creek and Seminole Wars, 1836–1838*, ed. James F. Sunderman (Gainesville: University of Florida Press, 1953), 120–23, 125, 129, 140, 277, and 280 for Uchee Billy, and 312 for "Uchee Indians."

6. King Philip was the principal leader of Seminoles living in the area of the middle St. Johns River and the father of the historically prominent warrior known as Wildcat or Cooacochee. See Sprague, *Florida War*, 98.

7. *Army and Navy Chronicle*, 18 September 1837.

8. J. R. Motte, *Journey into Wilderness*, 122–23.

9. *Army and Navy Chronicle*, 6 May 1837.

10. *Army and Navy Chronicle*, 6 May 1837.

11. *Army and Navy Chronicle*, 8 May 1837.

12. Sprague, *Florida War*, 438.

13. Sprague, *Florida War*, 440. Frank Laumer, ed., *Amidst a Storm of Bullets: The Diary of Lt. Henry Prince in Florida, 1836–1842* (Tampa FL:

University of Tampa Press, 1998), 70. Note that the spelling of Mickasukies follows Prince's spelling. Elsewhere in this chapter the more accepted spelling Mikasuki is used. The historic Mikasuki should not be confused with the modern Miccosukee Tribe.

14. Sprague, *Florida War*, 501

15. Cited as microfilm 640, roll 4, frames 720–21 under the heading of Seminole Emigration records on the website of the Seminole Nation of Oklahoma, www.seminolenation-indianterritry.org/provisions1842.htm (accessed 28 February 2006).

16. Sprague, *Florida War*, 510, 512.

17. Sprague, *Florida War*, 510, 512.

18. Sprague, *Florida War*, 510.

19. James W. Covington, *The Seminoles of Florida* (Gainesville: University Press of Florida, 1993), 115.

20. Jason Baird Jackson, "Yuchi," in *Handbook of North American Indians*, vol. 14: *Southeast*, ed. Raymond D. Fogelson (Washington DC: Smithsonian Institution, 2004), 415.

21. William Simmons, *Notices of East Florida with an Account of Seminole Nation of Indians by a Recent Traveller in the Province* (Charleston SC, 1822; repr. Gainesville: University of Florida Press, 1973), 59; and see Covington, *The Seminoles*, 48).

22. Charles H. Fairbanks, *Ethnohistorical Report on the Florida Indians* (New York: Garland, 1974), 230. This is an excellent source with many primary references for the era from the Spanish mission period through American rule leading to the 1823 Treaty of Moultrie Creek.

23. Fairbanks, *Ethnohistorical Report*, 204.

24. Fairbanks, *Ethnohistorical Report*, 230.

25. Fairbanks, *Ethnohistorical Report*, 230.

26. Chad O. Braley, *Yuchi Town (1RU63) Revisited: Analysis of the 1958–1962 Excavations* (Athens GA: Southeastern Archaeology Services, 1998).

27. Hugh Young, "A Topographic Memoire on East and West Florida with Itineraries of General Jackson's Army, 1818," *Florida Historical Quarterly* 13 (1934–35): 82–104, 82; Fairbanks, *Ethnohistorical Report*, 234.

28. Mark F. Boyd, "The Seminole War: Its Background and Onset," *Florida Historical Quarterly* 30 (1951): 3–115, 66.

29. M. M. Cohen, *Notices of Florida and the Campaigns*, (Charleston SC: Burges and Honour, 1836; Gainesville: University of Florida Press, 1964), 48, 163, 169, 170, and 213. This is a useful but highly idiosyncratic firsthand account of the events in first year of the Second Seminole War. Although Cohen

was wrong in identifying the corpse as Uchee Billy, his description does provide interesting details of dress and physical appearance and reveals popular attitudes of the time regarding Native Americans. In referring to the body of Euchee Billy or King Billy he writes (163) that "he is one of the most elegantly formed men I have ever beheld—chest broad and high, leg and ancle development beautifully rounded, the muscles being greatly developed by constant exercise." After noting small arms, strikingly small hands, and black hair clipped to form a "fowl's comb" on the top of the head, Cohen notes: "Billy is regularly marked with lines from the ancle to the hip. These scars are produced by scraping with the sharp teeth of the garr fish." Cohen heads this section with the title "Euchee Billy, or Billy Hicks, described," suggesting a possible source for Boyd's statement connecting Uchee Billy with the Mikasuki John Hicks. Cohen presents a phrenological analysis of Billy's "propensities," "sentiments," and "intellectual faculties" based on the examination of his skull (170–71).

30. Fairbanks, *Ethnohistorical Report*, 251–58.

31. James S. Dunbar, *Ponce de Leon Springs, Archaeological and Historic Resource Assessment, December 1980*, Florida Master Site File Survey Report #641, Tallahassee. James S. Dunbar, "The Kaskaskia Projectile Point: A Seminole Indian Metal Arrow Point Recently Recognized in Florida," *Florida Anthropologist* 31 (1981): 166–68; Archaeological Site Form for 8VO3441, Spring Garden 2, Florida Master Site File, Tallahassee; John M. Goggin, *Space and Time Perspective in Northern St. Johns Archeology, Florida*, Yale University Publication in Anthropology 47 (New Haven CT: Yale University Press, 1952), 90. Goggin briefly describes archaeological sites designated Vo 29, 30, and 31 in the presumed vicinity of the Yuchi settlement at Spring Garden but lists only artifacts and occupations attributable to late prehistoric groups.

32. Daniel T. Elliot and Rita F. Elliott, *The Yuchi Village at Mount Pleasant*, Lamar Institute Publication Series Report 137 (Savannah GA: Lamar Institute, 1997), 9–11.

33. John M. Goggin, "Seminole Pottery," in *Indian and Spanish Selected Writings*, ed. Charles H. Fairbanks, Irving Rouse, and William C. Sturtevant (Coral Gables FL: University of Miami Press, 1964). Goggin describes Yuchi pottery from the historic Southeast (206), cites Speck's study, and indicates an association between Yuchi and heavily brushed pottery with globular, constricted mouth vessel forms. Pottery vessels from the St. Johns River-Orlando-Kissimmee River region are shown (189, 193, 196).

34. Goggin, "Seminole Pottery," 182.

35. John K. Small, "Seminole Bread—The Conti," *Journal of New York Botanical Garden* 22 (1921): 121–37; Hale G. Smith, "The Ethnological and

Archaeological Significance of Zamia," *American Anthropologist* 53 (1951): 238–44.

36. Brent Richards Weisman, *Like Beads on a String: A Culture History of the Seminole Indians in Northern Peninsular Florida* (Tuscaloosa: University of Alabama Press, 1989); Brent R. Weisman, "Nativism, Resistance, and Ethnogenesis of the Florida Seminole Identity," *Historical Archaeology* 41 (2007): 195–208.

Contributors

~

Daniel T. Elliott is president of the Lamar Institute.

H. Thomas Foster II is an associate professor of anthropology at the University of Tulsa.

Steven C. Hahn is an associate professor of history at St. Olaf College.

Jason Baird Jackson is an associate professor of folklore and American studies at Indiana University.

Mary S. Linn is the associate curator of Native American Languages at the Sam Noble Oklahoma Museum of Natural History and an associate professor of anthropology in the Department of Anthropology, both at the University of Oklahoma.

Joshua Piker is an associate professor of history at the University of Oklahoma.

Brett Riggs is a research archaeologist in the Research Laboratories in Archaeology and an adjunct associate professor in the Department of Anthropology, both at the University of North Carolina–Chapel Hill.

Stephen Warren is an associate professor of history at Augustana College, where he also serves as department chair.

Brent R. Weisman is a professor of anthropology in the Department of Anthropology at the University of South Florida, where he also serves as department chair.

John E. Worth is an assistant professor of anthropology in the Division of Anthropology and Archaeology at the University of West Florida.

Index

~

Abeika. *See* Abihkas

Abihkas (Creek town or town grouping), 56, 174–75

Acmucieche (Creek leader), 146

active-stative (linguistic feature), 15
Adair, James, 173

agent-patient (linguistic feature), 7, 15

Alabama, state of, xiv, 33, 36, 39, 51, 60, 102–18, 103, 160, 177. *See also* Yuchi Town

Alabama language, 156

Alabama River, 51–52

Alabamas (as indigenous group, Creek town or town grouping), 67n39, 174–75, 193

Alachua FL, 223

Aleck (Cussita chief), 137–38, 143–44, 194–96, 199, 204, 209n12

Algic (language family), 13, 15

Algonkian-Ritwan (language family). *See* Algic

Algonquians (as linguistically and culturally related peoples of the Northeast), 129, 167, 172

amalgamation, 50

Ambrosino, Jim, 109

American Revolution, 69n53, 145, 178

Andres, Usanaca (Timucuan chief), 130

Anglican Church, 149n21, 162

animacy and inanimacy (linguistic feature), 5

Apalachees, 55, 70n59, 128, 132, 167–68, 170

Apalachicola (as a Creek town), 105–6, 132, 133, 146. *See also* Pallachacolas

Appalachian Mountains, xiv, xxiii, 33, 46, 126, 178

Arbika. *See* Abihkas

Archdale, John, 166

architecture, xix, 76, 89, 99n49, 111–13, 116, 165, 169, 172, 191. *See also* house, war; square, town

areal linguistic features, 4

Ashley River, 166

assimilation, xv,

Atakapa language, 15, 22

Atasi (Creek town), 68n42

Athabaskan (language family), 17, 23

Atkin, Edmond, 157, 176

Atlantic world, the, xvi, xxvii, 49

Augusta GA, 51, 78–79, 127, 142–45, 164–66, 170, 202, 210n19. *See also* Fort Moore

Ayers, Thomas, 136

Ballard, W. Lewis, 7

Barnard, Edward, 204

Barnard, John, 80–81, 204

Barnard, Timothy, 81, 116, 204

Barnard, Timpoochee (Yuchi leader), 81, 116, 203–4, 227n2

Barnard, William, 81

food and foodways, 87, 89, 98n44, 173, 198, 217, 226. *See also* fasting
Fort Benning, 97n34, 107–9, 118, 173
Fort Brooke, 219, 221
Fort Gibson, 219
Fort King, 219
Fort Ligonier (archaeological site), 89
Fort Marion, 220
Fort Mellon, 218
Fort Mitchell, 116
Fort Moore, 75, 149
Fort Picolata, 79, 143, 145
Fort Prince George, 75, 89
Foster, Thomas, 150n24
fragmentation, social process of, 224
Frederica GA, 98n42, 135, 137, 142
French, xxiii, 34, 53–54, 127–28, 164, 168, 175, 178, 197
French and Indian War, 143–44, 174–75
French Broad River, 36

Gallatin, Albert, 12
Gallay, Alan, xxii
Galphin, George, 75, 202, 204
Galphin Trading Post Site (archaeological site), 93n5
Gatschet, Albert, 13, 178
gender: sociocultural concepts of, xxxivn25, 172–73; and Yuchi grammar, 7
genocide, xv, 158
Georgia, xiv, 33–34, 39, 52, 73–91, 98n42, 102–18, 123–47, 171–72, 189, 191–206
Georgia Assistants, 125
Germans, xv, 77, 79, 87, 171–72. *See also* Salzburgers
gifts. *See* exchange
Glen, James, 106, 175–78
Glover, Charlesworth, 132–34, 170–71, 173
Godin, David, 175–76
Gravier, Jacques, 161
Great Lakes (region), 164, 172
green corn ceremony, xxiv–xxv, xxxivn24, 44, 61n10, 76–77, 90,

95n17, 99n49, 145–46, 160, 220. *See also* dances; ritual
Grey, William, 142
Guale (province), xxiii
Gulf (language family), 15–16
Gulf Coast (region), 51, 168, 220
guns and gun parts, 89, 112, 132, 142, 164, 167, 217

Haas, Mary R., 11, 15, 17, 21–22, 23
hair and hairstyles, 44, 98n42, 161–63, 165, 230
Halburta Harjo (Seminole or Yuchi man), 219
Hamilton, Christopher, 108
Hamilton, T. M., 112
Handbook of North American Indians, xxii, xxvii
Hargrave, Michael, 109
Hawkins, Benjamin, xxi, 104, 106–7, 113, 116–17, 137–38, 178, 192, 195, 204, 209n12
head-marking (linguistic feature), 3, 10
Hewitt, James, 201
Hicks, John (Seminole chief), 221–23
Hitchiti (as a Creek town), 105, 146
Hitchiti (as sociolinguistic affiliation among the Creek), 101–3, 110, 113–14, 117–18
Hitchiti language, 156, 160
Hiwassee (Cherokee town), 60n9
Hiwassee River, 36, 46, 50–51, 53, 57, 96n34
Hodge, Fredrick, 45
Hokan (language family), 18
Hokan-Siouan (language family), 14, 18, 21, 23
honorific marking (linguistic feature), 6
house, war, 45, 169. *See also* architecture
Howard, James H., 99n49
Hudson, Charles, 48
Hughes, Price, 44
hunting, 87, 98n42, 130, 161, 176
Hurt, Wesley, 107
Huscher, Harold, 107, 111–12, 118

Martyn, Benjamin, 125
Maryland, 166–67, 170, 173
McGillivray, Alexander, xxxn5
McNeil, John Winfield Scott, 216
Mekoche (Shawnee division), 163
Memphis TN, 161
Methodists, Yuchi, xxxn5. *See also* Christianity
Miccosukee Tribe of Indians of Florida, 220, 228n13
"Mico of the Uchesses" (Yuchi chief), 194
migration, xv, 50, 77, 103, 105–6, 126, 142, 155–179
Mikasukis (native affiliational group in Seminole-period Florida), 219, 221, 223, 228n13
Milford, Louis LeClerk de, 164
militarization, 50, 68n43
Miller, John, 202
Mingo Ouma (Chickasaw chief), 171, 192
Mississippian (archaeological culture), 35–37, 43
Mississippi River, 50, 161
Mississippi Valley (region), 21, 49
Mobile Bay (region), 21
Monroe, Lake, 218
Moon (as a being), xxiv
Mooney, James, 69n53
Moore, James, 166–67
Moore, William, 79
morphology, linguistic, 6
mother towns: Creek, 133; general concept, 114–15; Yuchi, 96n34, 114–17, 145–46, 173. *See also* towns
Mount Pleasant (Yuchi townsite), 75–92, 171, 197–99, 201, 204, 210n19
mourning wars. *See* Iroquois Wars
Mouse Creek (archaeological site), 48, 97n34
Mouse Creek (watercourse), 48
Mouse Creeks (archaeological phase), 48–49, 64n25
Muccalassee (Alabama/Creek town), 174–75

multilingualism, 160–62. *See also* language
Muscogee (as a sociolinguistic affiliation among the Creek), 101, 113–14, 117, 156, 172
Muscogee (Creek) Nation, xiv, xviii, 90, 123. *See also* confederation and confederacies; Creek Indians
Muskingum River, 176
Muskogean (language family), 4, 12, 14, 156, 172
Muskogee (Creek) language, 156, 160, 190. *See also* language; Yuchi language
mythology, xxiv–xxv, 90, 142, 155. *See also* narrative, traditional; cosmology

Nairne, Thomas, 44, 53, 60n9, 69n52, 115, 157, 170
Napochin (town and chiefdom), 37
narrative, traditional, xxiv, 3–4, 142, 155, 159, 190
Natchez, xxxn5, 68n44, 156
Natchez language, 15
Natchez-Muskogian (language family sub-group), 14
nation: concept of, xvii, xxixn7; Yuchi as, xviii, xxixn7. *See also* Muscogee (Creek) Nation; confederation
Naucooche (Cherokee town), 56
New Ebenezer GA, 77
New Windsor GA, 79
New York, 177
Nichols, Johanna 10–11
Nicklas, T. Dale, 8
Norris Basin (region), 37–38
North Carolina, xiv, 128, 166, 168. *See also* South Carolina
noun class systems (linguistic feature), 5
noun incorporation, 3
Nuyaka (Creek town), xx

Ocala FL, 219
Ochese Creek, 127–28
Ocmulgee (as a people), 109
Ocmulgee (Creek town), 68n42, 105, 126–28

www.ingramcontent.com/pod-product-compliance
Ingram Content Group UK Ltd.
Pitfield, Milton Keynes, MK11 3LW, UK
UKHW040823120325
456138UK00003B/152